IMAGES
of America
SAN FRANCISCO'S PORTOLA

Rayna Garibaldi

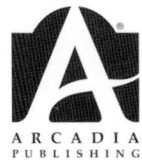

ARCADIA
PUBLISHING

Copyright © 2007 by Rayna Garibaldi
ISBN 978-0-7385-4715-2

Published by Arcadia Publishing
Charleston SC, Chicago IL, Portsmouth NH, San Francisco CA

Printed in the United States of America

Library of Congress Catalog Card Number: 2006934438

For all general information contact Arcadia Publishing at:
Telephone 843-853-2070
Fax 843-853-0044
E-mail sales@arcadiapublishing.com
For customer service and orders:
Toll-Free 1-888-313-2665

Visit us on the Internet at www.arcadiapublishing.com

IMAGES
of America

SAN FRANCISCO'S
PORTOLA

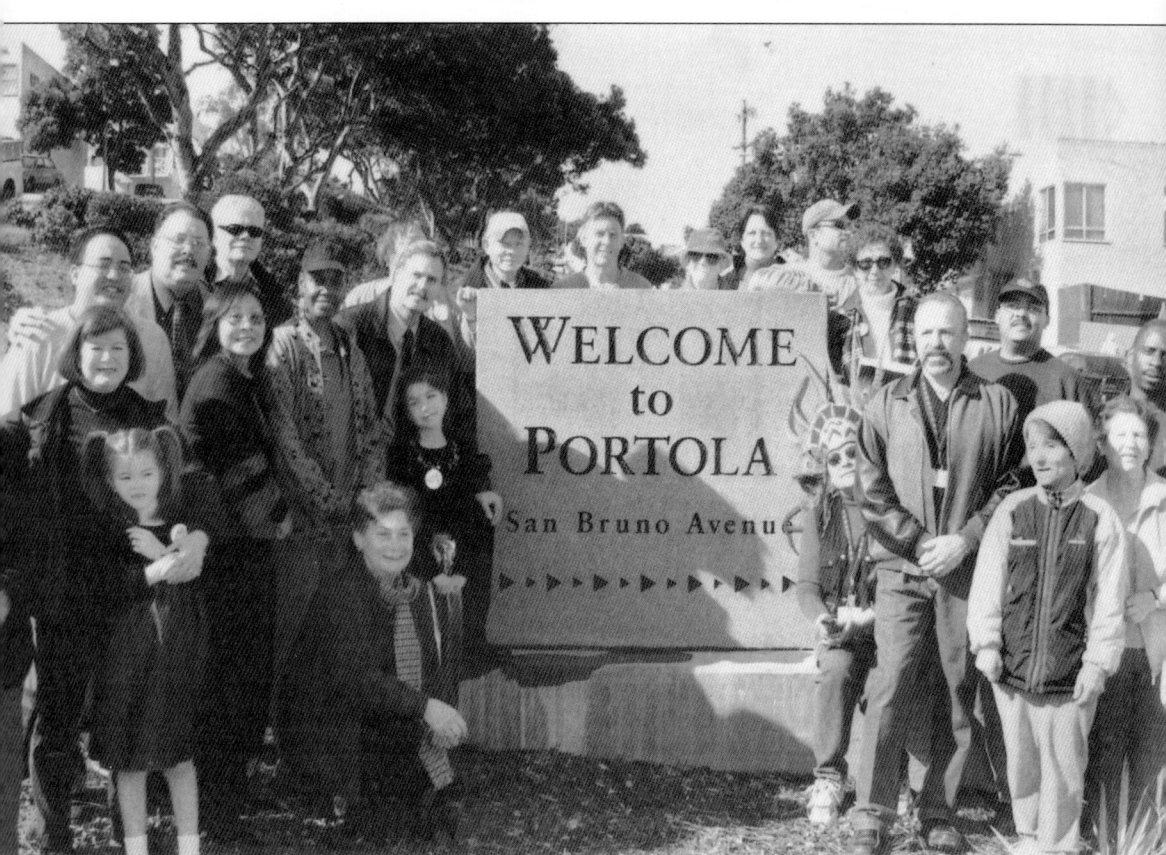

On February 28, 2000, the "Welcome to Portola" monument was installed at Mansell Street. Pictured are members of the St. Elizabeth/San Francisco Organizing Project (SFOP), the Community Alliance for Portola and Silver Terrace (CAPS), community leaders and residents, and city leaders. Another monument can be found at the Alemany/San Bruno Avenue circle. (Courtesy of Dwayne and Terezinha Jusino.)

ON THE COVER: Portola children gather at 405 Brussels Street on September 2, 1935, to celebrate a birthday. (Courtesy of June Blut Conlon.)

Contents

Acknowledgments		6
Introduction		7
1.	Nurseries	11
2.	Churches and Schools	31
3.	San Bruno Avenue	51
4.	People	93
5.	Neighborhood Sports	115
Bibliography		127

ACKNOWLEDGMENTS

I would like to thank all the people who helped to make this book a reality. Many thanks to everyone who so generously shared their photographs. To my cousin, Gerald Garibaldi, for his help in recreating the history of the nurseries. To Irene Crescio and Barbara Fenech for their diligent efforts in locating pictures of San Bruno Avenue. To the San Francisco Public Utilities Commission: Maureen Barry, Katherine Dutiel, Beverly Hennessey, and Frank Kukula. To the Portola residents who contributed historical information: Tom Assereto, Joellyn Bischeri, Roz Chang, June Blut Conlon, Kate Connell, Laura Luttringer, Franco Mancini, Angelo Meneguzzi, Chris Ortiz, Jack Parodi, Beverly Putnam, Mrs. Harry Swinkels, and Silvio Scocca. Those who donated funds to obtain photographs from the San Francisco library collection: Irene Crescio, Barbara Fenech, the Garibaldi family, Barbara Harrington, and Dwayne and Terezinha Jusino. To my nephew, David R. Mehrwein, for his photographic assistance. To Barbara Harrington for suggesting I undertake this project. To John Poultney, my editor at Arcadia, for his help in guiding me through this project. And lastly, to my family for their love and support in this and all my endeavors.

INTRODUCTION

San Francisco's Portola looks at the early days of the neighborhood, including the nurseries, San Bruno Avenue, and the churches, schools, and people that built the area. The Portola is believed to be named in honor of Gaspar de Portola (1723–1784), a Spanish soldier and explorer who carried out a land expedition into Alta (Upper) California. The expedition's goal was to map the land route from Baja (Lower) California to Monterey Bay. The 64-person expedition set out from San Diego on July 14, 1769, traveling in a northward direction and keeping as near to the coast as possible. On October 31, 1769, the expedition reached the top of Montara Ridge (in Pacifica) from where they could see the San Francisco Bay. Portola and his company then realized they had traveled too far north. They spent a few days camping out in a valley (now Linda Mar) before returning to San Diego. A statute of Gaspar de Portola can be found in a public parking lot near Highway 1 and Crespi Drive in Pacifica.

The geography of the Portola, throughout much of its prehistory, included large regions abundant with birds, deer, rabbit, and other small game animals. Much of the area was populated by small groups of native peoples known as the Ohlone. The Ohlone tribe specific to the Portola was the Yelamu, and they traveled up and down the peninsula trading with other tribes. Many of the Ohlone tribal groups were decimated within the first 25 years after contact with the Spanish. By 1810, less than 2,000 Ohlone inhabited the San Francisco/Monterey Bay region with their numbers continuing to decline throughout subsequent years.

Mexico gained its independence from Spain in 1821, and California became a state in 1850. Later, large land grants were given to individuals, many of whom were working in the cattle industry. The Portola fell within the jurisdiction of Grant No. 153, the Rincon de las Salinas y Potrero Viejo, which was granted on December 31, 1857, and encompassed 4,446 acres. The southernmost boundary of the land grant extended through present-day McLaren Park.

In its earliest days, the Portola encompassed a much larger area. Before the construction of Highway 101, the Portola included areas east of Bayshore Boulevard. The current borders of the Portola are defined as Alemany Boulevard/Interstate 280 to the north, Mansell Street to the south, Bayshore Boulevard to the east, and LeGrande Street to the west.

Among residents, there has been a long, ongoing debate about the correct pronunciation of the district's name. A December 1988 article in the *San Francisco Examiner* listed "the first way as pore-tow-la with the first syllable rhyming with 'more' and the last two with 'cola.' Then there's the right way according to the residents. They pronounce it port-a-la with the first two syllables rhyming with 'sorta.'" Longtime residents omit the second "o" altogether and pronounce it as one syllable "portla." It is also rumored that residents born in the Portola in the 1920s and 1930s possess a somewhat "Brooklyn" accent that is undetectable to themselves but has been known to fool even native New Yorkers. Neighborhood slang has developed as far as references to the shopping district on San Bruno Avenue is concerned. One merely has to say they will be "down the road" to mean they are going anywhere along San Bruno Avenue.

In the 1800s, the Portola was simply known as "the flat" because for the most part the land was flat, although University Mound Hill is listed as one of the 43 hills of San Francisco with an elevation of 265 feet. University Mound Hill's western boundary is McLaren Ridge, which has a height of 515 feet. The development of the Portola district can be traced back to 1869 when the University Homestead Association filed a permit with the city to develop the land and began to name many of the streets for eastern universities and colleges. Dartmouth Street can trace its name origins not only to the college of the same name but back to the Second Earl of Dartmouth, whose ancestral home lies at the mouth of the River Dart in Southern England. Felton Street was named for Charles Felton who came to California in the gold rush and later made his fortune from investments in the Nevada Comstock lode. Bowdoin Street was named for the college in Maine, which was named for James Bowdoin, a political leader during the American Revolution and member of the Constitutional Convention.

In its earliest days, the Portola was home to a large Jewish population, earning it the nickname "Little Jerusalem." San Bruno Road was home to two major synagogues. The congregation of Ahabat Achim moved to Girard and Burrows Streets in 1919 and eventually bought its own building on Girard and Felton Streets. In 1907, the congregation of Mokum Israel was founded and was located on Silliman and Brussels Streets. In 1918, many Jewish immigrants met at the San Bruno Settlement House at 2574 San Bruno Avenue (which later would become the site of the Boys Club.) The Settlement House, built by the San Francisco Section of the National Council of Jewish Women, was run by Grace Weiner. In this settlement house, wives learned the American way of life, and young girls could learn to sew. Boys used the settlement house for gym and shop classes. The clubhouse was also the site of weddings, confirmations, and dances and used by Temple Emanu-El to conduct religion classes. Kosher delicatessens, butcher shops, and a variety of businesses could be found in the neighborhood. During these early years, many of the Jewish residents of the Portola left the area to settle elsewhere in the city. The Portola then began to be settled by Maltese families, many of whom came from Mosta, Malta. Some Italian families came from towns in Italy, while others came from parts of North Beach in San Francisco.

During the 1920s, the Portola became home to as many as 19 different family-owned nurseries. These nurseries grew most of the flowers sold in the city. Some of the names of these nurseries were California Evergreen, DePaoli, DeMilla and Parodi, Fatima, Ferrari Brothers, Ferrari Orchid, Gemignani, Granara, Gregoire Brothers, Olivera, Restani, Silver Terrace, Siri, Somerset, University Mound (Garibaldi Brothers), Vic Pardini, Victoria Pardini, and Winant. Each nursery grew its own specialty flowers such as azaleas, begonias, carnations, Easter lilies, French marigolds, orchids, poinsettias, roses, snapdragons, and assorted plants. Neighborhood children were often enlisted to help the nursery workers pull weeds. The greenhouses' characteristic white color was achieved by whitewashing them every year to protect the plants inside from sun damage. During World War II, when flower production was deemed nonessential, many nurserymen raised chickens or grew vegetables to supplement their incomes.

In 1926, the San Francisco Board of Supervisors voted to acquire 550 acres in the Portola for a park, which was to be named in honor of John McLaren, who was considered the father of the city's park system. In 1928, a bond issue to acquire more property within McLaren Park failed and the board began to purchase land. Over the years, park acreage has fluctuated from its original planned 550 acres to its current size of 317 acres. Until 1953, the city had spent close to $800,000 buying private McLaren Park lots as boundaries changed.

Pauline Des Roches, of 1323 Woolsey Street, owned one of the largest amounts of private property within McLaren Park. Her land was a little more than two acres, which is about two city blocks or approximately 40 of the 25- by 120-foot lots. Her nurseryman father had settled into the area around 1880. In 1957, the city began to file condemnation suits, a legal maneuver used to appropriate private property for public use. Once a suit had been filed, the real estate department would try to negotiate with the property owner. Des Roches fought a long battle to retain her property or at least get a more equitable price for her land than what the city was offering her. Many of the nurserymen with property surrounding areas that would become the

University Mound Reservoir system faced similar hurdles. Although many landowners tried to retain their land through legal action, in the end they were unsuccessful and moved to other parts of the area.

Residents have celebrated the Portola Festival, which was observed throughout the city to commemorate San Francisco's recovery from the earthquake and fire of 1906. The first festival occurred on October 19, 1909, and festivals were also held in 1913 and 1948. In 1948, the queen of the Portola Festival for the Portola district was Frances Monterosso.

San Bruno Road was one of the last major city streets to be paved. It was then that it went from its designation of road to avenue. To this day, it continues to be referred to it as "the Road." From 1900 until 1910, the Golden City Nickelodeon could be found on San Bruno Avenue showing popular short films of the day. Popular establishments such as Etalo Market, the Avenue Sweet Shop, the Avenue Theatre, O'Connors, and the San Francisco Public Library have been the places where Portola residents met for shopping, dining, and entertainment.

Early education in the Portola district included the South End School located on Somerset Street (between Burrows and Felton). It was closed in 1910 with the opening of Portola School, which was later transformed into a junior high school when Edward Robeson Taylor Elementary School opened. Portola Junior High School was renovated in 1983, keeping only the auditorium and gymnasium intact and renaming it Martin Luther King Jr. Elementary School. In 1955, Simpson Bible Institute moved from its location in Seattle, Washington, to 801 Silver Avenue and was renamed Simpson Bible College. It remained at that location until 1989, and the site is now used by Cornerstone Academy. Along with the remaining public elementary and secondary schools, the neighborhood also includes private schools such as St. Elizabeth Catholic School and Cornerstone Academy.

In data taken from the Portola Community Library Needs Assessment San Francisco Public Library document, Section F, the 2000 Census figures show that the Portola is a culturally diverse community—53 percent of the community is Asian/Pacific Islander, 22 percent is Hispanic/Latino, 17 percent white, 5 percent African American, and .16 percent Native American. Median home prices in the Portola as of August 2006 were $722,500, with the median price in San Francisco being $832,000.

The Portola maintains a strong community group, the St. Elizabeth/San Francisco Organizing Project (SFOP), which has been instrumental in promoting the neighborhood and campaigning to enact programs to beautify the neighborhood. In 1996, SFOP was able to negotiate with the California Department of Transportation (CalTrans) and the city of San Francisco to reopen three of the four Silver Avenue freeway off-ramps that were closed due to the 1989 Loma Prieta earthquake and subsequent freeway retrofit.

SFOP was also key to the installation of the "Welcome to the Portola" monuments. One is located at Mansell Street and San Bruno Avenue and the other at the Alemany Circle at the foot of San Bruno Avenue. In March 2006, the Mayor's Office of Neighborhood Services and the Department of Elections officially recognized the Portola, and beginning with the June 2006 election, results reported by neighborhood will include the Portola. Neighborhood projects, which included the planting of additional trees on San Bruno Avenue, have been mostly completed, and there are current plans to place all overhead wires below ground. Plans are also currently underway to relocate the library at 2450 San Bruno Avenue for a new library, which will occupy the corner of Bacon and Goettingen Streets. The Ahabat Achim Synagogue is now the Apostolic Assembly of the Faith in Christ Jesus Church. One has to only look at the stained-glass Star of David on the Girard Street side of the building to remember its early roots. The Mokum Israel Synagogue has become the Ukrainian Catholic's Parish of the Immaculate Conception. The San Bruno Avenue Street Fair, which began in 2000, has continued to bring the community together to celebrate diversity. The Portola continues to change and grow with a new sense of community and multicultural pride.

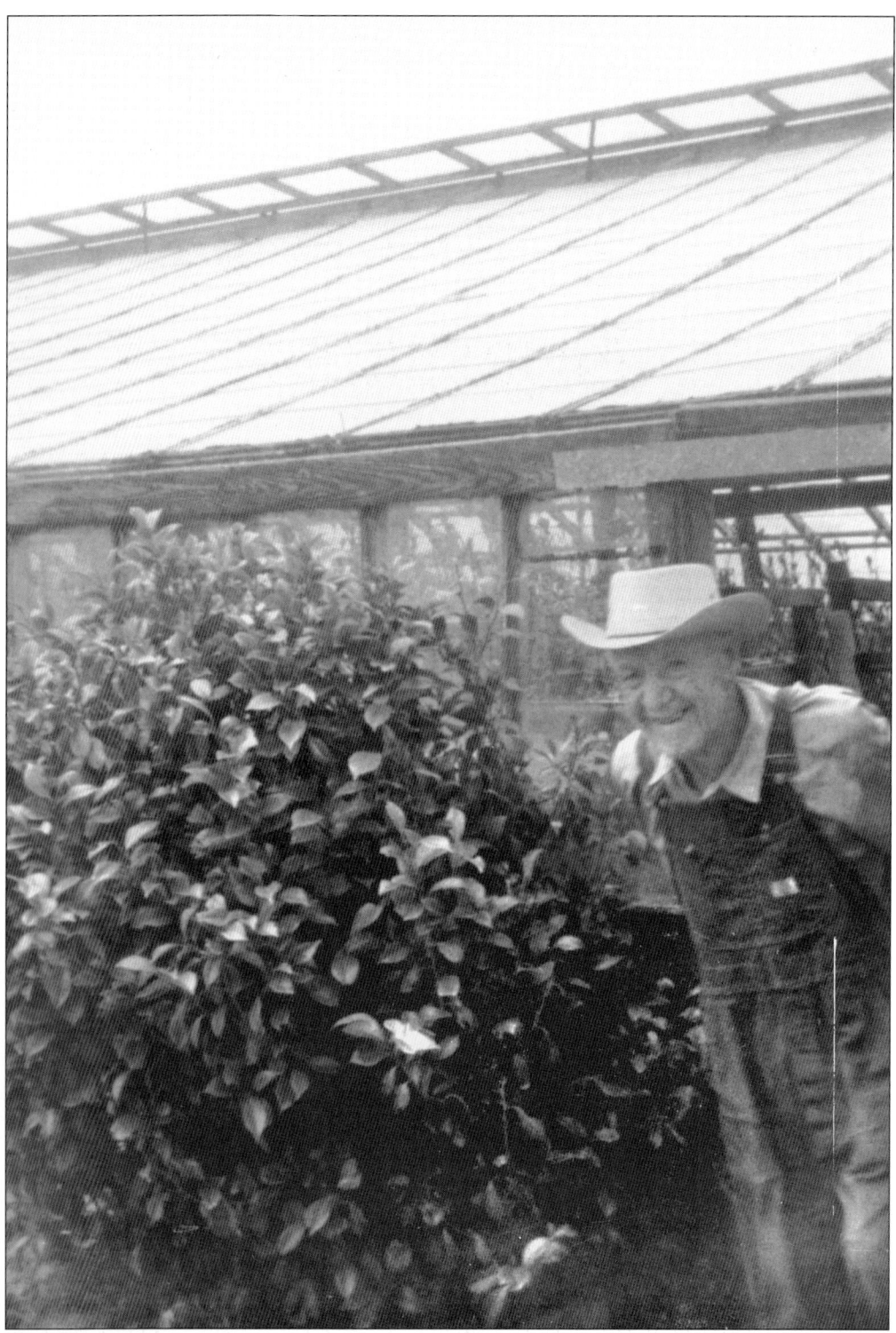
This photograph from 1960 shows Joseph Winant in front of one of his greenhouses at Cambridge and Felton Streets. (Courtesy of Claire Winant O'Sullivan.)

One
NURSERIES

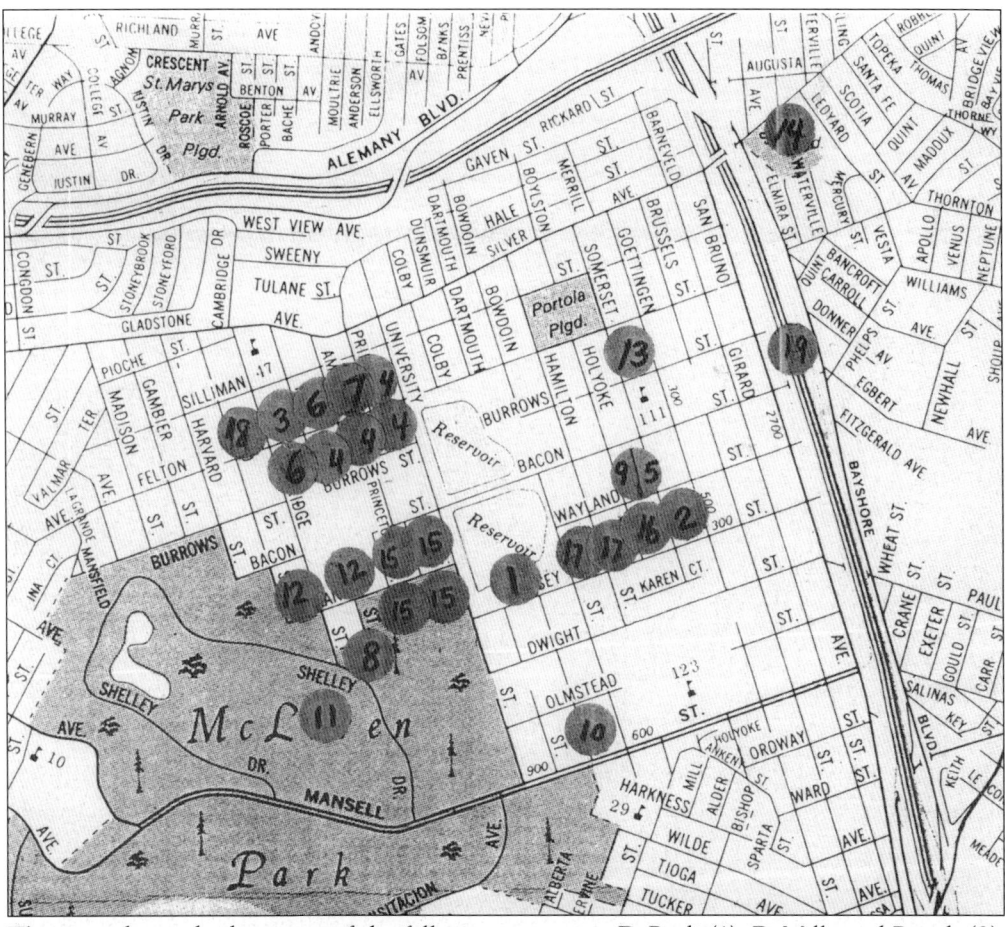

This map shows the locations of the following nurseries: DePaoli (1), DeMilla and Parodi (2), Ferrari Orchid (3), Ferrari Roses (4), Granara (5), Gregoire (6), Gregoire (7), Gemignani (8), Olivera (9), Victor Pardini (10), Victoria Pardini (11), Restani (12), California Evergreen (13), Silver Terrace (14), Siri (15), Somerset (16), University Mound (17), Winant (18), and unidentified (19). (Courtesy of Gerald Garibaldi.)

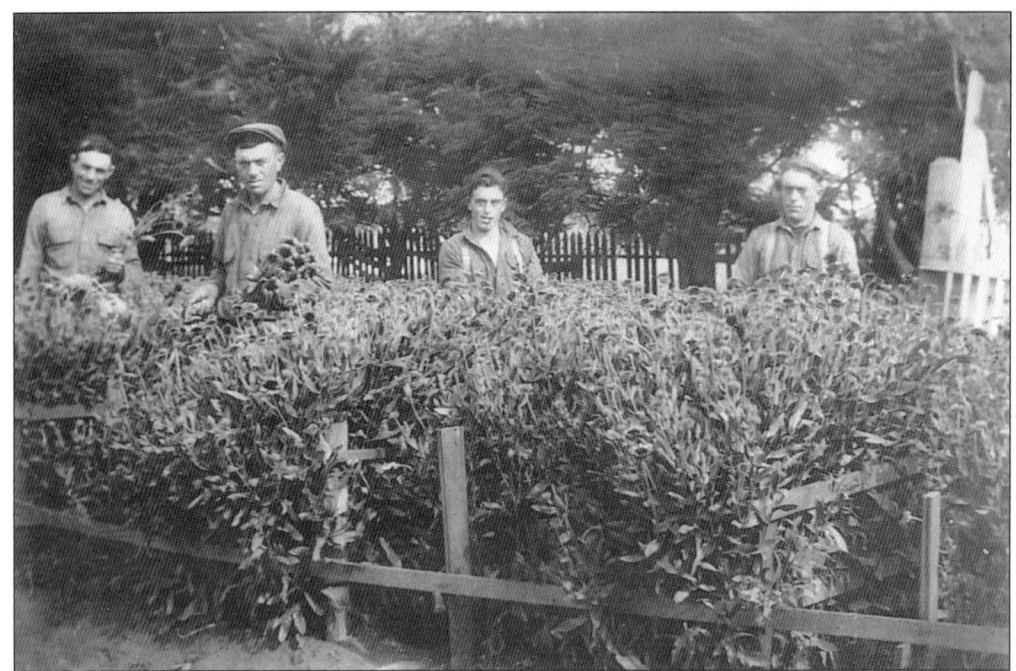

In this 1920s photograph, the founders of the University Mound Nursery are pictured in the field where they grew French marigolds. From left to right are Giovanni, Andrew, Ernesto, and GioBatta Garibaldi. (Courtesy of Gerald Garibaldi.)

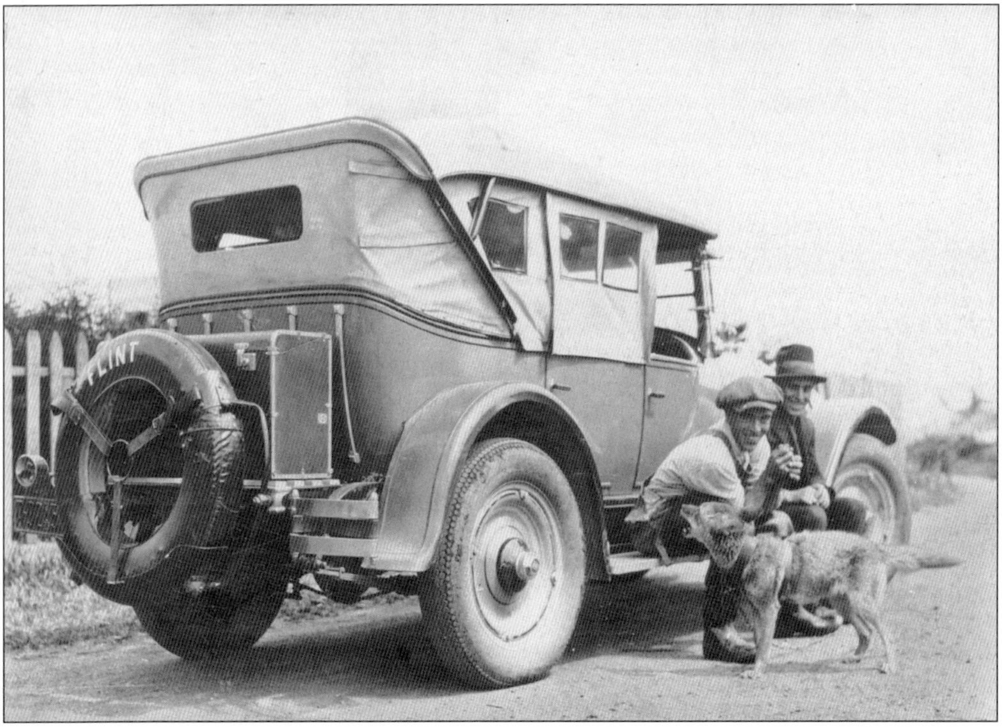

The University Mound Nursery kept an unnamed coyote as a pet. Pictured here in the 1920s are brothers GioBatta and Ernesto Garibaldi. (Courtesy of Gerald Garibaldi.)

In this view looking north in 1924, Margaret "Maggie" Garibaldi is pictured with her son Victor at the University Mound Nursery on Hamilton Street. (Courtesy of Gerald Garibaldi.)

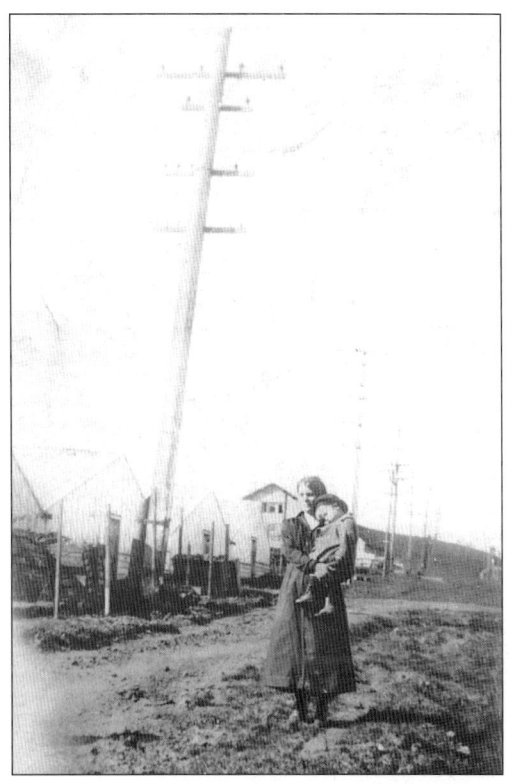

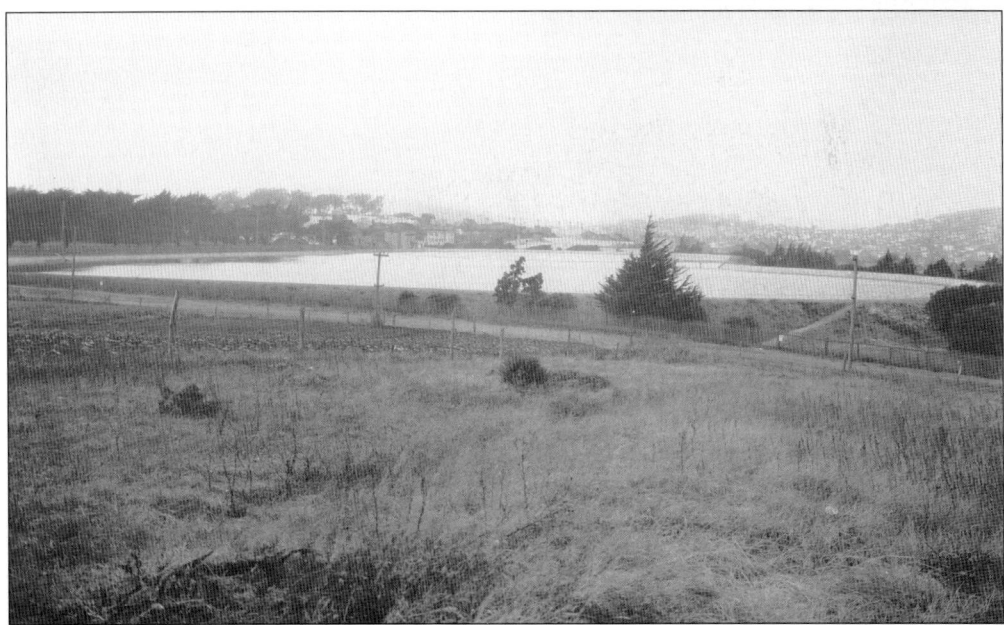

Constructed by Hermann Schussler of the Spring Valley Water Company in 1885, the uncovered North Basin of the University Mound Reservoir is pictured here as it appeared on September 14, 1925. The University Mound Reservoir is one of three terminal reservoirs in San Francisco's water system. The water in it flows by gravity from the Hetch Hetchy Reservoir. (Courtesy of George Fanning/San Francisco Public Utilities Commission.)

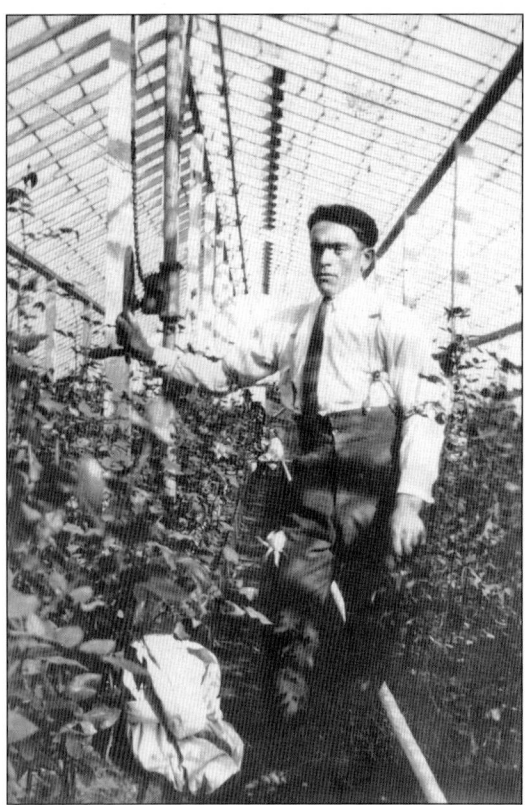

One of the founders of the University Mound Nursery, GioBatta Garibaldi works inside the greenhouse in this 1930 photograph. The roses needed to be constantly monitored to ensure they did not get too cold or too warm. (Courtesy of author.)

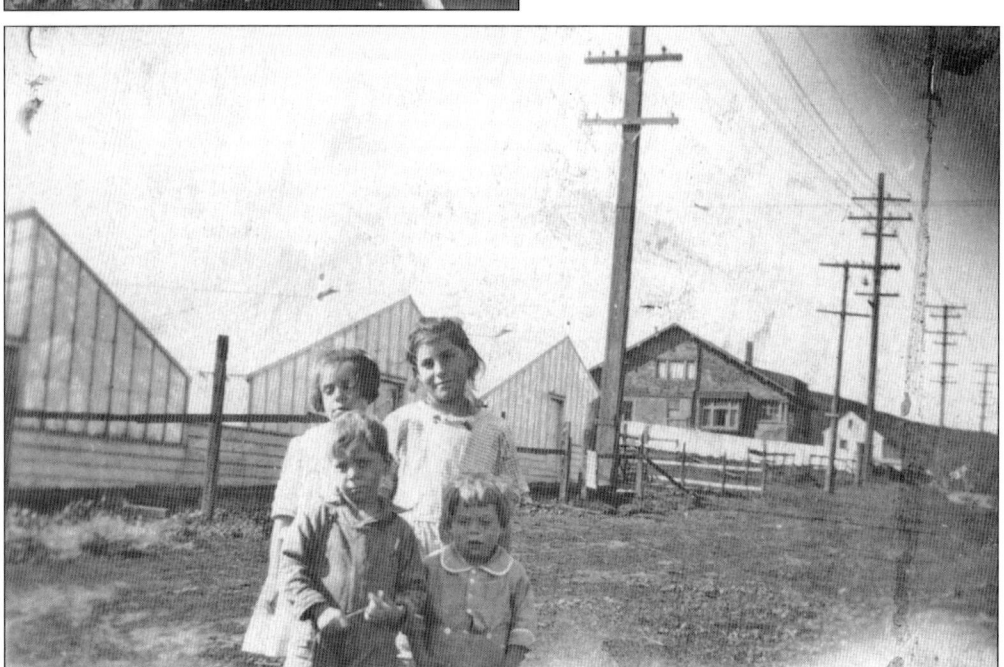

Children stand in front of the University Mound Nursery on Hamilton Street in the 1920s. Pictured from left to right are (first row) Ernest and Victor Garibaldi; (second row) Aileen and Bernice Garibaldi. The Colbert house can be seen in the background. (Courtesy of Gerald Garibaldi.)

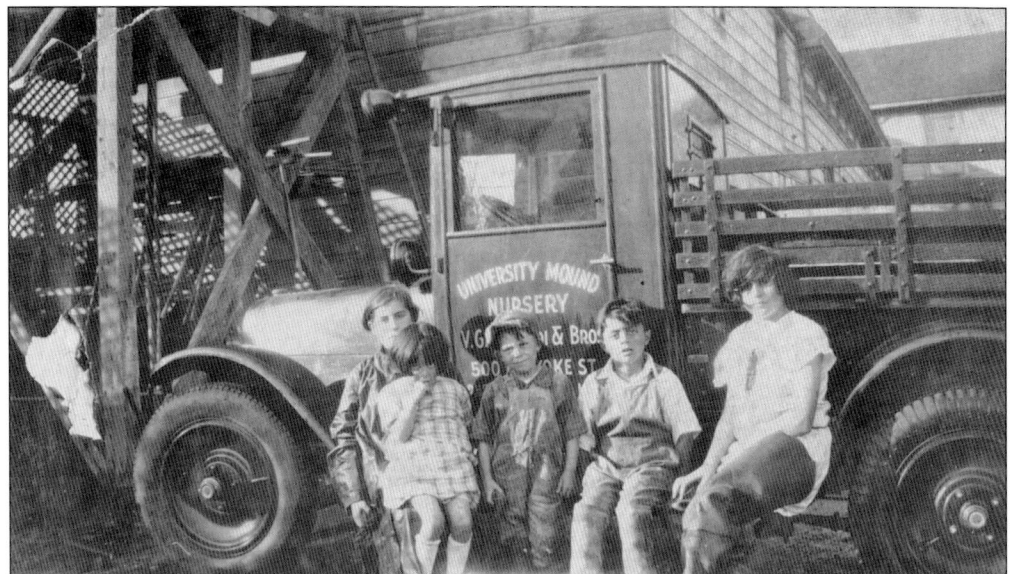

The Garibaldi children pose for a photograph in front of the University Mound Nursery truck during the 1920s. The children of the nurserymen were often enlisted to perform tasks such as picking weeds. Pictured from left to right are Aileen, Angie, Victor, Andrew, and Mary. (Courtesy of Gerald Garibaldi.)

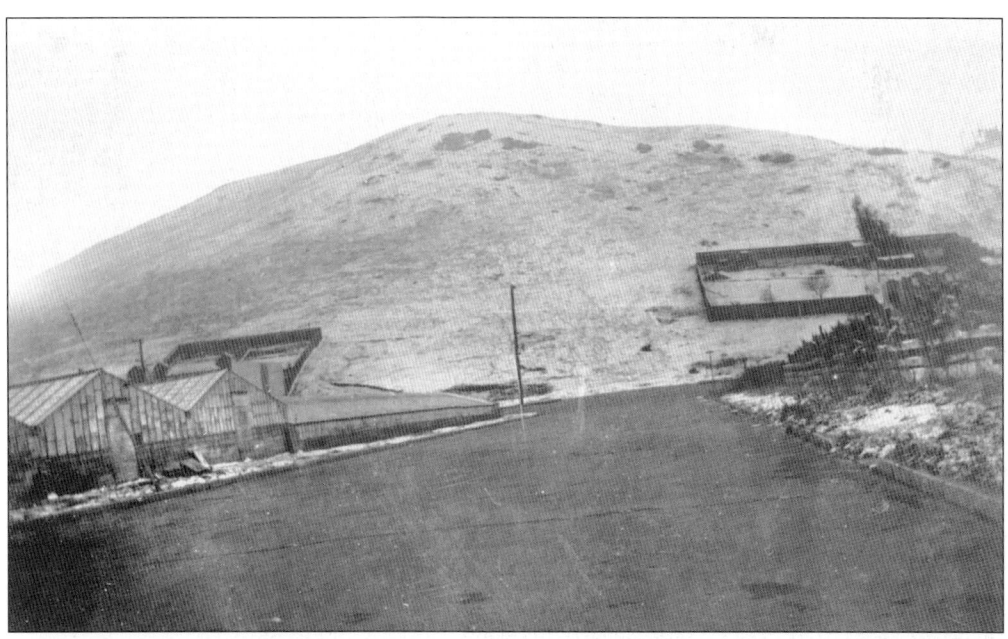

Looking south towards Woolsey Street, Holyoke Street is seen here in the 1930s. The hill would later be developed for homes and include Dwight Street and Karen Court. (Courtesy of Gerald Garibaldi.)

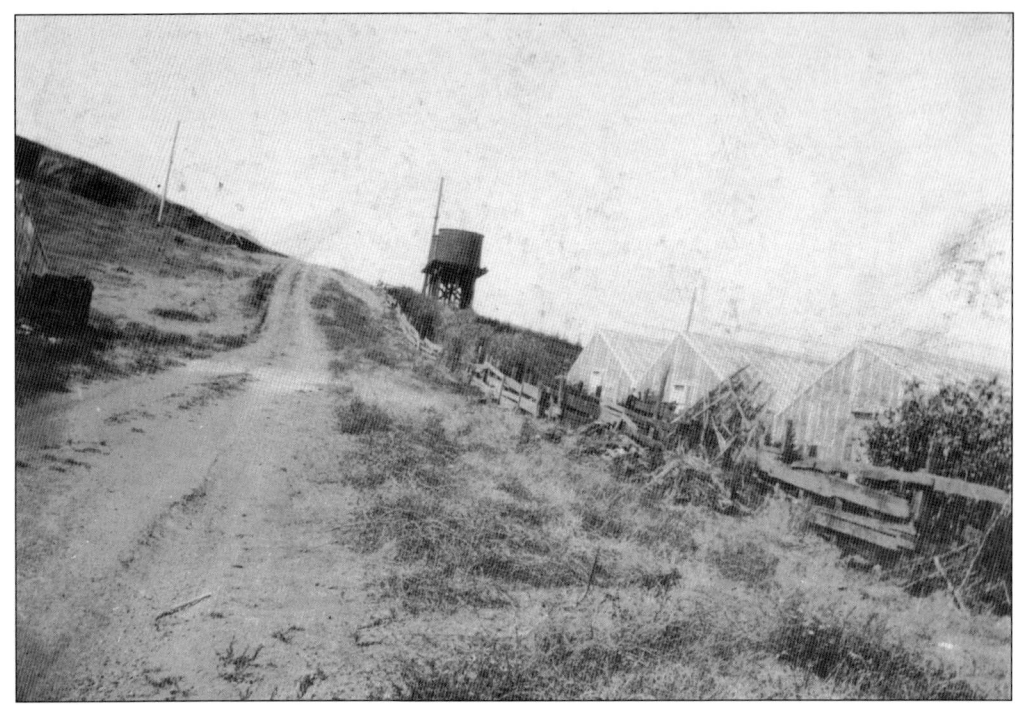
An artesian well was the source for the water tanks at the University Mound Nursery. This view of the tanks is seen from Bowdoin and Woolsey Streets around 1930. (Courtesy of Gerald Garibaldi.)

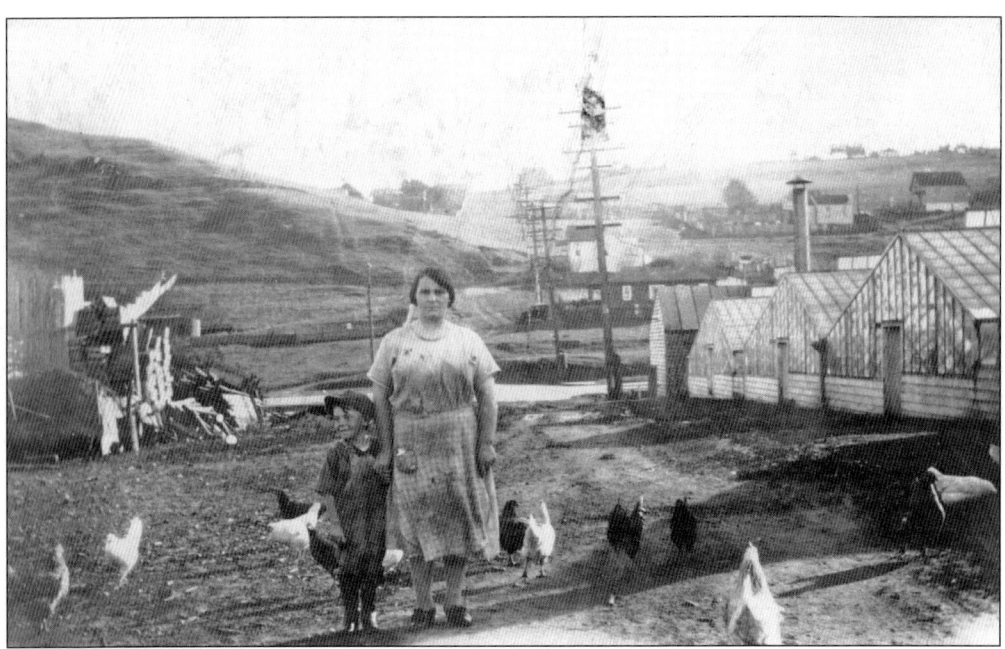
Margaret "Maggie" and Victor Garibaldi walk down Hamilton Street by the University Mound Nursery in the 1920s. (Courtesy of Gerald Garibaldi.)

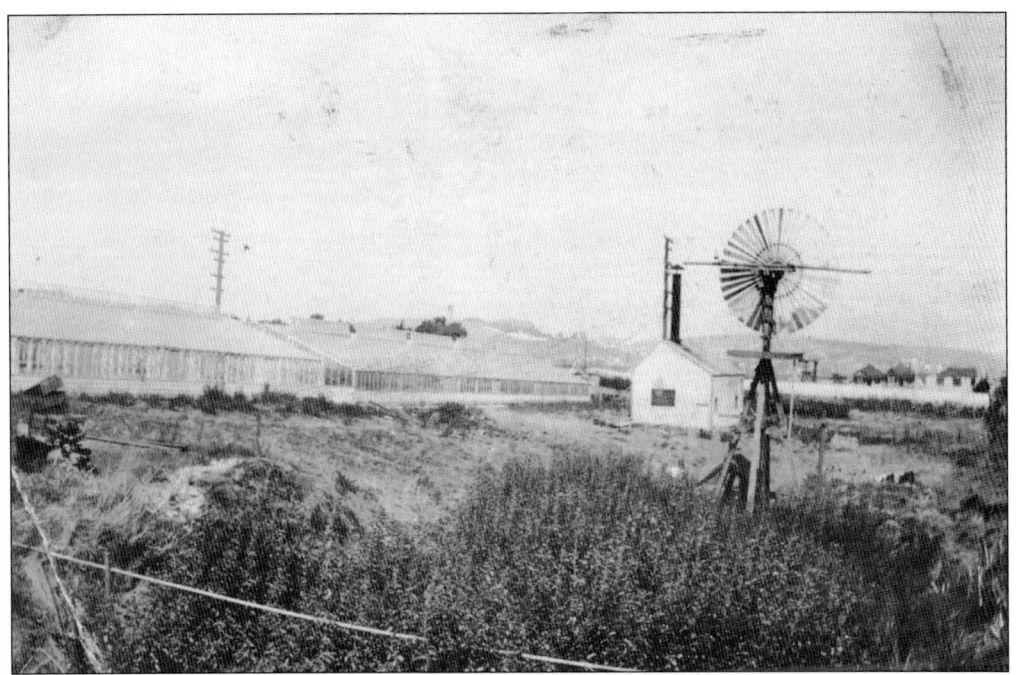

The University Mound Nursery is visible in this 1930s photograph from the corner of Bowdoin and Woolsey Streets. (Courtesy of Gerald Garibaldi.)

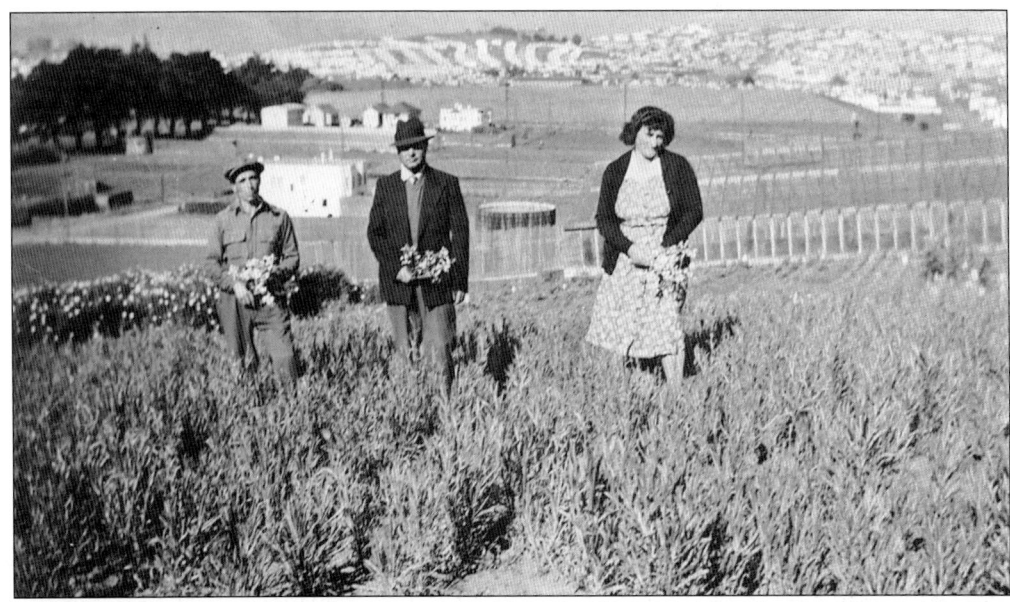

Frederico, Frank, and Maria Gemignani stand in the flower field at the Gemignani Nursery, which bounded Woolsey, Wayland, and Cambridge Streets in the 1930s. (Courtesy of the Gemignani family.)

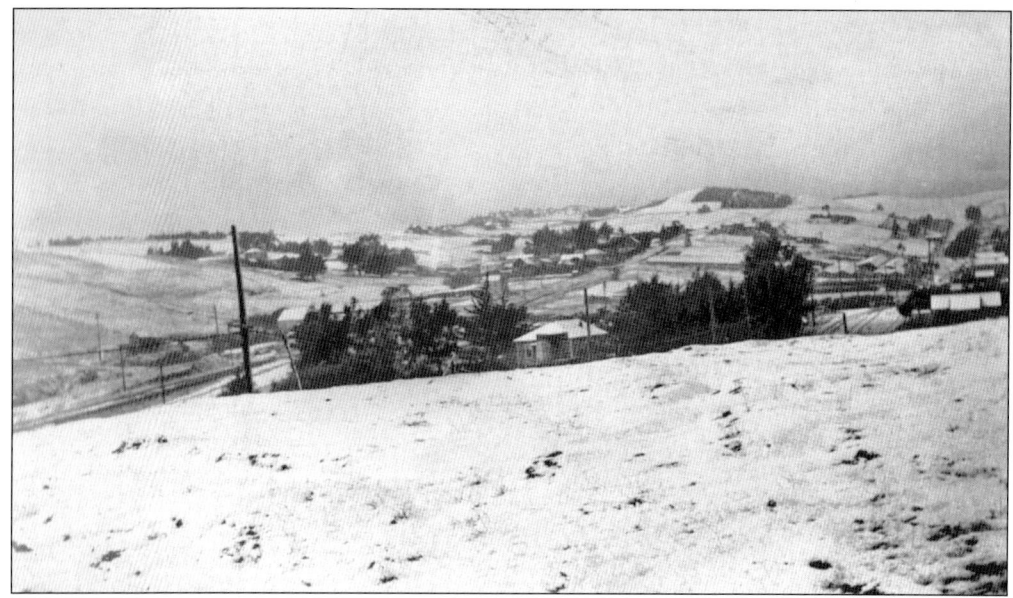
Although infrequent, snow has been an occasional visitor to San Francisco. This photograph from 1932 overlooks the neighborhood. (Courtesy of Gerald Garibaldi.)

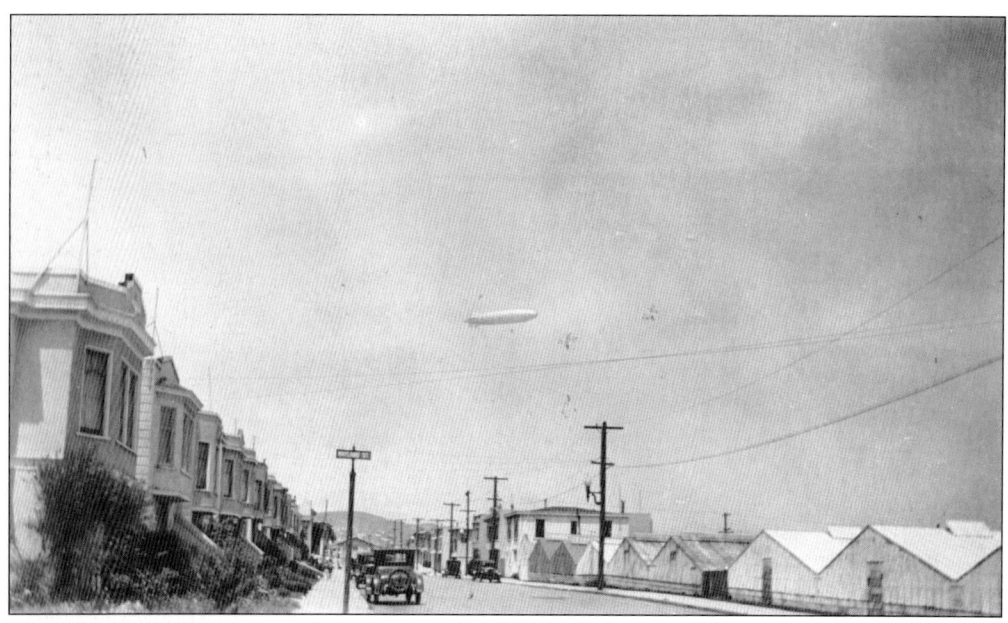
This May 20, 1932, photograph looks northward down Holyoke and Wayland Streets. The naval airship *Akron* can be seen in the background. (Courtesy of Gerald Garibaldi.)

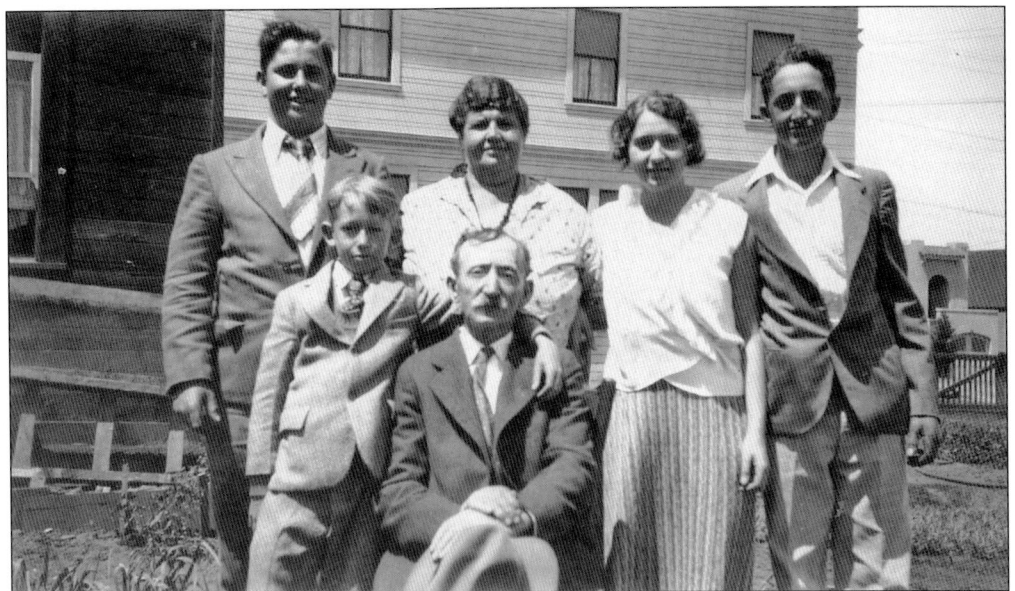

Joseph and Irma (Champion) Gregoire founded Gregoire Flowers in 1897. This August 10, 1931, family photograph was taken in front of the family home on Colby Street. Pictured from left to right are (first row) Paul and Joseph; (second row) Louie, Irma, Pauline, and Leon. (Courtesy of the Gregoire family.)

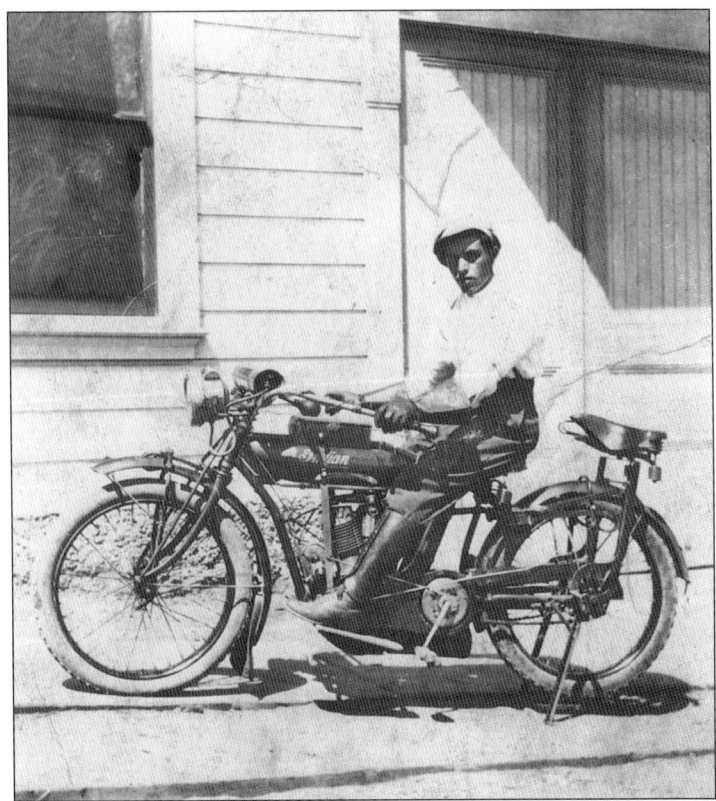

The motorcycle was a popular mode of transportation around the nurseries. Here Ernesto Garibaldi poses on his Indian motorcycle. (Courtesy of Gerald Garibaldi.)

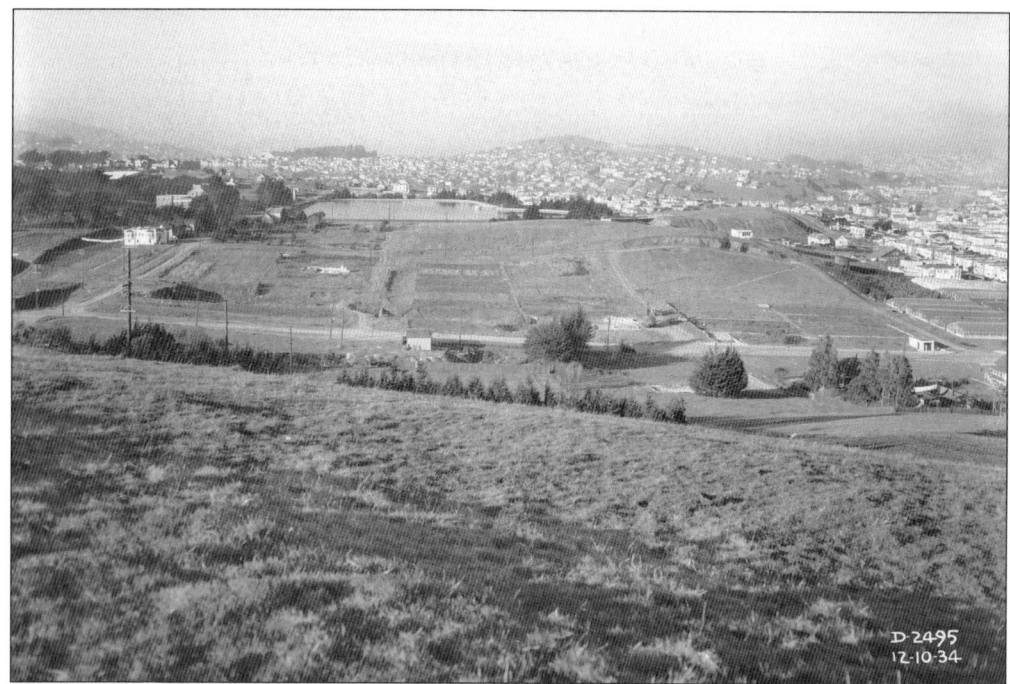

This photograph overlooks the Portola district on December 10, 1934. The uncovered North Basin of the University Mound Reservoir can be seen in the distance. (Courtesy of George Fanning/San Francisco Public Utilities Commission.)

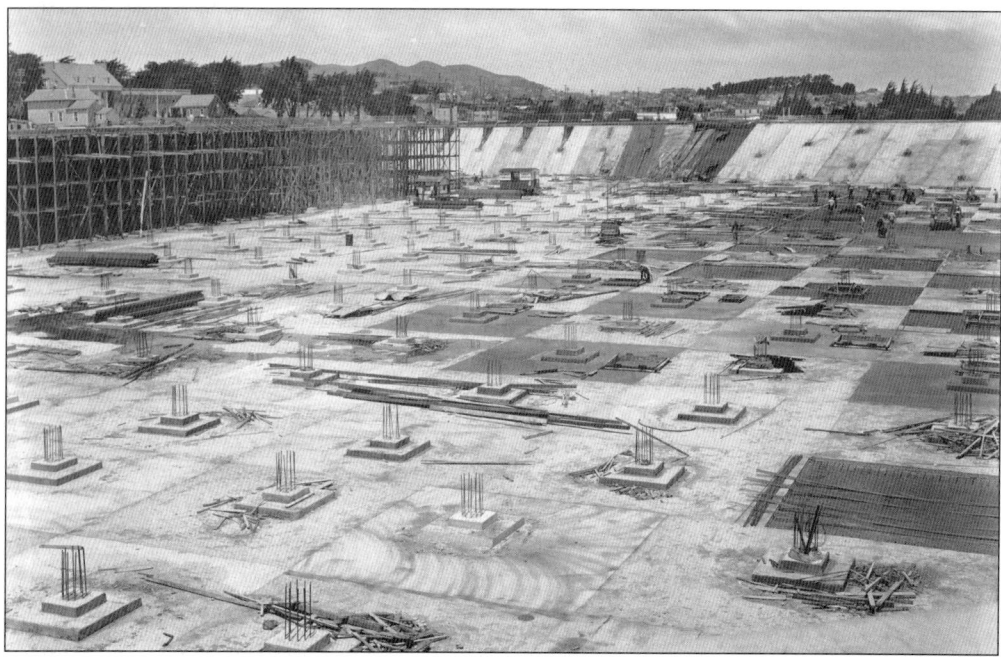

The construction of the South Basin of the University Mound Reservoir is depicted in this July 13, 1937, photograph. Both the North and South Basins serve San Francisco, including parts of Bayview, Mission, South of Market, downtown, North Beach, Marina, and Treasure Island. (Courtesy of George Fanning/San Francisco Public Utilities Commission.)

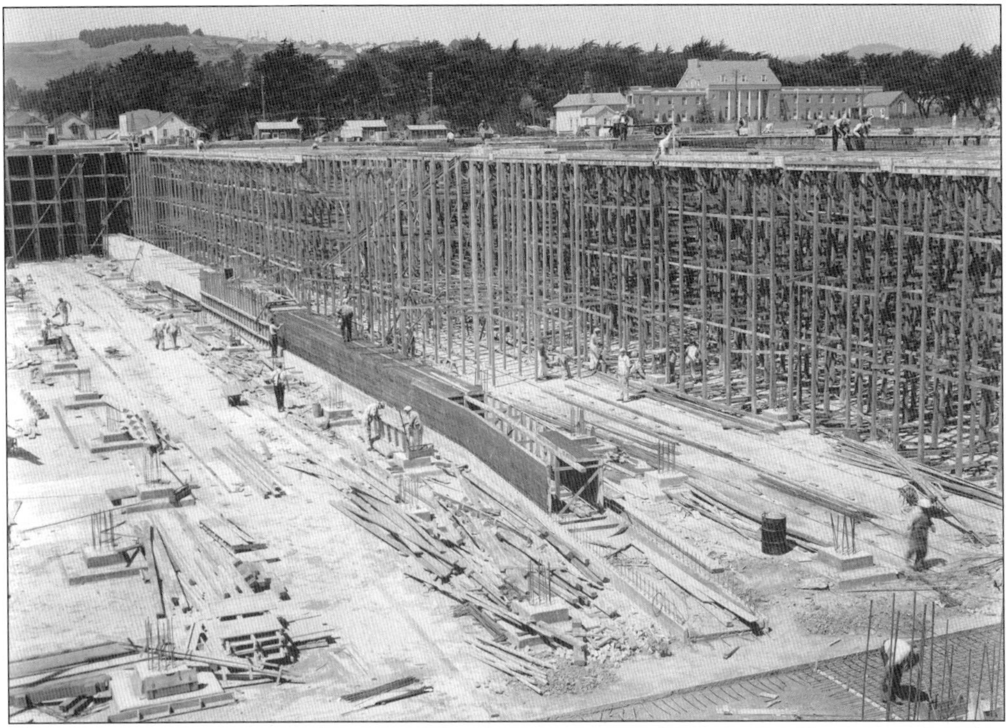

The construction of the South Basin of the University Mound Reservoir is documented in this August 24, 1937, photograph. The University Mound Ladies Home can be seen in the upper right. (Courtesy of George Fanning/San Francisco Public Utilities Commission.)

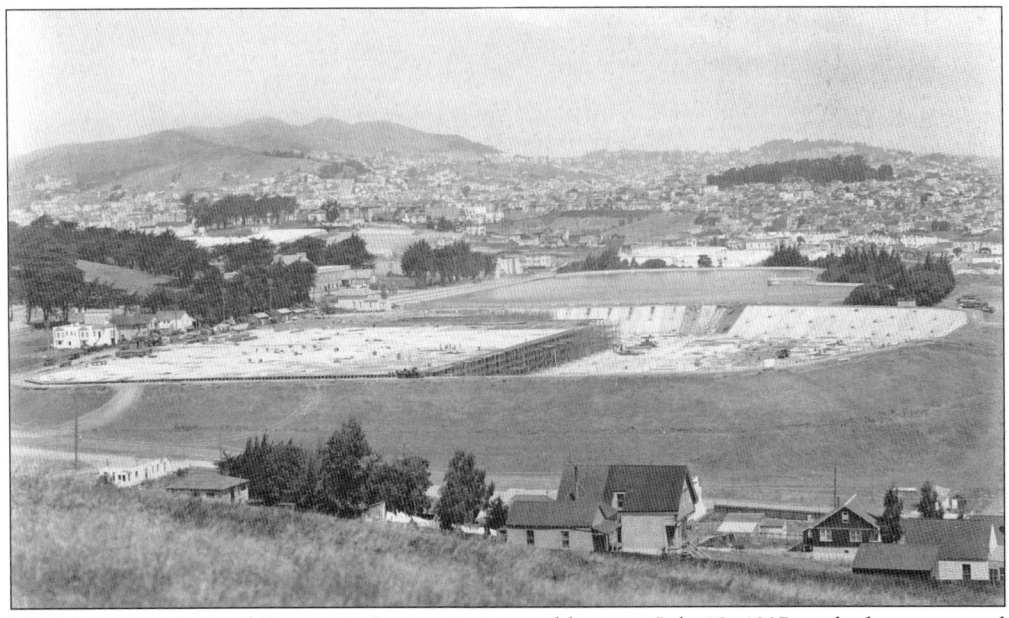

The University Mound Reservoir System is pictured here on July 13, 1937, with the uncovered North Basin located in the background. The South Basin was under construction at this time, with half of the concrete roof installed. Both the North and South Basins each cover approximately 10 acres of land. (Courtesy of George Fanning/San Francisco Public Utilities Commission.)

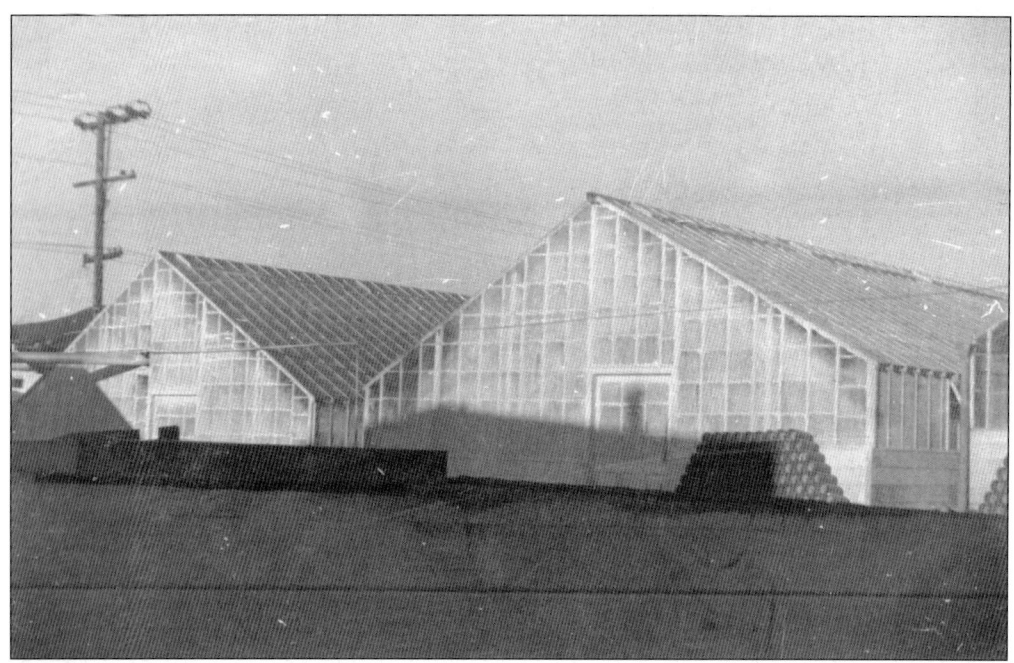

This is an outside view of the greenhouses at the California Evergreen Nursery. This nursery grew a variety of plants. (Courtesy of Irene Crescio.)

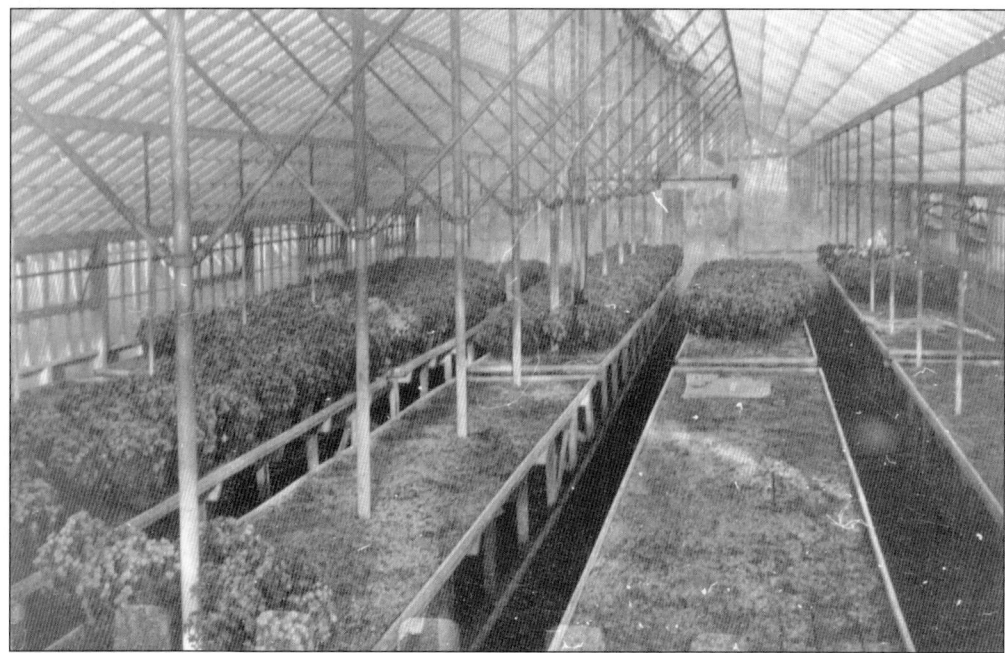

California Evergreen Nursery, established in the 1920s, occupied one square block bounded by Goettingen, Burrows, Felton, and Somerset Streets. The business was a partnership of several families, including the Rolleries, Crescios, Merlos, Romanos, Mateos, and the Fagaries. California Evergreen Nursery eventually sold their property in the Portola to Hayman Brothers Construction, who built homes on the site. This photograph shows the inside of the nursery. (Courtesy of Irene Crescio.)

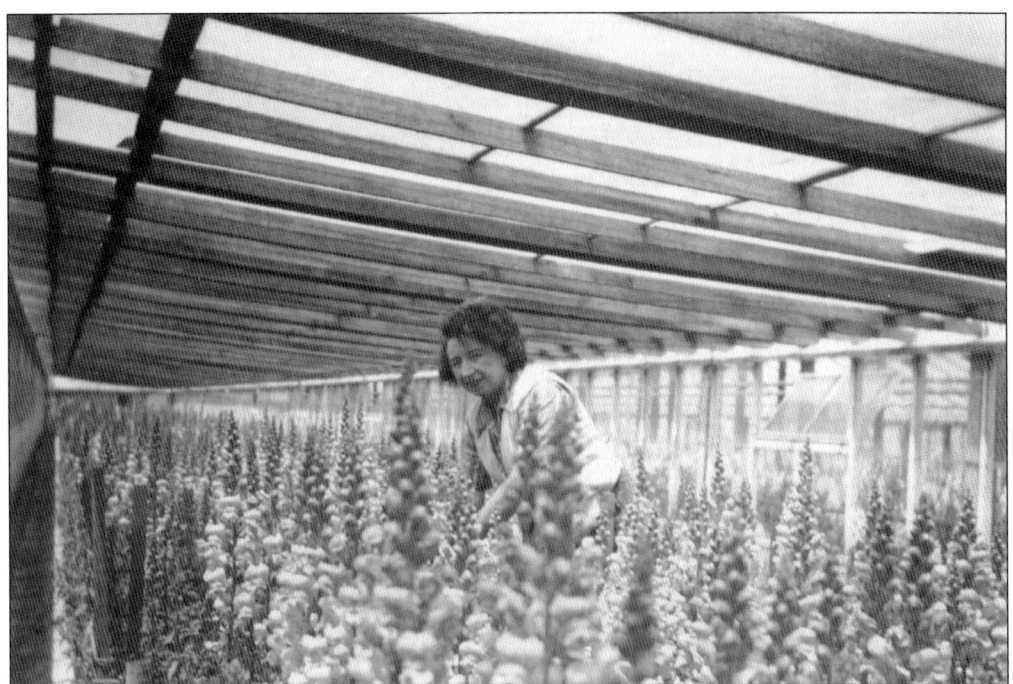

Here Josephine Winant picks snapdragons in the Winant Nursery. (Courtesy of Claire Winant O'Sullivan.)

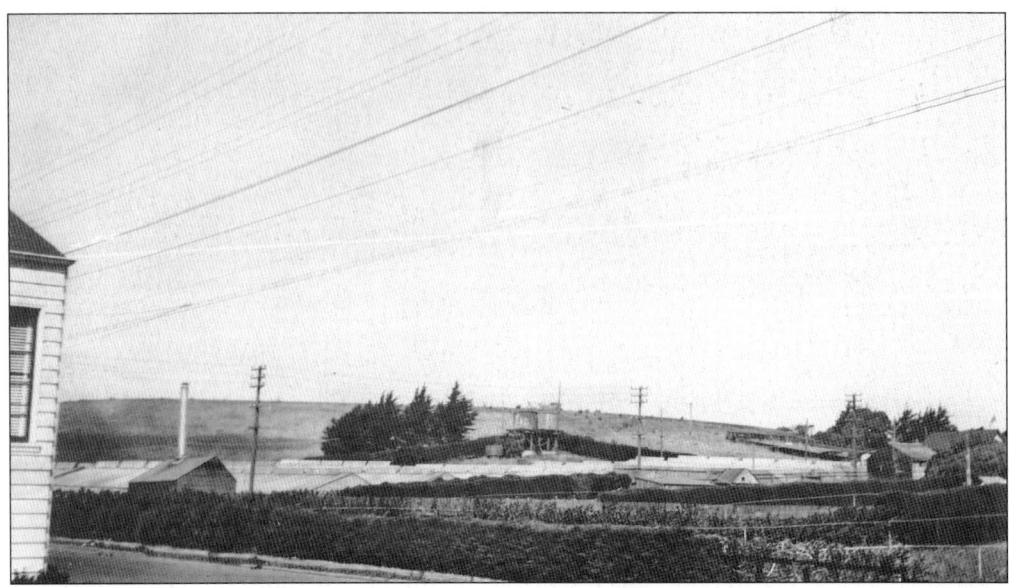

This 1940 photograph of the University Mound Nursery looks towards Woolsey Street. (Courtesy of Gerald Garibaldi.)

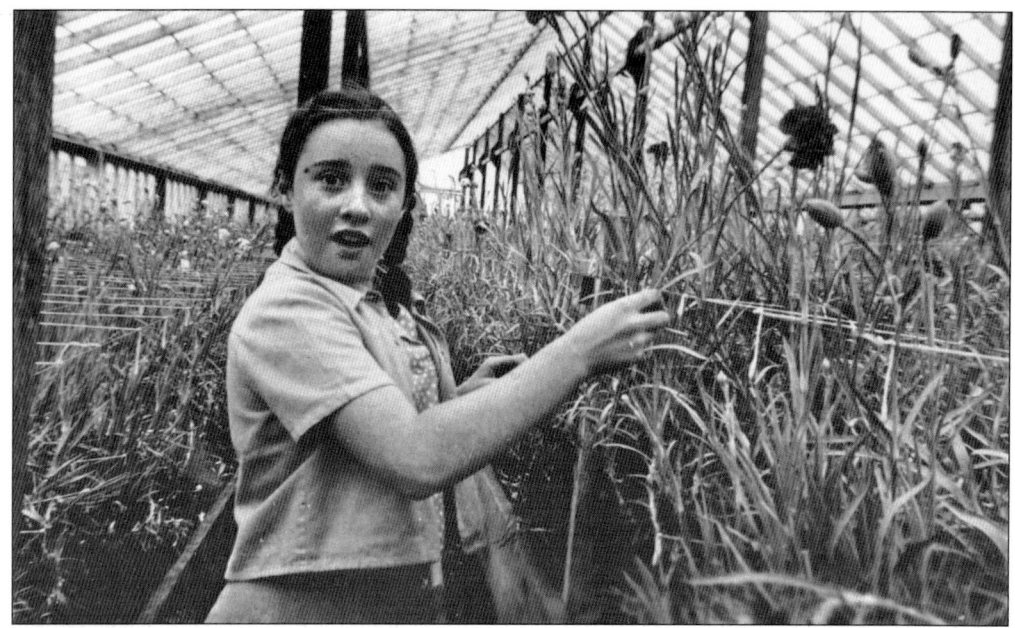
Claire Winant poses with carnations in the Winant Nursery around 1941. (Courtesy of Claire Winant O'Sullivan.)

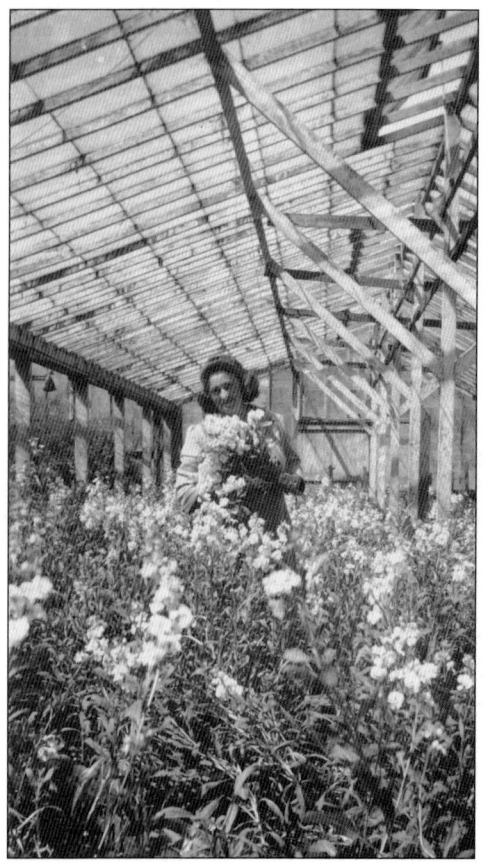
Blanche Gemignani is pictured inside the Gemignani Nursery around 1941. (Courtesy of the Gemignani family.)

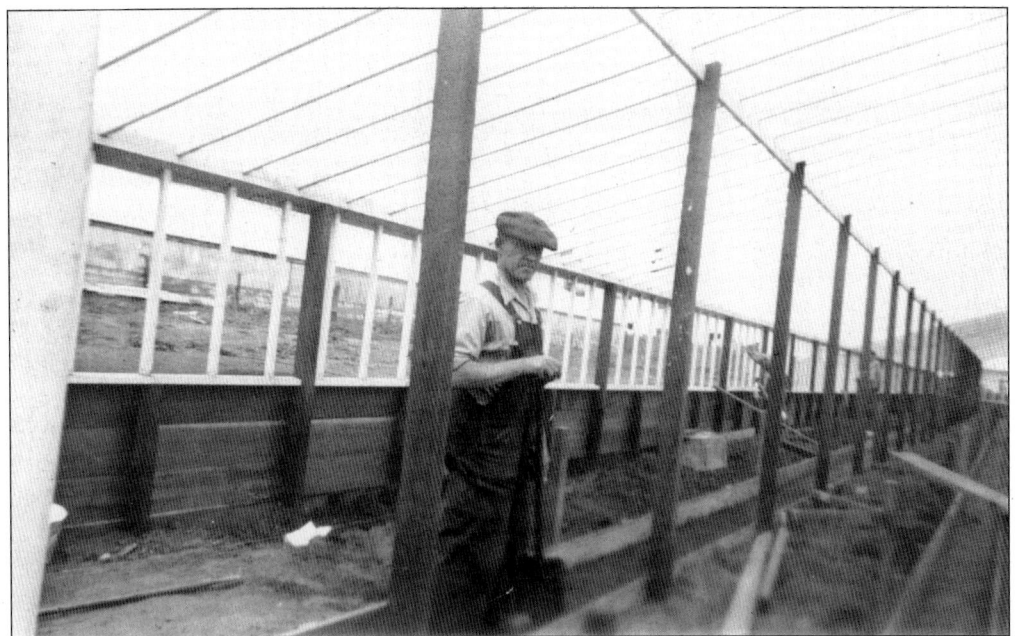
In this 1942 photograph, Joseph Winant builds a greenhouse. The Winant Nursery, located on Cambridge Street between Felton and Silliman Streets, was founded by Leon Winant. (Courtesy of Claire Winant O'Sullivan.)

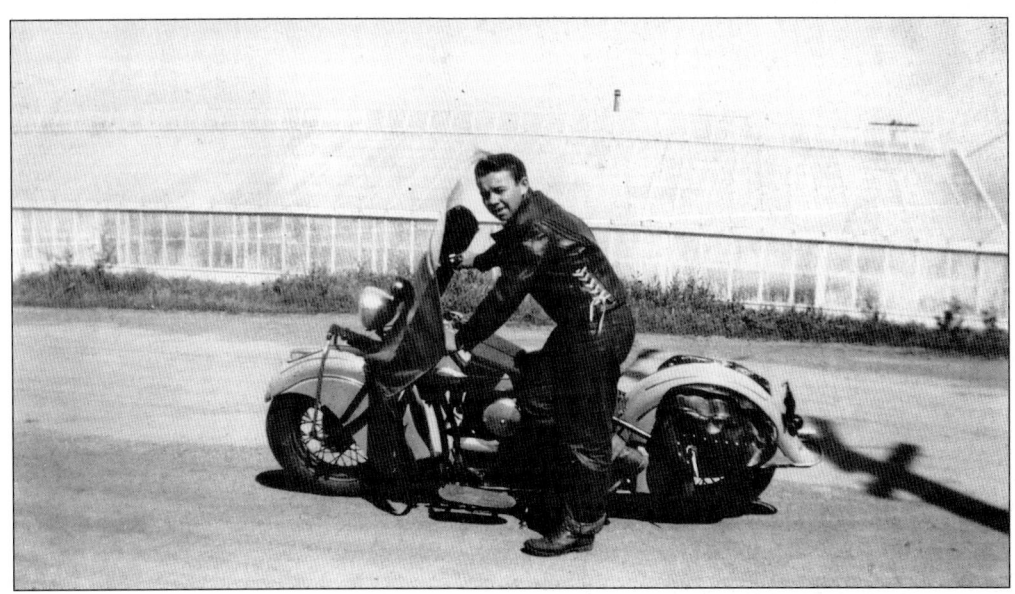
Leon "Joe" Winant poses on his 1941 Indian motorcycle in front of the Winant Nursery at Cambridge and Felton Streets around 1944. (Courtesy of Claire Winant O'Sullivan.)

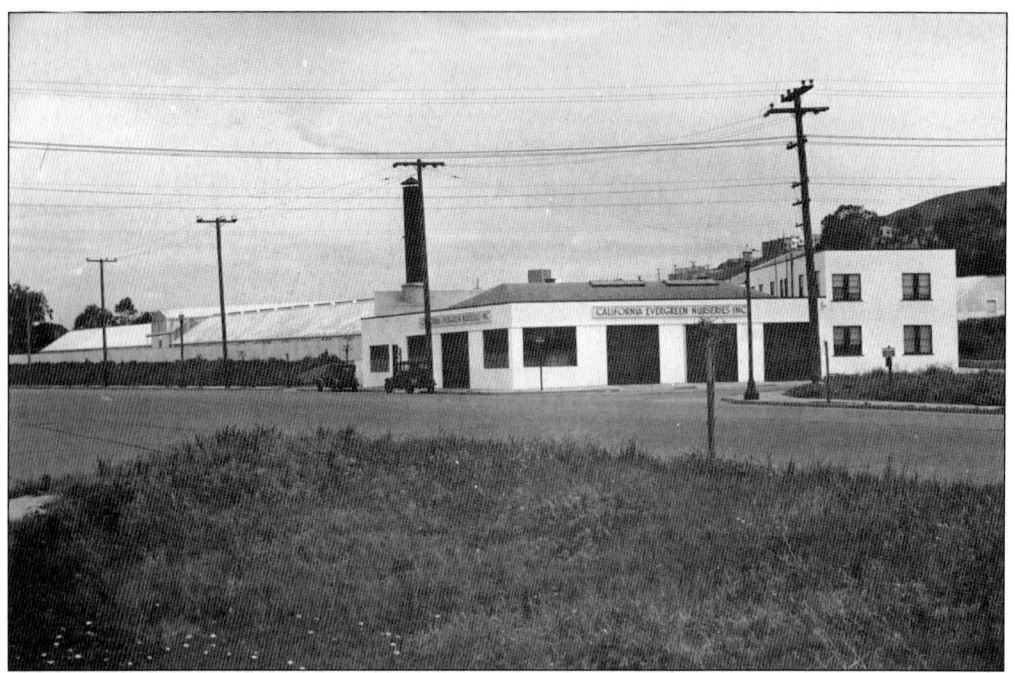

In the 1940s, the California Evergreen Nursery moved from its location in the Portola to Alemany Boulevard. (Courtesy of Albert Rolleri.)

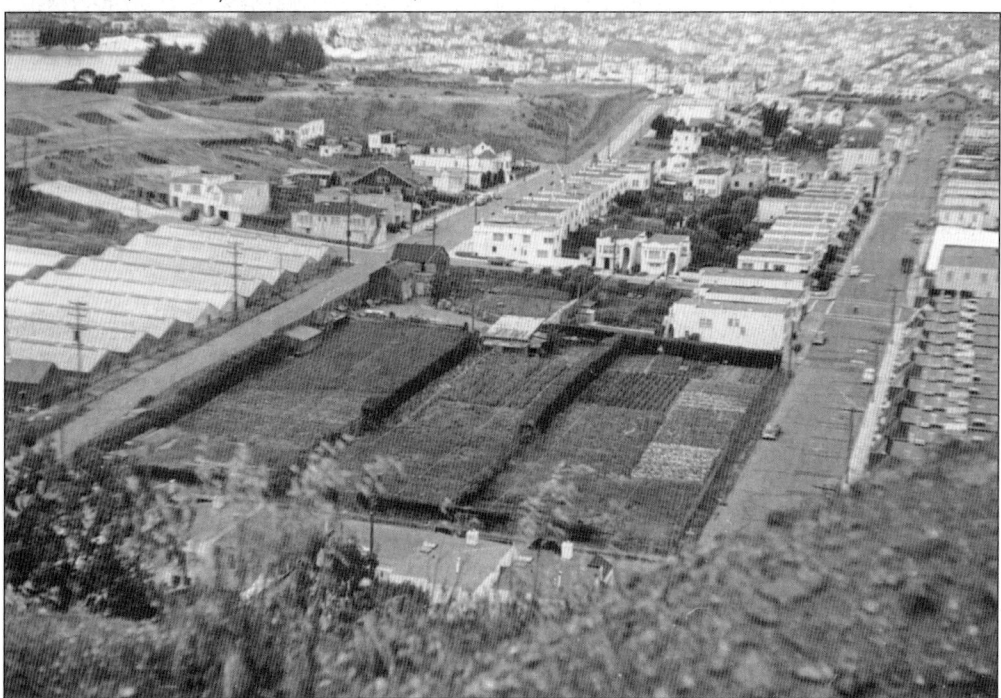

This photograph shows Dwight Street overlooking Hamilton and Holyoke Streets in 1952. The University Mound Nursery can be seen to the left, and a glimpse of the University Mound Reservoir, in its uncovered state, can be seen in the upper left corner. Assorted flowers were grown in the fields. (Courtesy of Gerald Garibaldi.)

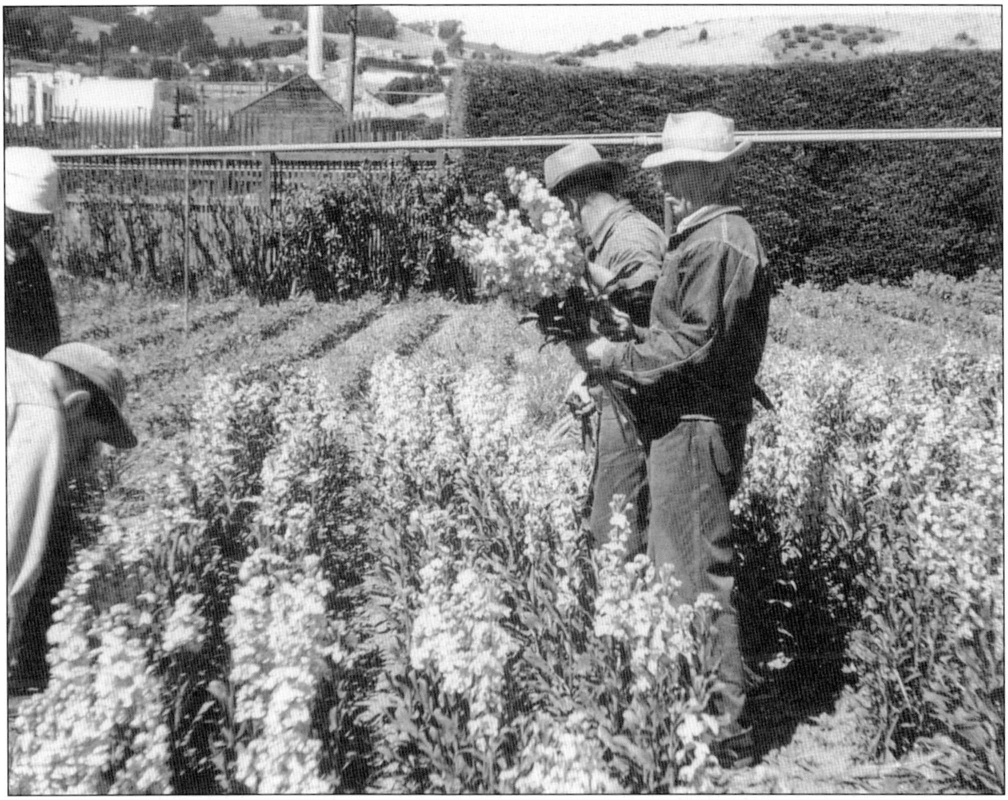

This view of the University Mound Nursery field of stock flowers on Holyoke Street looks west towards Hamilton Street. In 1955, the self-employed nurserymen began signing up for the Social Security program. This meant that they would now have to pay three-percent tax on their earnings, but they would also be eligible to receive benefits when they reached retirement age. Pictured in this 1952 photograph are, from left to right, Antonio Garibaldi, Andrew Garibaldi, Ernesto Garibaldi, and Frank Ferrando. (Courtesy of Gerald Garibaldi.)

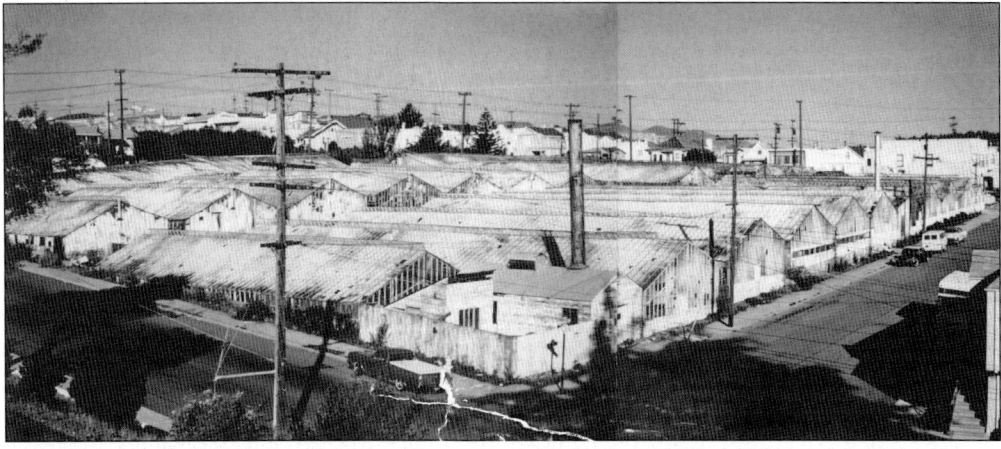

This photograph shows the Gregoire Nursery, established in 1897, at Felton and Colby Streets where carnations were grown. (Courtesy of the Gregoire family.)

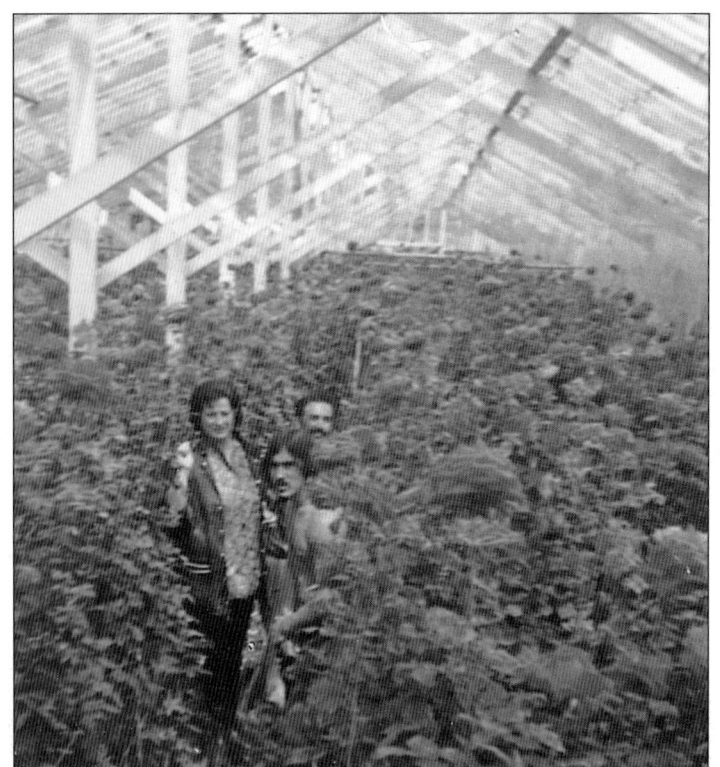

Located at Wayland and Cambridge Streets, the Restani Nursery, established in 1949 by Albert Joseph Restani, grew roses, while the Fatima Nursery, also located at Wayland and Cambridge Streets and run by the Restani family, grew carnations. Albert Joseph Restani named the Fatima Nursery, established in 1959, in honor of Our Lady of Fatima. He often donated flowers to his parish church for holy days. In this c. 1968 photograph of the Restani Nursery are, from left to right, Ann Restani, Jerry Restani, and Jube Esparza (the nursery's foreman). (Courtesy of the Restani family.)

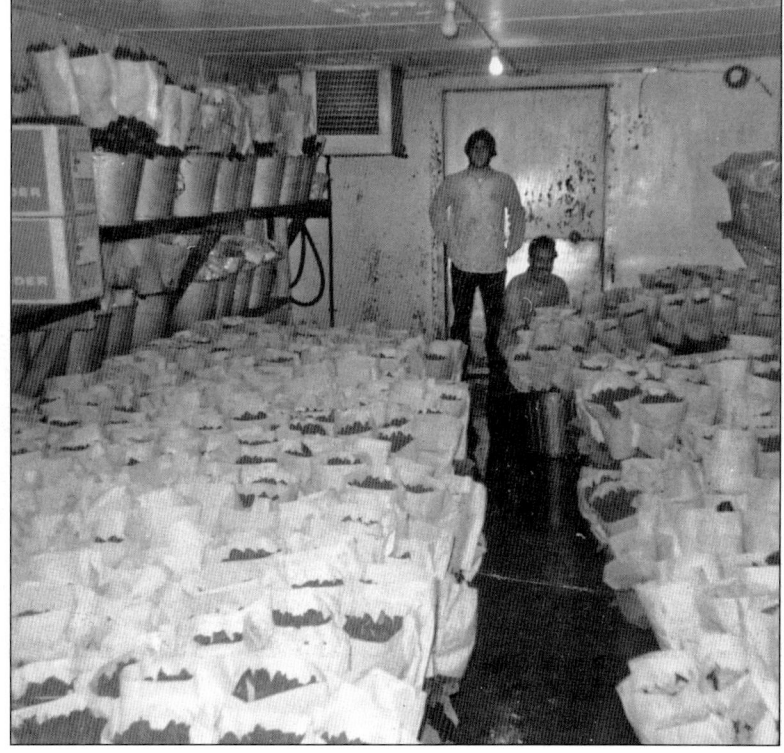

In this April 1971 photograph, the roses of the Restani Nursery that have been graded and bunched are sent to one of two refrigeration units before they go to market. Pictured are, from left to right, Tom Restani and Jube Esparza. (Courtesy of the Restani family.)

This c. 1968 photograph depicts the installation of a second boiler in the Restani Nursery at Wayland and Cambridge Streets. The boilers were used to keep the roses warm in the winter. The man at bottom center in front of the door is Mark Restani. (Courtesy of the Restani family.)

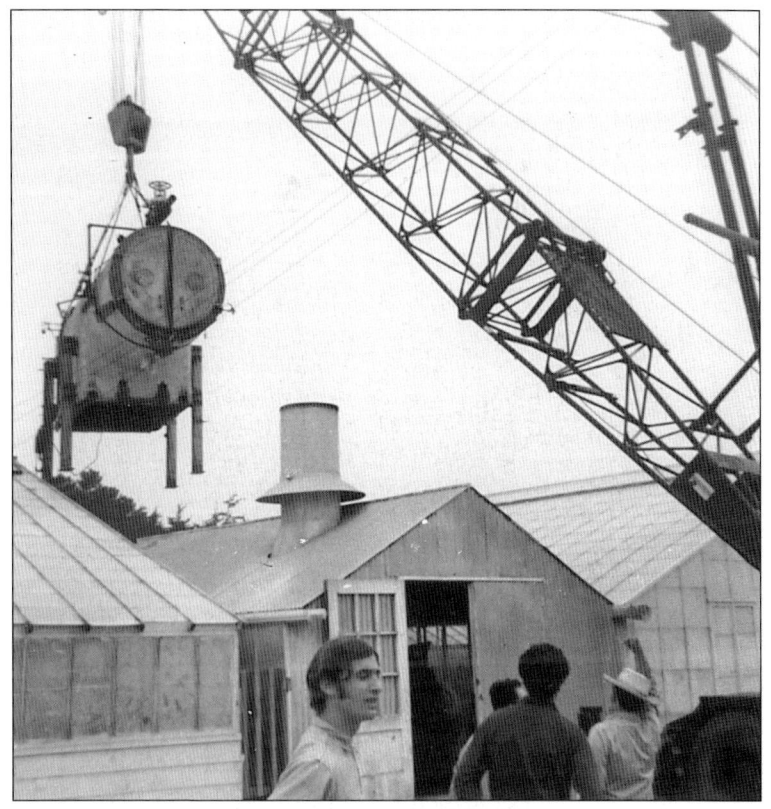

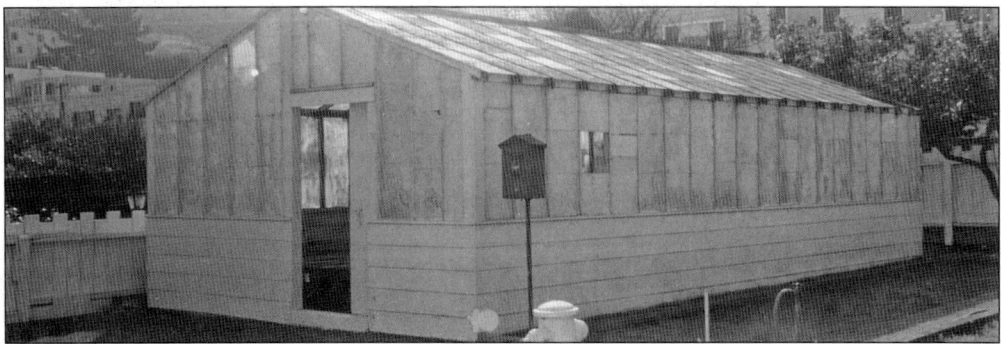

This private greenhouse in a Holyoke Street backyard was used to grow lemon trees. The greenhouse was taken down in 2003 after rotting timbers made it unsafe to occupy. (Courtesy of Mary Lou Garibaldi.)

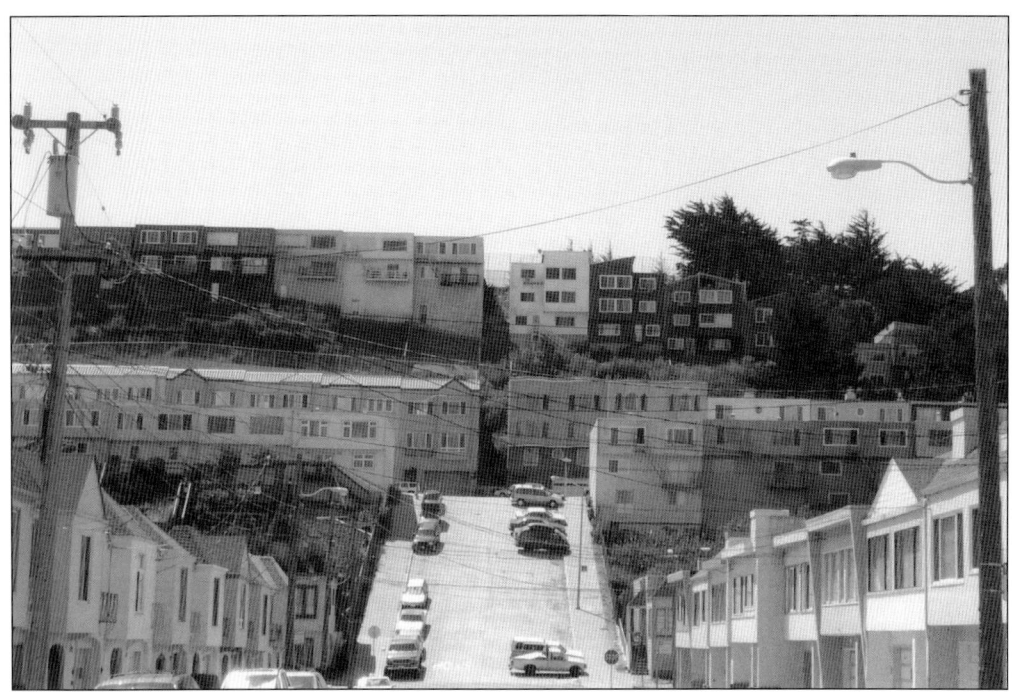
This view of Holyoke Street looks south towards Woolsey Street in 2006. This is the same view as seen on the bottom of page 15, which is from the 1930s. (Courtesy of David R. Mehrwein.)

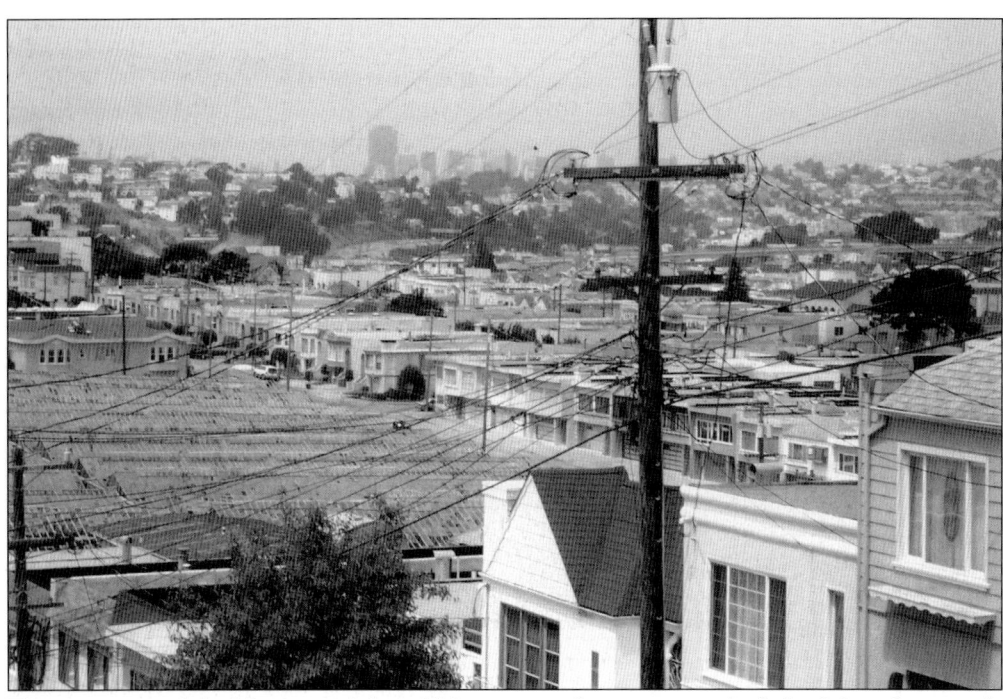
The remnants of the University Mound Nursery can been seen to the left of this photograph taken in July 2006 from the top of Bowdoin and Dwight Streets. Housing has replaced all of the nurseries. (Courtesy of David R. Mehrwein.)

Two
CHURCHES AND SCHOOLS

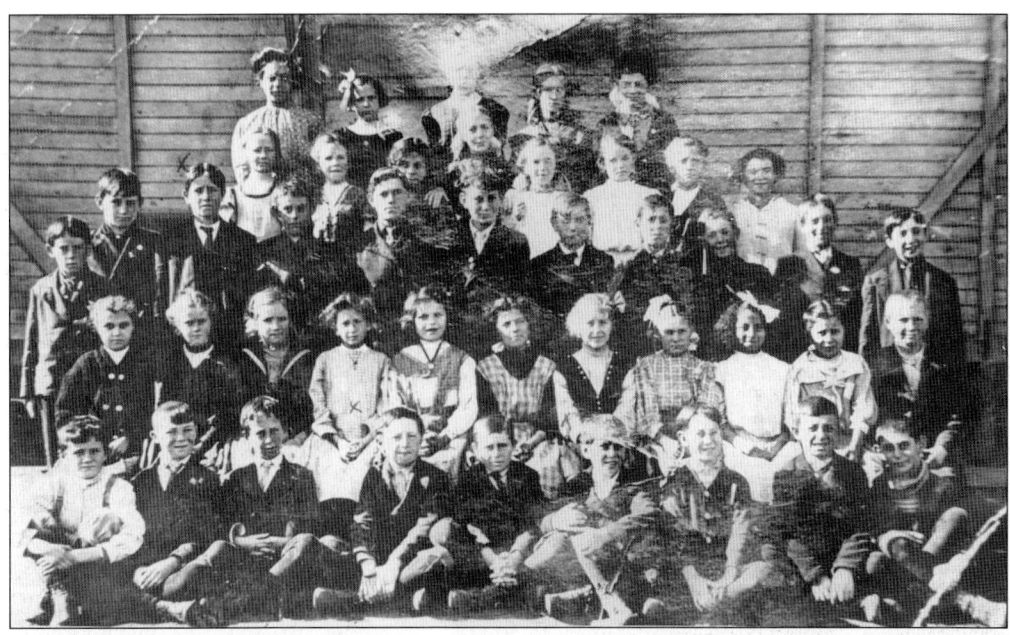

The South End School is depicted here in an undated class photograph. The school was a one-story frame building containing two classrooms and was located at Somerset and Burrows Streets. It opened on July 9, 1877, with an enrollment of 81 students, and Miss R. B. Birdsall was the principal. The South End School closed in 1910 with the opening of Portola Grammar School. (Courtesy of June Blut Conlon.)

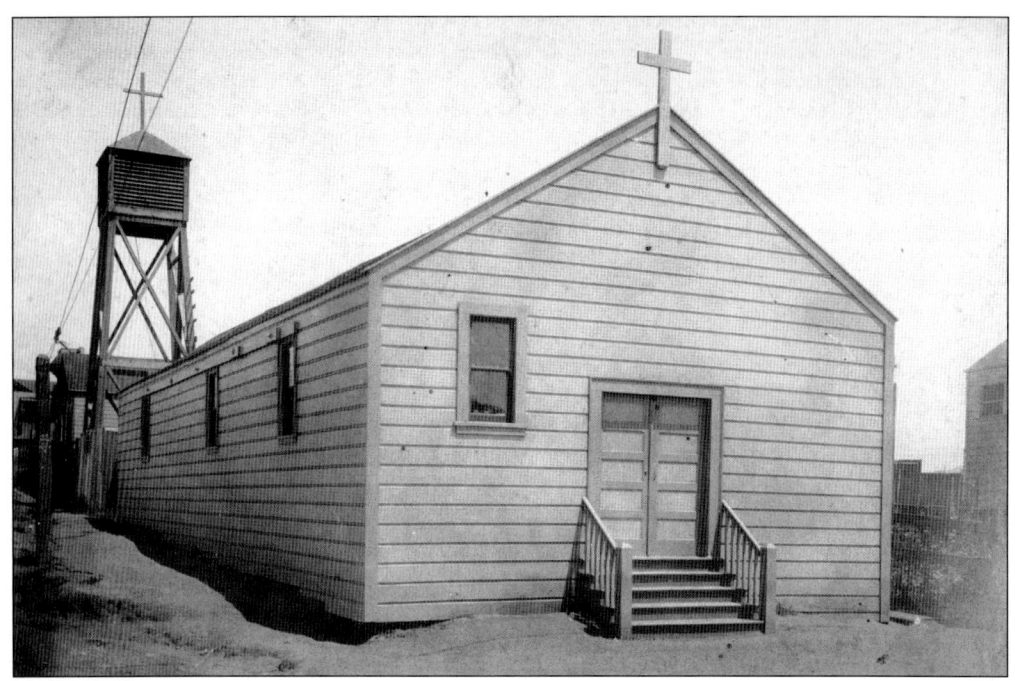

St. Elizabeth parish's first church began as a mission in 1907 at the corner of Berlin and Wayland Streets. Built as a temporary place of worship, it cost $450 to construct and could seat 200. Between 1907 and 1912, it was enlarged twice. During World War I, Berlin Street was renamed Brussels Street. (Courtesy of St. Elizabeth Church.)

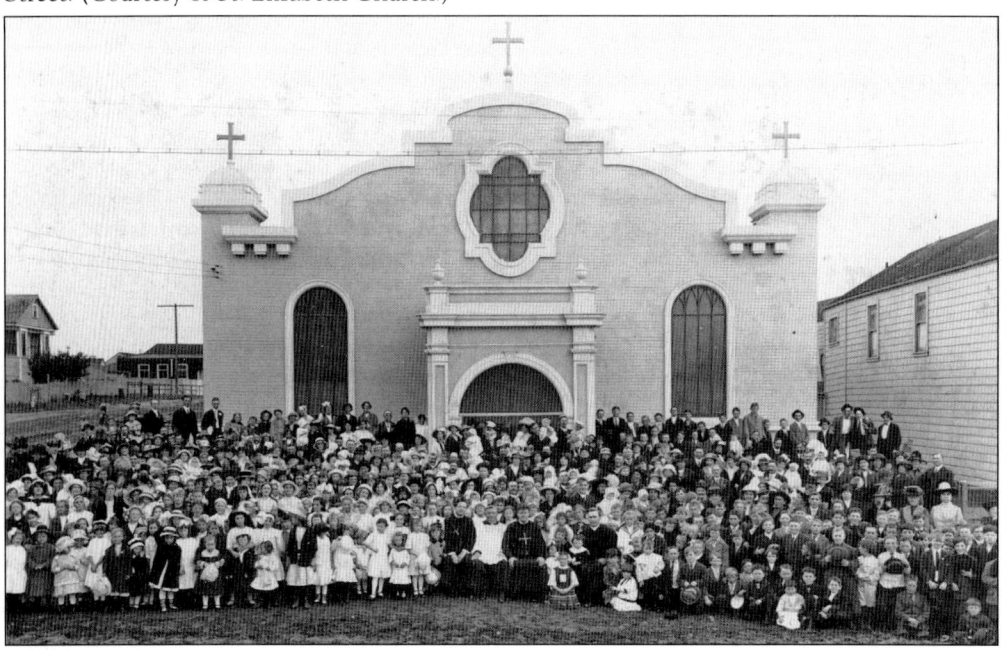

Newly built to hold 400 people and costing $6,000, St. Elizabeth Church at Brussels and Wayland Streets is pictured here with its parishioners on May 24, 1914. The church was officially dedicated on June 17, 1914, by Archbishop Edward Hanna. Rev. Thomas McNaboe, the pastor, and Rev. Richard Ryan, the assistant pastor, are seated here. (Courtesy of St. Elizabeth Church.)

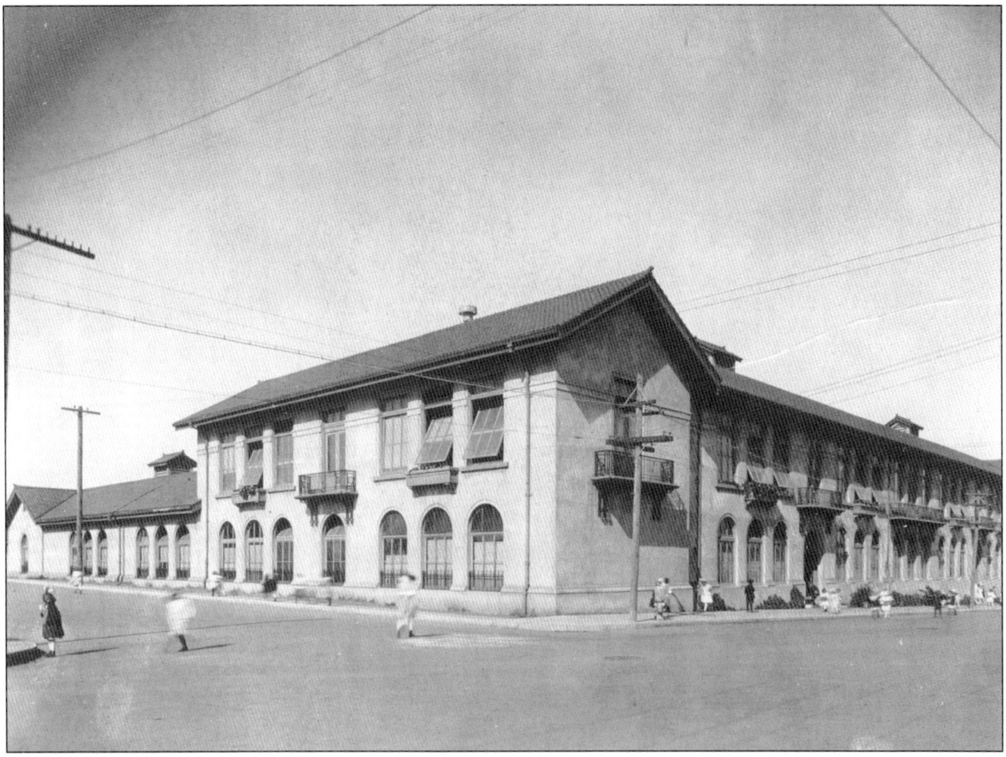

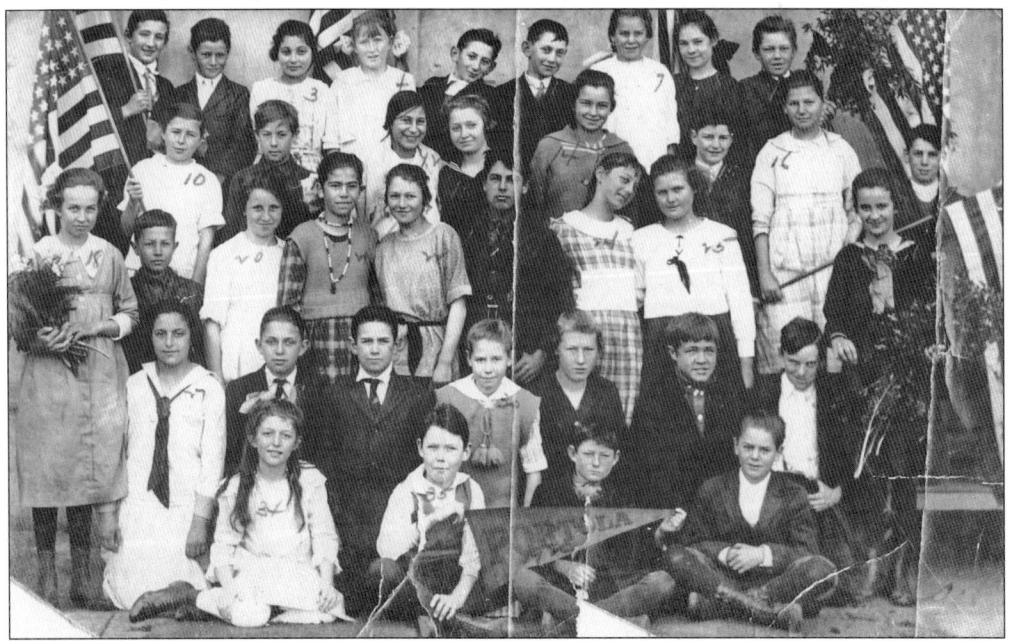

Located at Brussels and Bacon Streets, Portola Grammar School is pictured here in 1917. After Edward Robeson Taylor School was built, Portola became a junior high school, one of the first in the nation. (Courtesy of the San Francisco History Center, San Francisco Library.)

Before becoming a junior high school, Portola School was a grammar school. In this 1920 photograph, grade 6B poses for a class picture. (Courtesy of June Blut Conlon.)

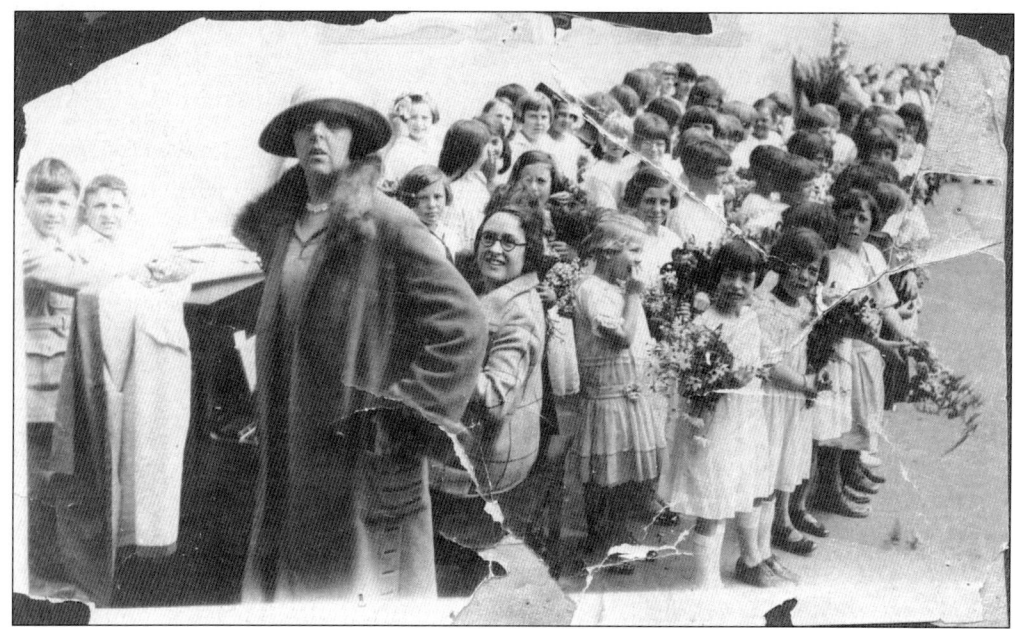
Edward Robeson Taylor School students are depicted at a graduation performance in 1921. From left to right are teachers Miss Tepping and Miss Downey (at the piano). (Courtesy of John Fenech.)

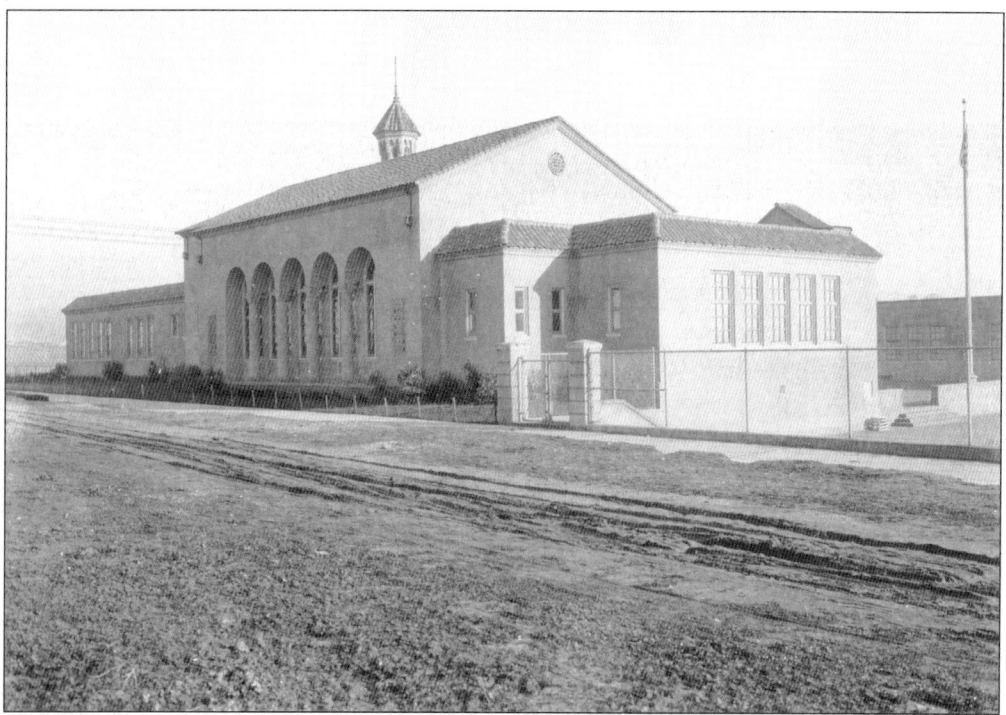
Edward Robeson Taylor School at 423 Burrows Street was photographed here on December 23, 1924. Referred to as E. R. Taylor by local residents, this public grammar school was where many Portola children were educated. The school is still in operation. (Courtesy of the San Francisco History Center, San Francisco Public Library.)

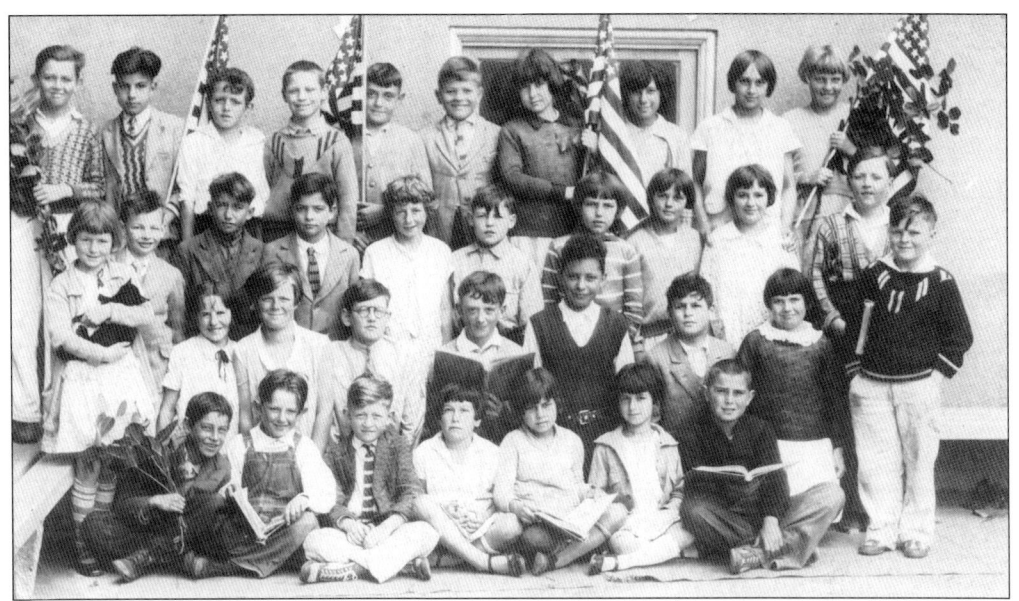
The class of 1929 at E. R. Taylor School pose for this picture. (Courtesy of Jim Grady.)

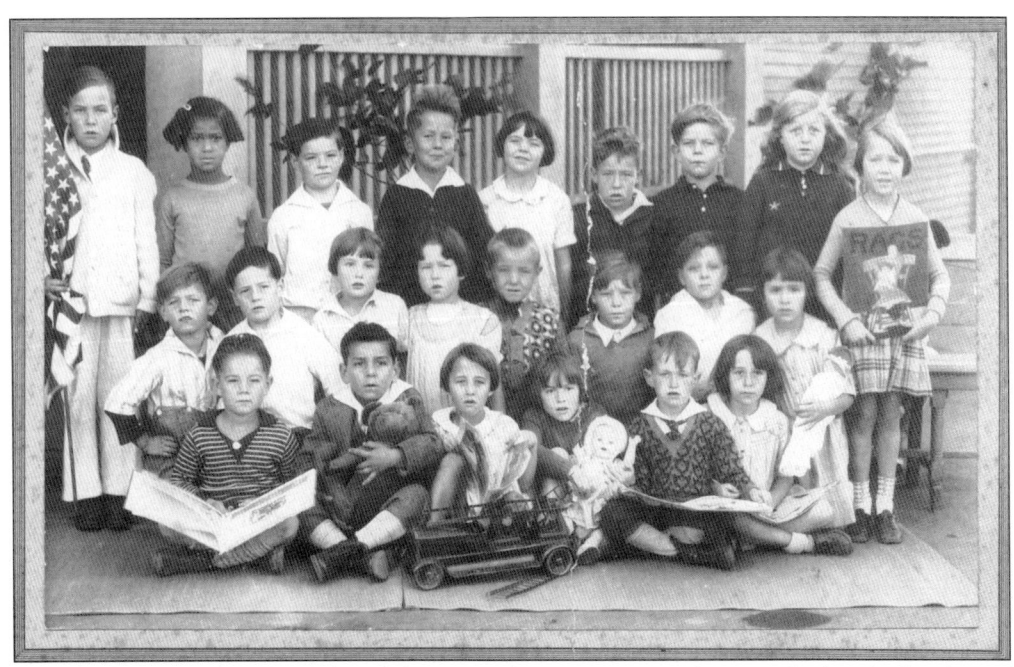
Hillcrest Elementary School, located at 810 Silver Avenue, is photographed with the class of 1930. (Courtesy of the Macchia family.)

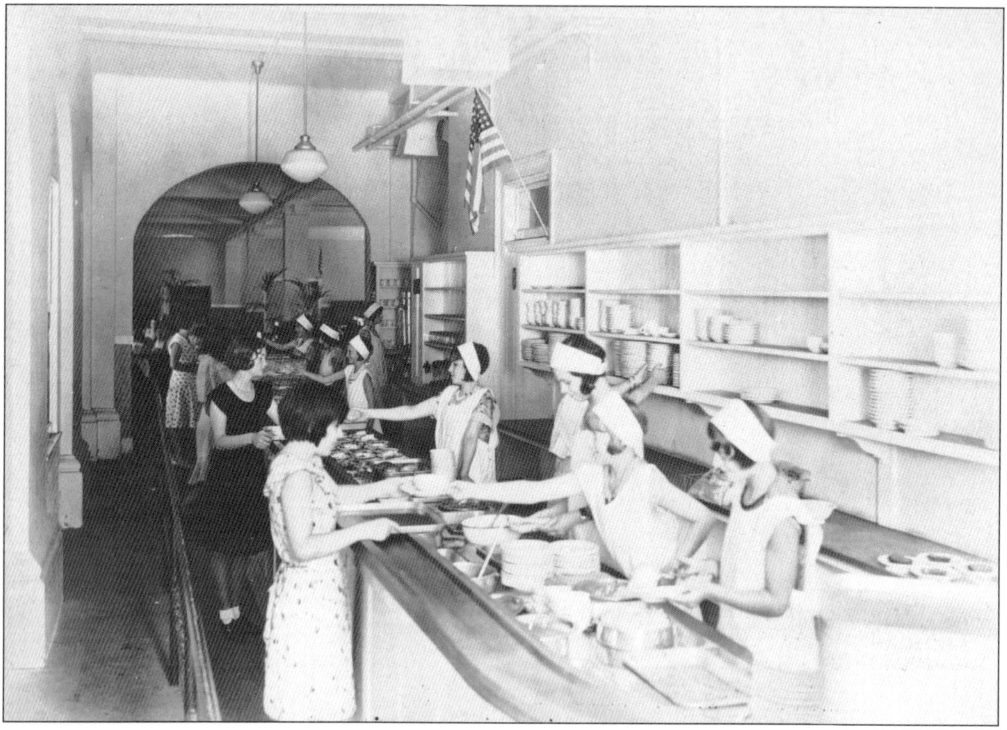

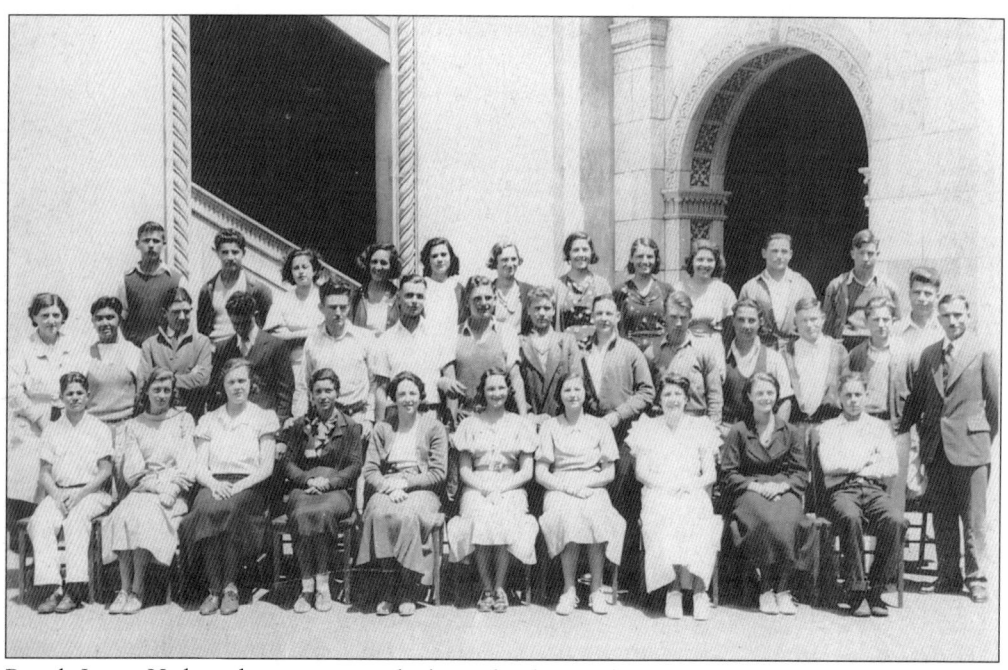

Portola Grammar School was the school that Portola residents attended before the establishment of E. R. Taylor. In this undated photograph, students at Portola Grammar School help in the cafeteria. (Courtesy of the Carraro family.)

Portola Junior High students pose outside their school around 1932. (Courtesy of Catherine Raugi.)

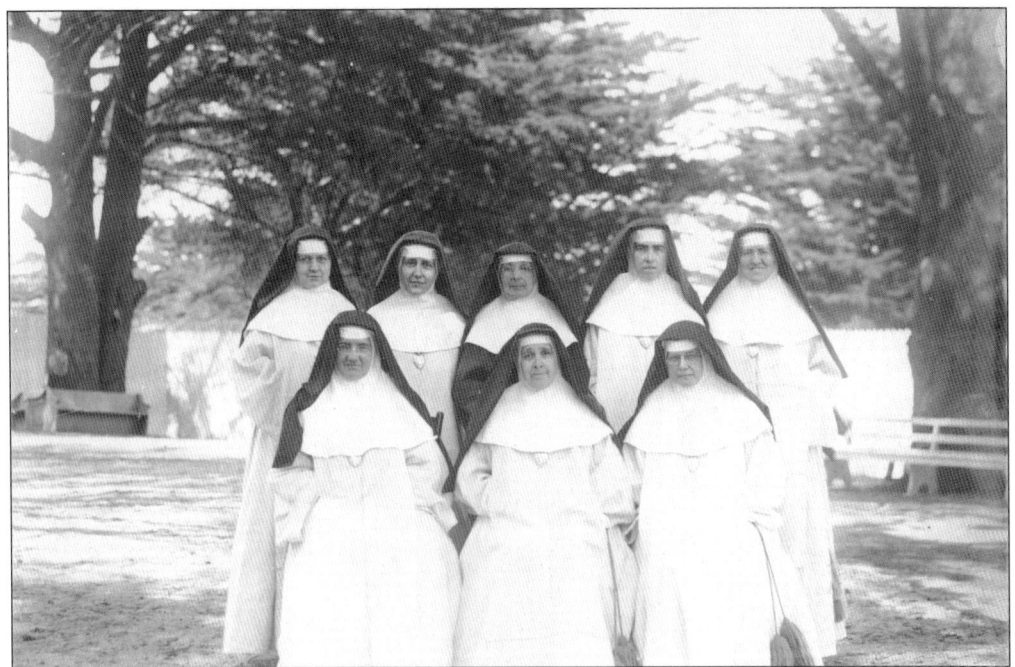

This photograph from 1932 shows the eight founders of the Convent of the Good Shephard. Pictured are Mother M. of the Annunciation (Superior), Sister Mary Martha Moore, Sister M. Divine Shephard, Sister Mary of Our Lady of Victory, Sister M. Passion Nally, Sister M. of St. Rene Dundon, Sister M. Germaine Egan, and Sister Marie Consolata. (Courtesy of the Sisters of the Good Shephard.)

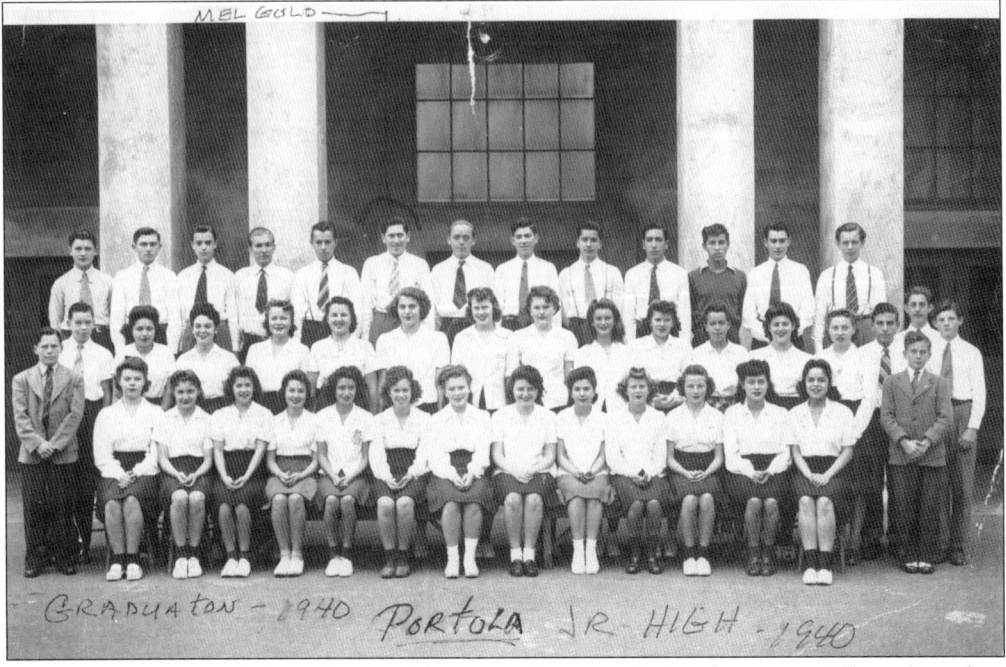

The Portola Junior High class of 1940 celebrates graduation with this class picture. The only student identified is Mel Gold, who is sixth from the left in the back row. (Courtesy of Mel Gold.)

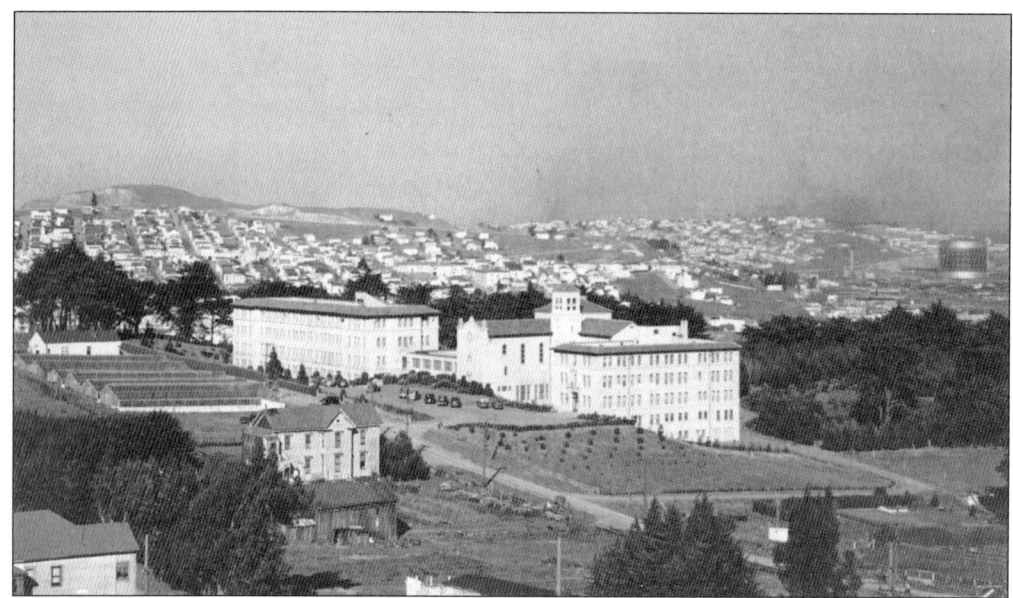

The Convent of the Good Shephard at 501 Cambridge Street, which was located on University Mound Hill, is seen in this 1942 photograph. The site was a portion of what had once been the University Mound College grounds, run by the Presbyterians in 1863. The upper half of the grounds were sold to the Sisters of the Good Shephard in 1931, and they maintained a home for pre-delinquent girls there. The Good Shephard Sisters have continued their mission in their current location at 1310 Bacon Street, ministering to adult women in need. The site on Cambridge Street is now the home to Cornerstone Academy. The Winant Nursery can be seen in the left corner of the photograph. (Courtesy of the Sisters of the Good Shepard.)

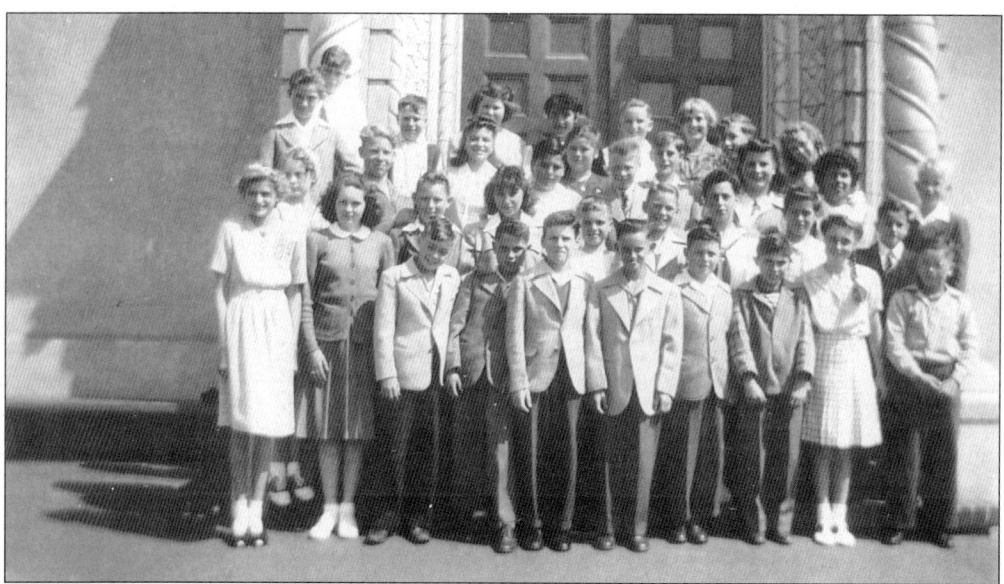

Sixth-grade teacher Miss Grimm, pictured in the back row sixth from the left, and her students pose for a photograph to commemorate their graduation day at E. R. Taylor School in June 1946. (Courtesy of Jane M. Landucci.)

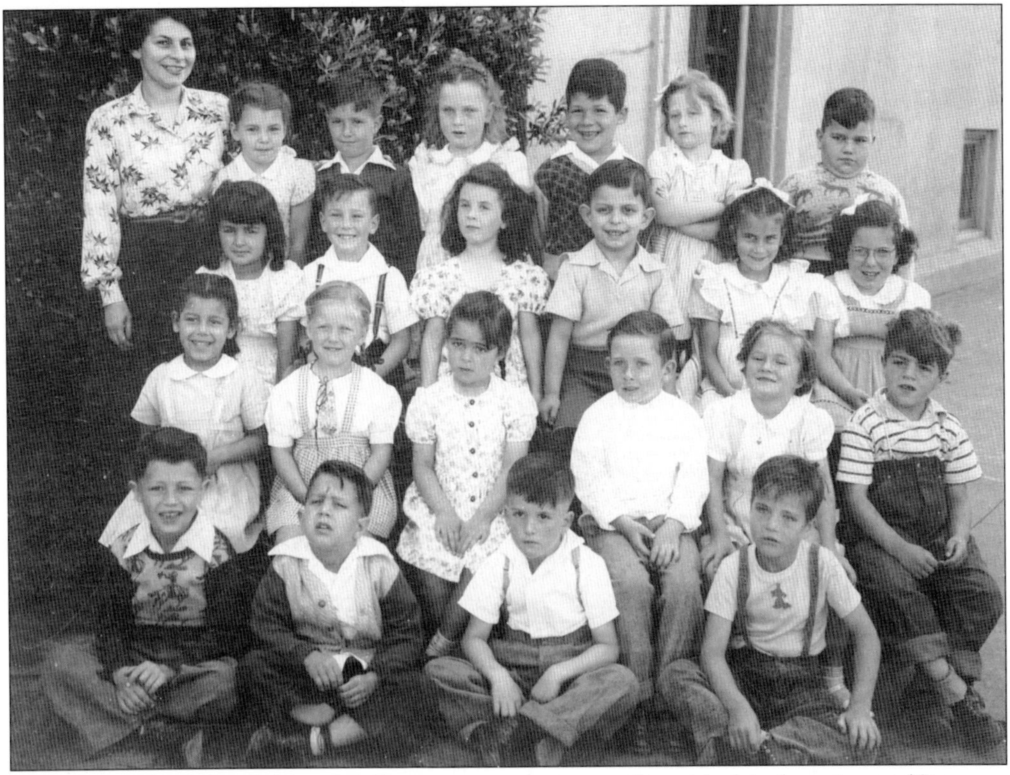

The E. R. Taylor School class of 1947 captures an important day with this class picture. (Courtesy of Patricia Semenero.)

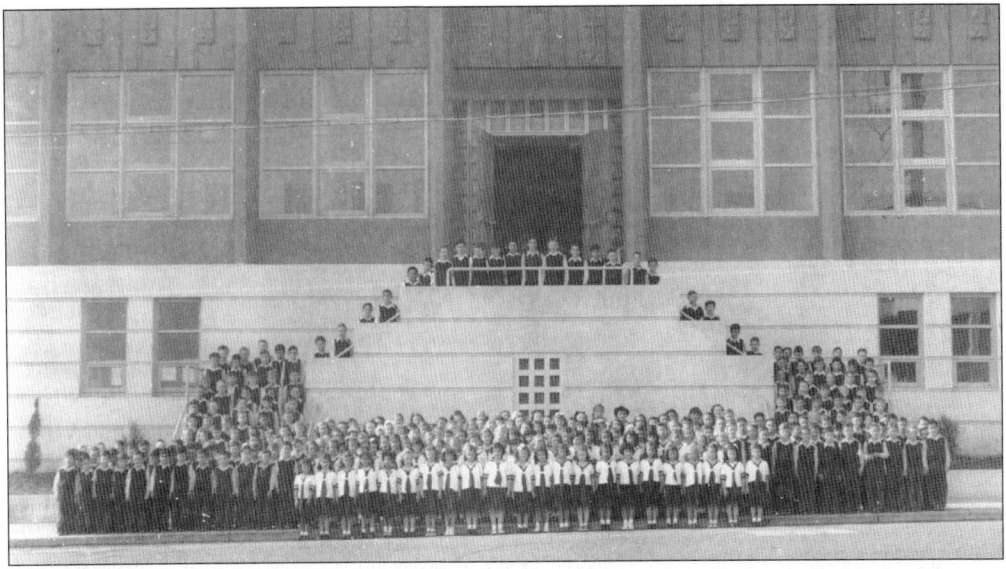

Located at 450 Somerset Street, St. Elizabeth School, with its first class of students in grades one through five, was photographed on November 27, 1949. Parishioners held fund-raising activities to help fund the building of the school, which cost between $400,000 and $500,000. The school was officially dedicated on December 11, 1949, by Archbishop John Mitty. (Courtesy of St. Elizabeth School.)

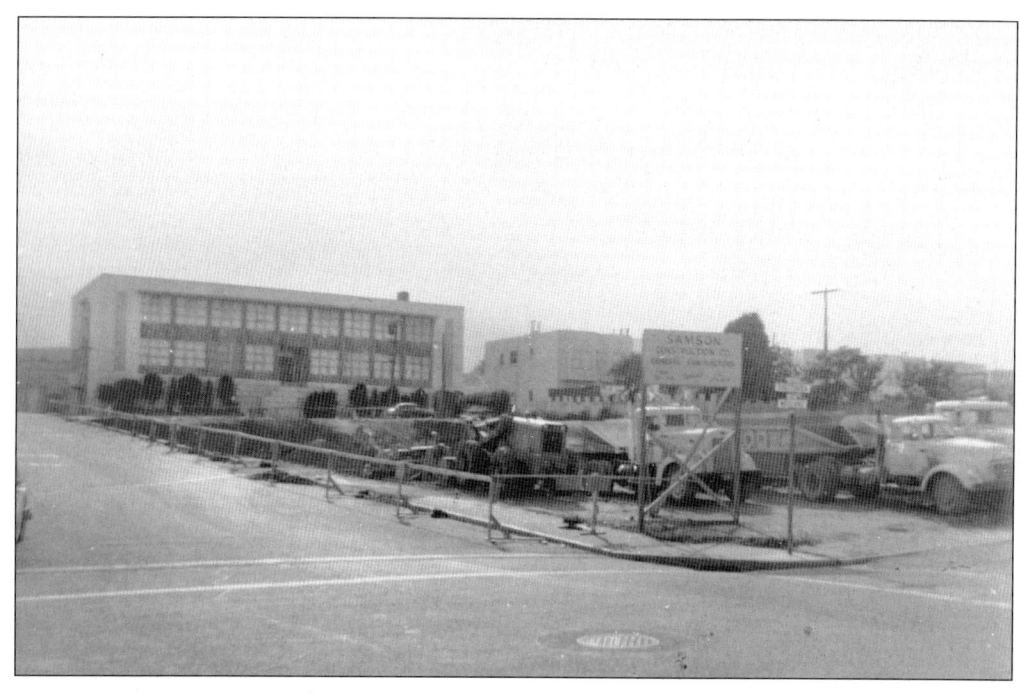

These photographs depict the building of St. Elizabeth Church at Somerset and Wayland Streets. The church was officially dedicated in August 1961 by Archbishop John Mitty. (Courtesy of St. Elizabeth Church.)

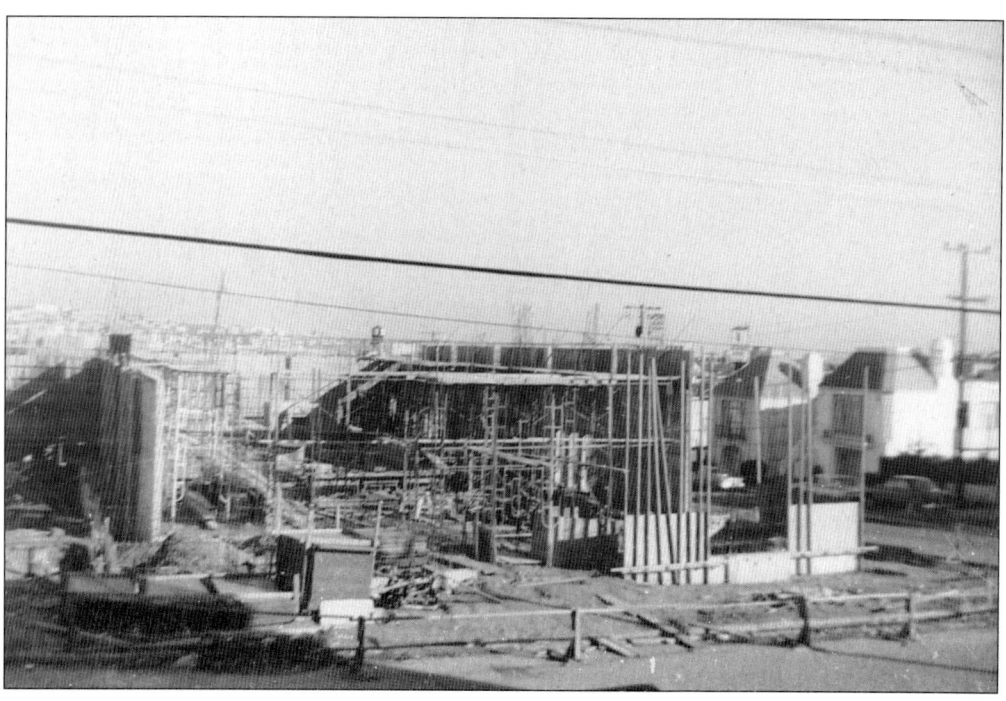

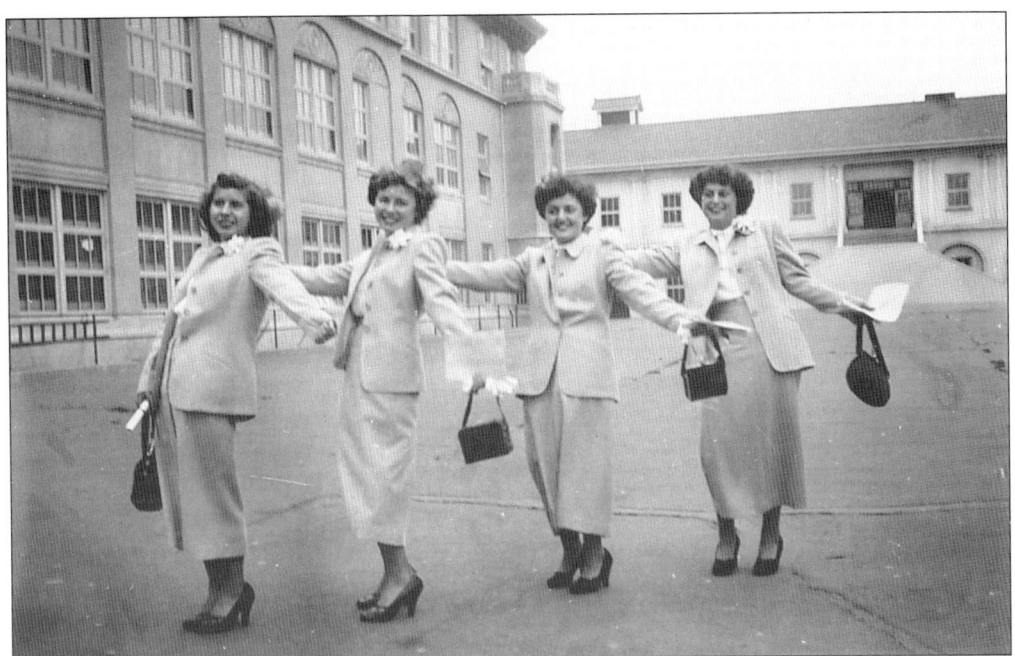

Friends Chris, Betty, Nancy, and Lucy celebrate graduation day at Portola Junior High School in 1950. (Courtesy of Patricia Semenero.)

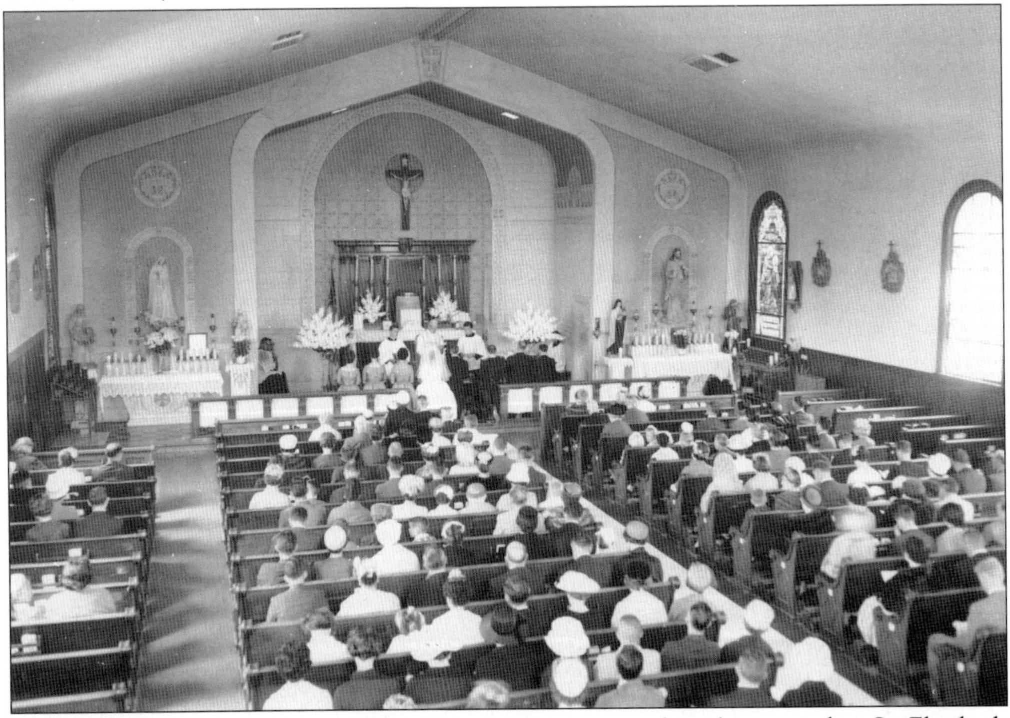

June Blut and Thomas "Tommy" Conlon were the last couple to be married in St. Elizabeth Church at Brussels and Wayland Streets on August 26, 1961, because the new church at Somerset and Wayland Streets was being used. The old church was demolished in 1972. (Courtesy of June Blut Conlon.)

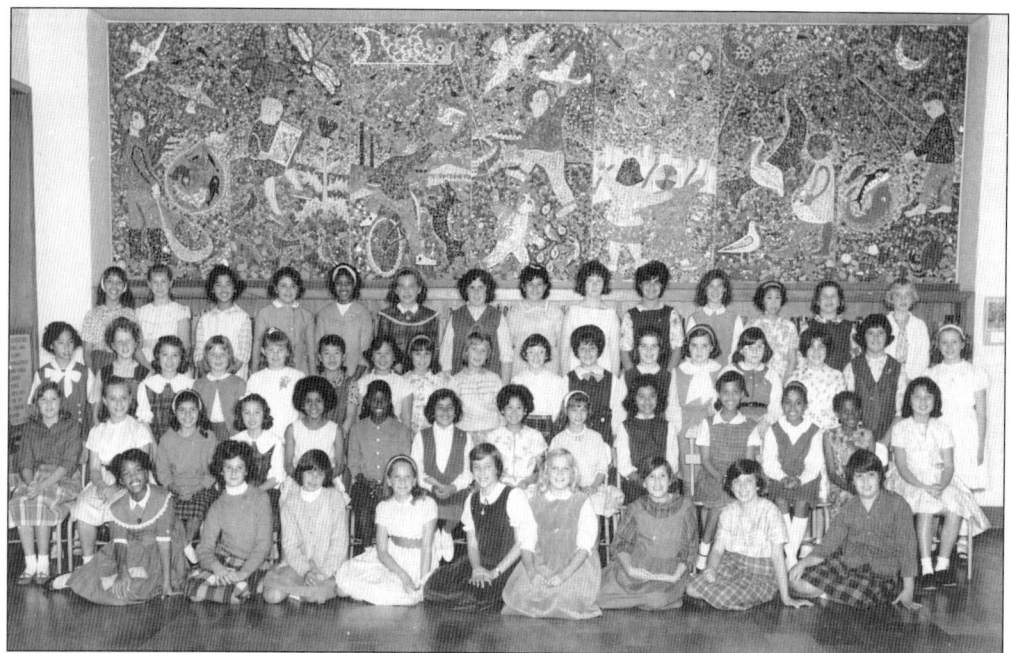

The Girls Service Club of Hillcrest School, located at 810 Silver Avenue, are pictured here in the library in October 1964. At this time, girls were not permitted to be on traffic patrol so they acted as hall monitors inside the school. Behind them is a mural by artist Ruth Asawa, who also sculpted *Andrea*, the mermaid fountain at Ghirardelli Square. (Courtesy of the Macchia family.)

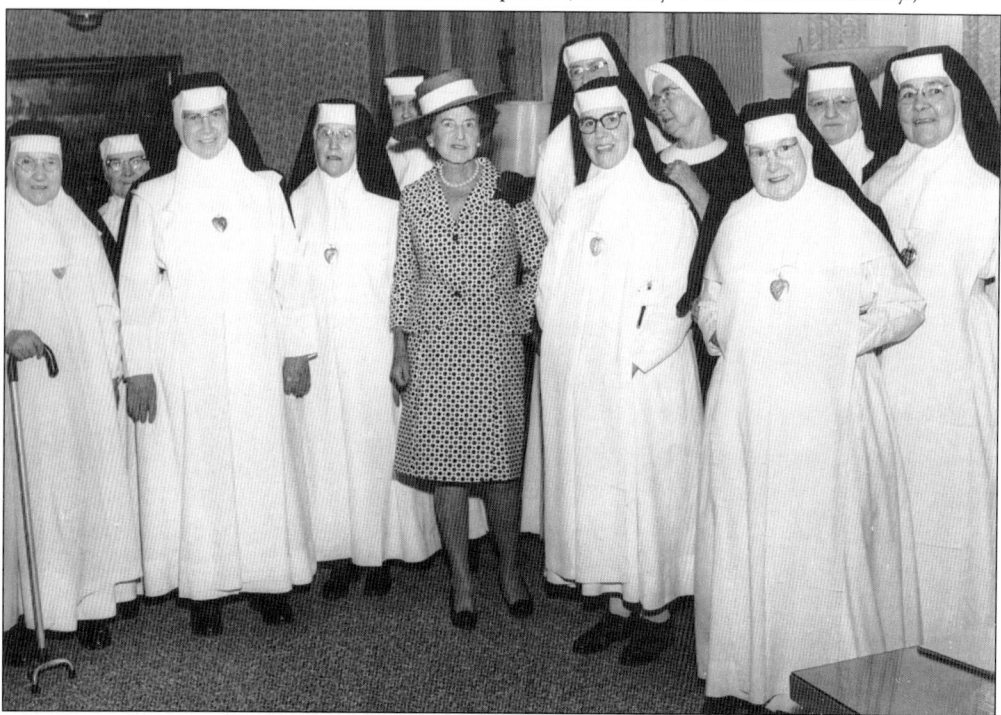

Rose Kennedy visits the Convent of the Good Shephard in 1968. She was a personal friend of one of the founders, Sister M. Passion Nally. (Courtesy of the Sisters of the Good Shephard.)

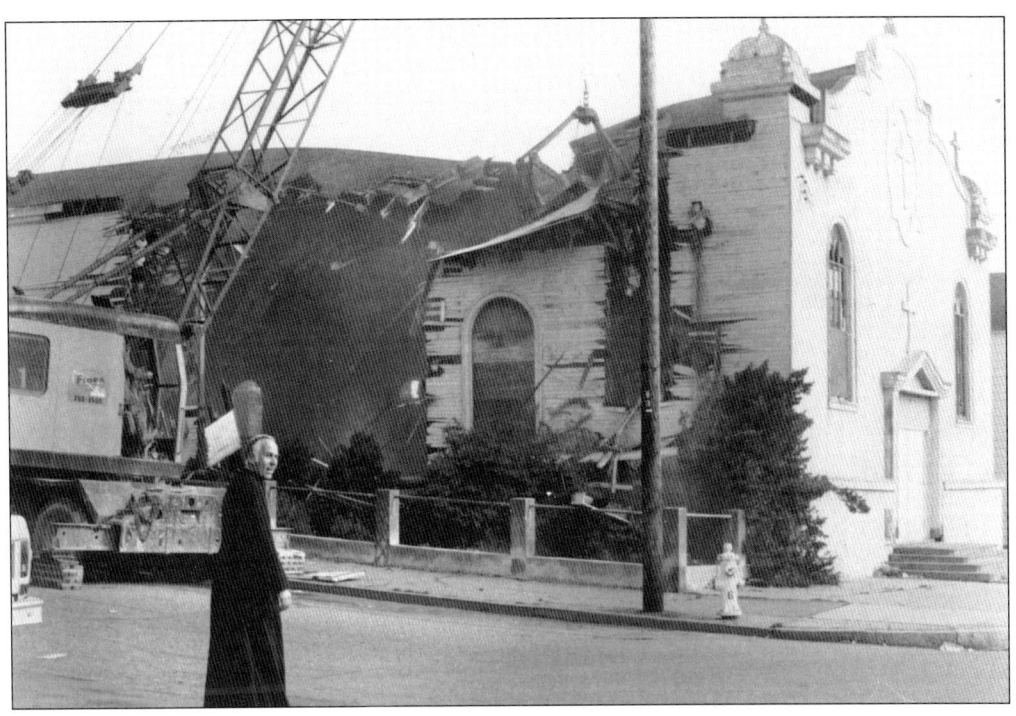

Pastor Howard Rasmussen oversees the demolition of St. Elizabeth's Church at Brussels and Wayland Streets, which was completed on February 14, 1972. (Courtesy of St. Elizabeth Church.)

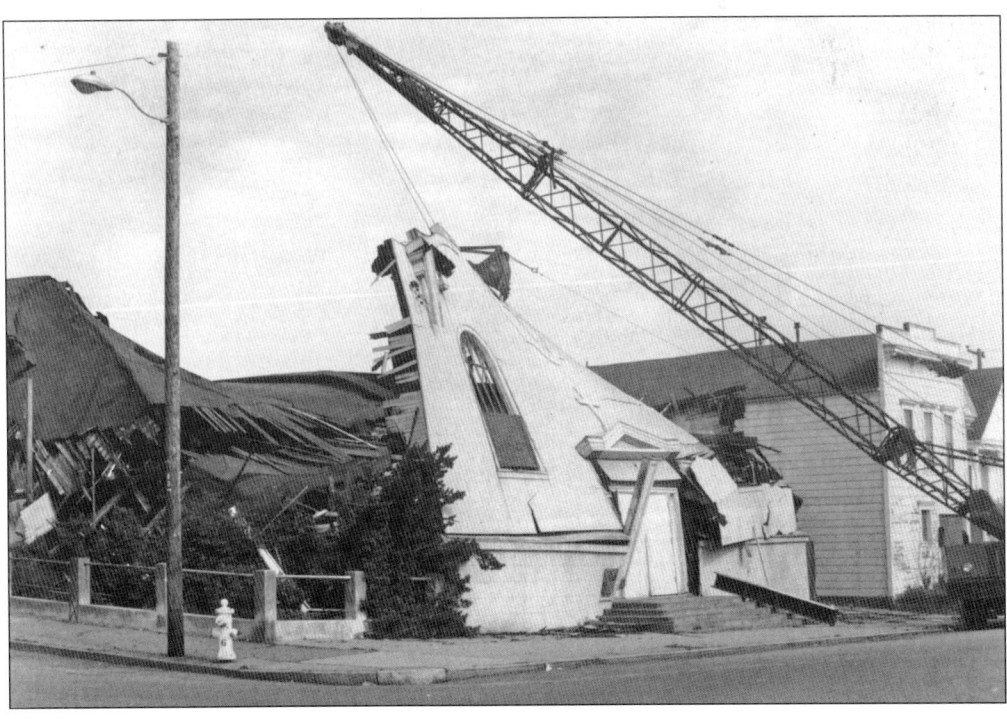

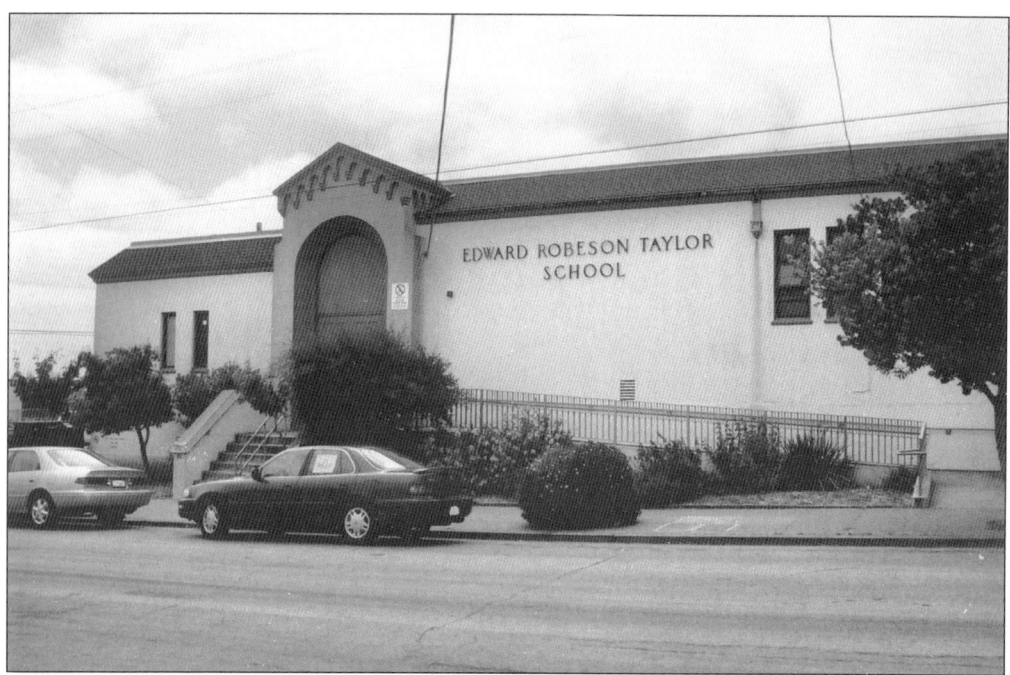

Portola residents refer to Edward Robeson Taylor School as E. R. Taylor. The school, located at 423 Burrows Street, is pictured here in 2006. (Courtesy of David R. Mehrwein.)

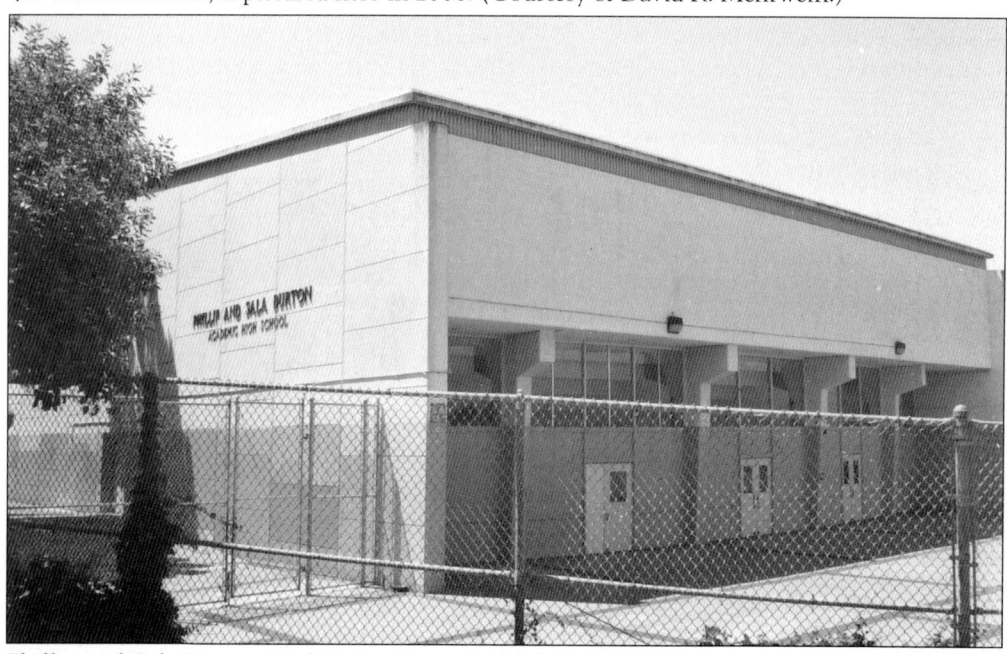

Phillip and Sala Burton High School was established in 1984 because of a consent of decree between the city of San Francisco and the National Association for the Advancement of Colored People (NAACP). Originally situated in the Silver Terrace neighborhood, it was relocated to the former site of Woodrow Wilson High School at 400 Mansell Street in 1996. The school was named for Phillip Burton, a democratic member of the California Assembly from 1957 to 1964 and a U.S. Representative of California from 1964 to 1983. (Courtesy of David R. Mehrwein.)

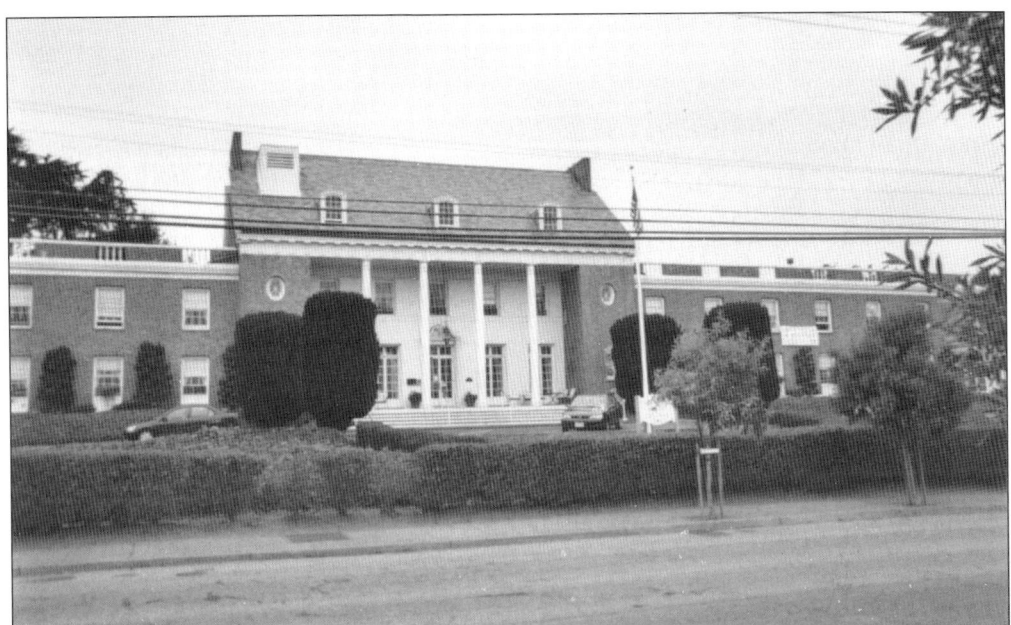

The University Mound Ladies Home at 350 University Street was founded by California pioneer and philanthropist, James Lick. Before his death, Lick appointed trustees to distribute his estate. After his death in 1876, the trust provided $100,000 to establish a home for women over the age of 60. The home opened in 1884, occupying a two-story frame building that once housed Presbyterian University. However, the old-frame building was eventually considered unsafe, and the building seen in this current photograph was constructed in 1932. (Courtesy of author.)

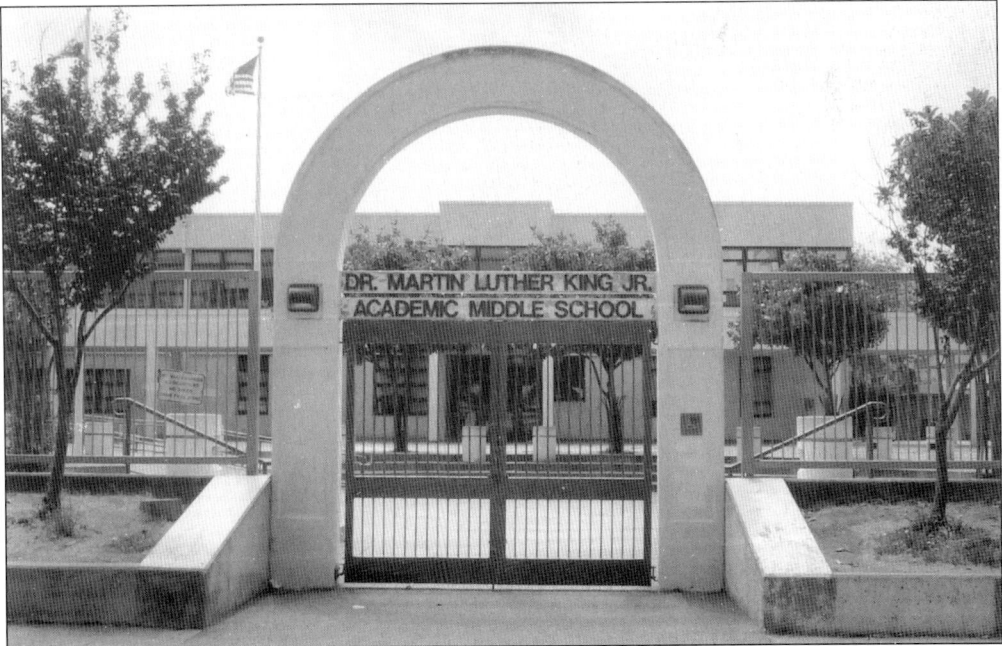

Established in 1983, Martin Luther King Jr. Middle School occupies the former site of Portola Junior High School at 350 Girard Street. The only sections of Portola Junior High that remain are the auditorium and the gymnasium. (Courtesy of David R. Mehrwein.)

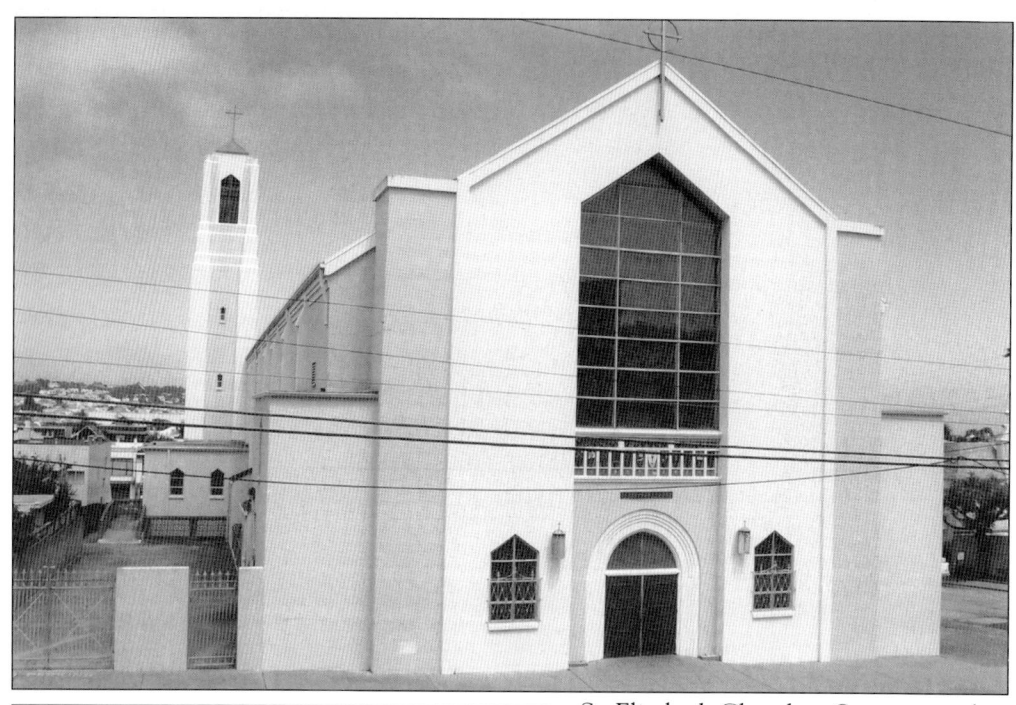

St. Elizabeth Church at Somerset and Wayland Streets is pictured here in July 2006. (Courtesy of David R. Mehrwein.)

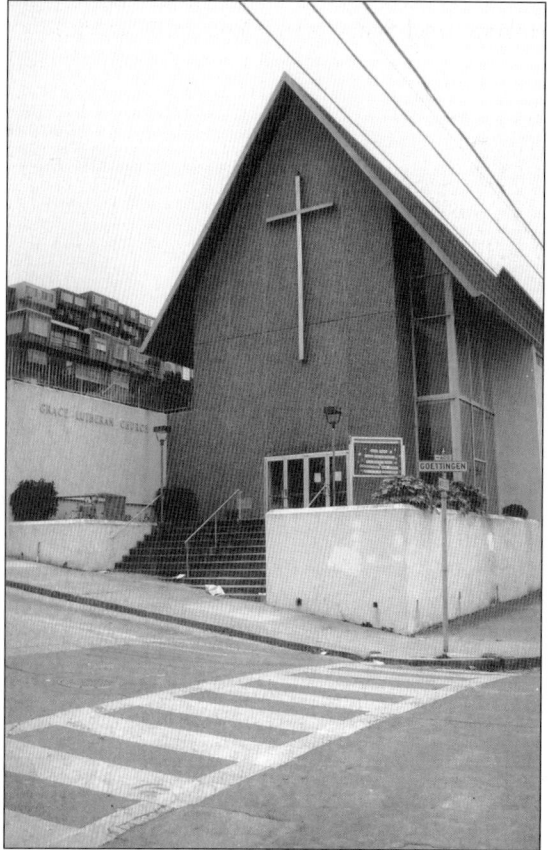

The Grace Lutheran Church, at 465 Woolsey Street and Goettingen, has been a Portola institution since 1908. Located on the corner of Berlin (now Brussels) and Bacon Streets, the lot for the first church was purchased for $1,500, and it cost $8,000 to build. It was dedicated on September 22, 1912. In 1960, ground was broken for a new church on Woolsey Street, costing $260,000 in total. It was dedicated on September 10, 1961. (Courtesy of David R. Mehrwein.)

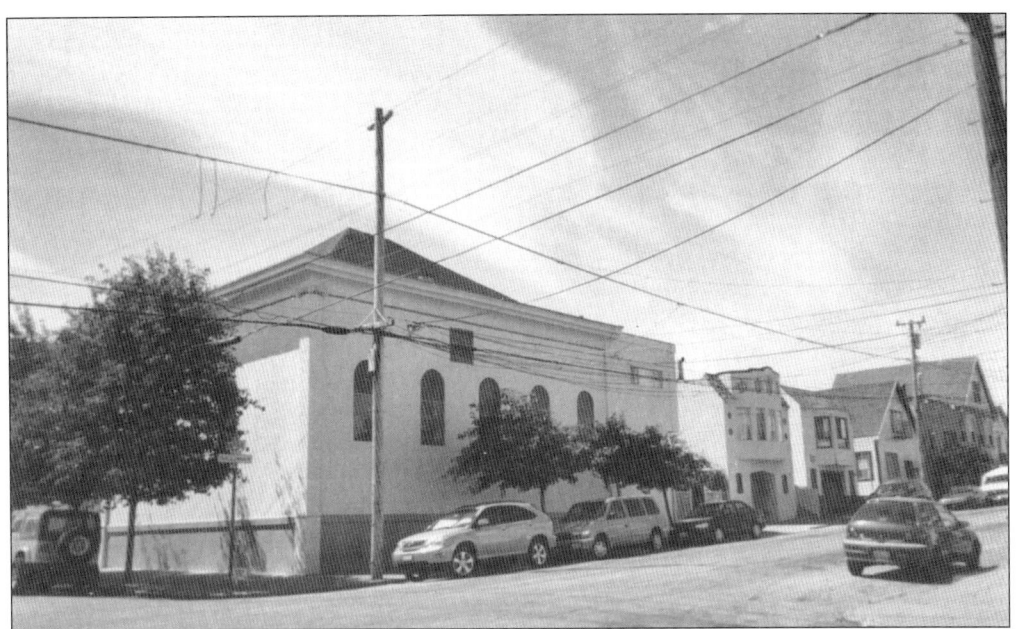

As the Ukrainian population in the Portola grew, they built their first church—the Immaculate Conception Ukrainian Catholic Church—located at 857 Girard Street and constructed at a cost of $15,000. As the parish continued its growth, it moved to 215 Silliman Street in April 1968. The church occupies the former site of the Mokum Israel Synagogue. (Courtesy of author.)

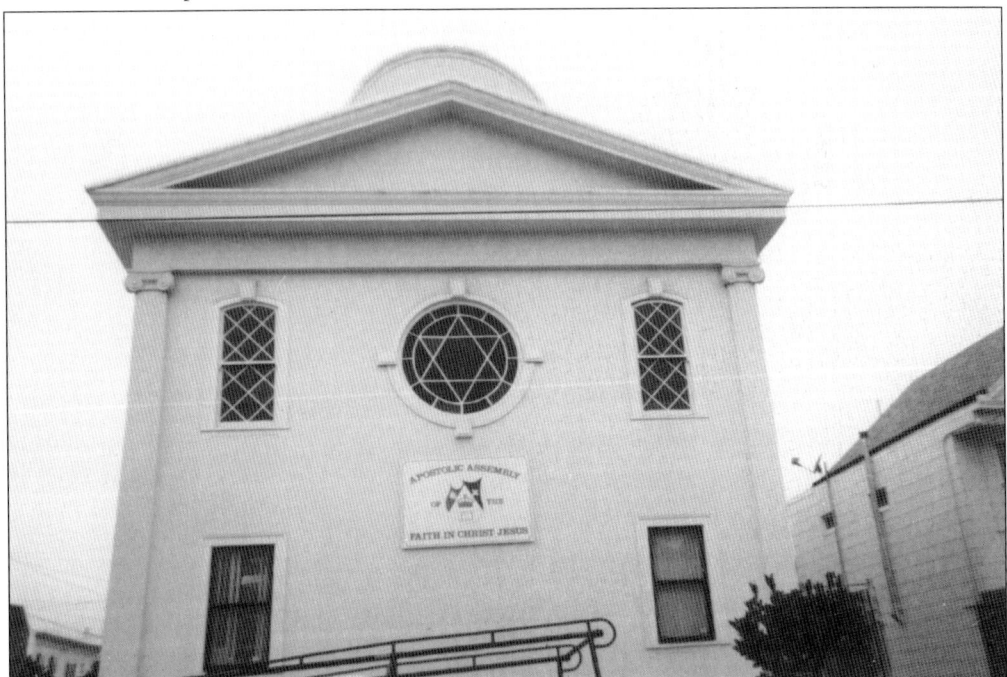

Located at 100 Felton Street, the Apostolic Assembly of the Faith in Christ Jesus Church sits on what was once the site occupied by the Ahabat Achim Synagogue. On the Girard Street side of the building, the stained-glass Star of David from the synagogue remains intact. (Courtesy of Barbara Fenech.)

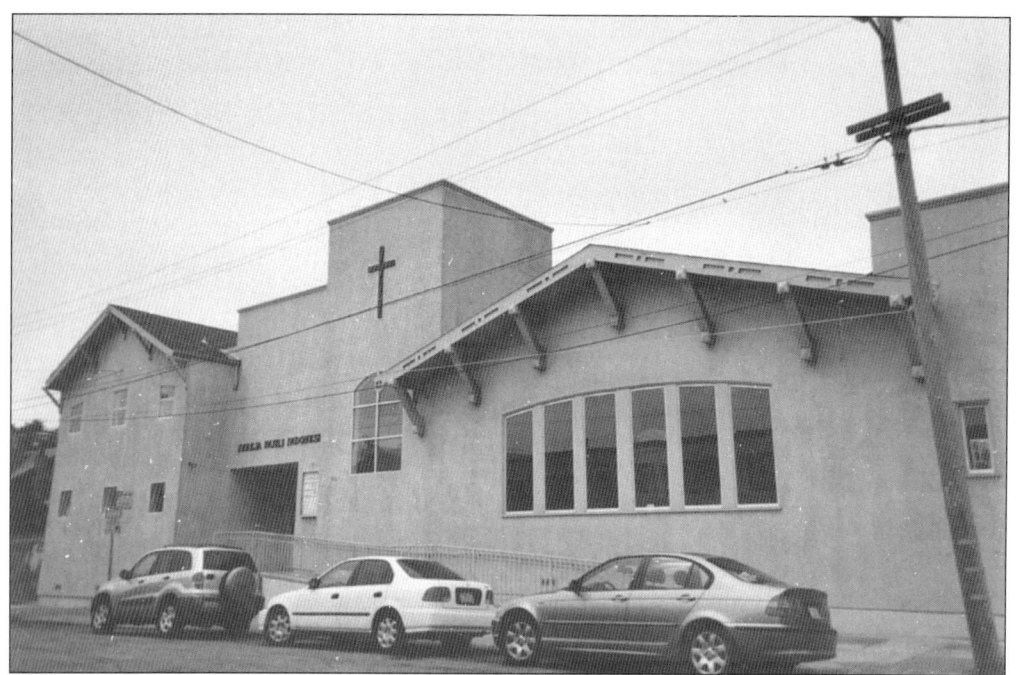

Located at 400 Brussels Street, the Christian Evangelical Mission in America Church, which houses the Indonesian Evangelical Church, the Chinese Evangelical Church, and the Christian Evangelical Chinese School, was the former site of Grace Lutheran Church. (Courtesy of author.)

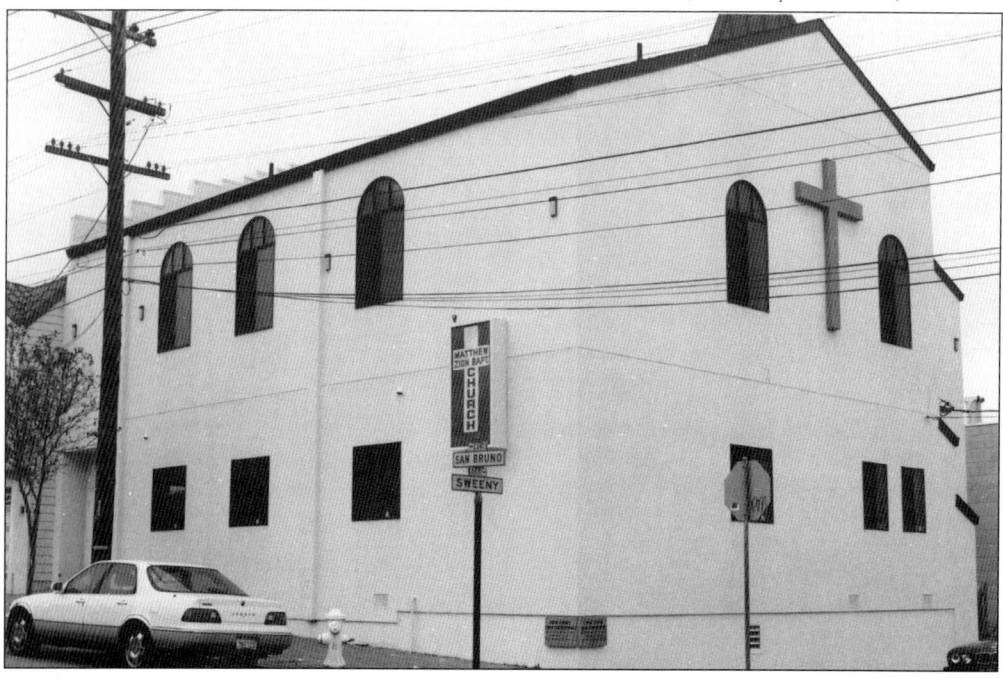

Matthew Zion Missionary Baptist Church, Inc., founded in 1955, was located at 1643 O'Farrell Street. In 1970, the church moved to 857 Girard Street and later relocated to its current home at 2340 San Bruno Avenue in 1983. Pastor Marlon D. F. Washington Sr. heads the church, and the congregation celebrated in 50th anniversary in 2005. (Courtesy of Jean Harrell.)

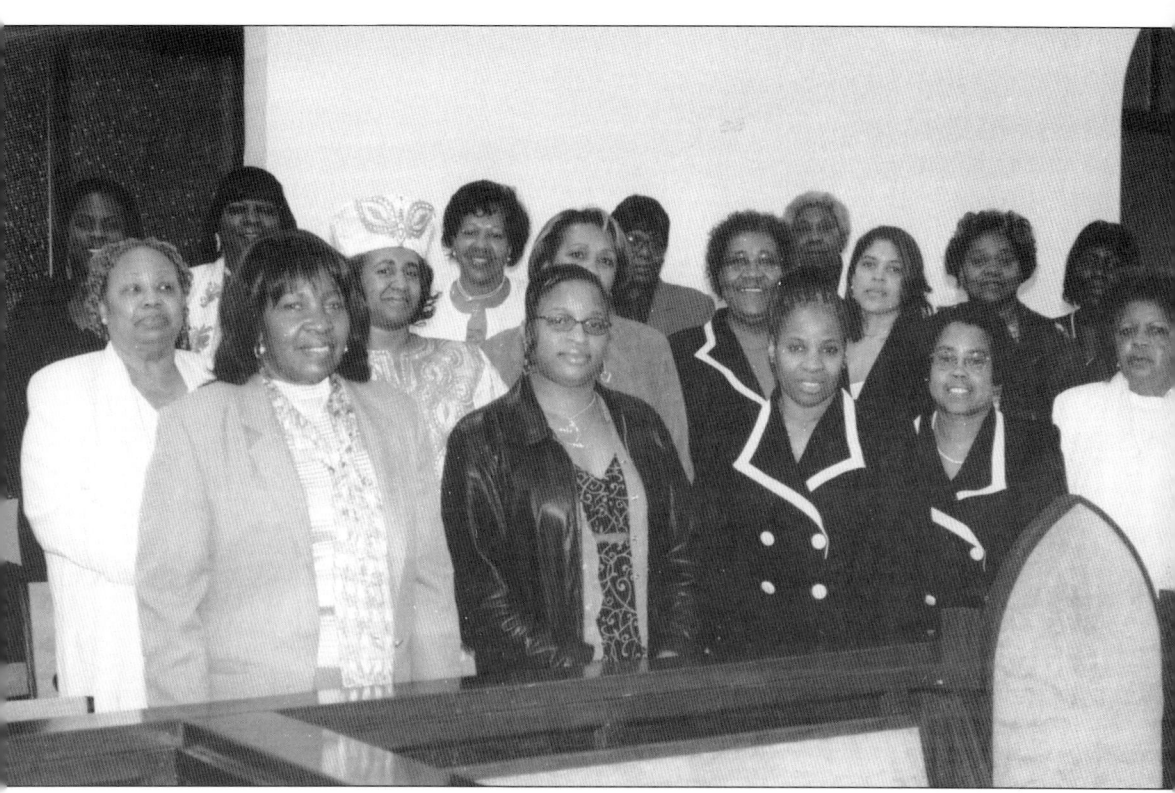
The Women's Auxiliary Ministry of the Matthew Zion Missionary Baptist Church, Inc. works with young women to develop positive self-esteem and also aids those wishing to return to the faith. (Courtesy of Jean Harrell.)

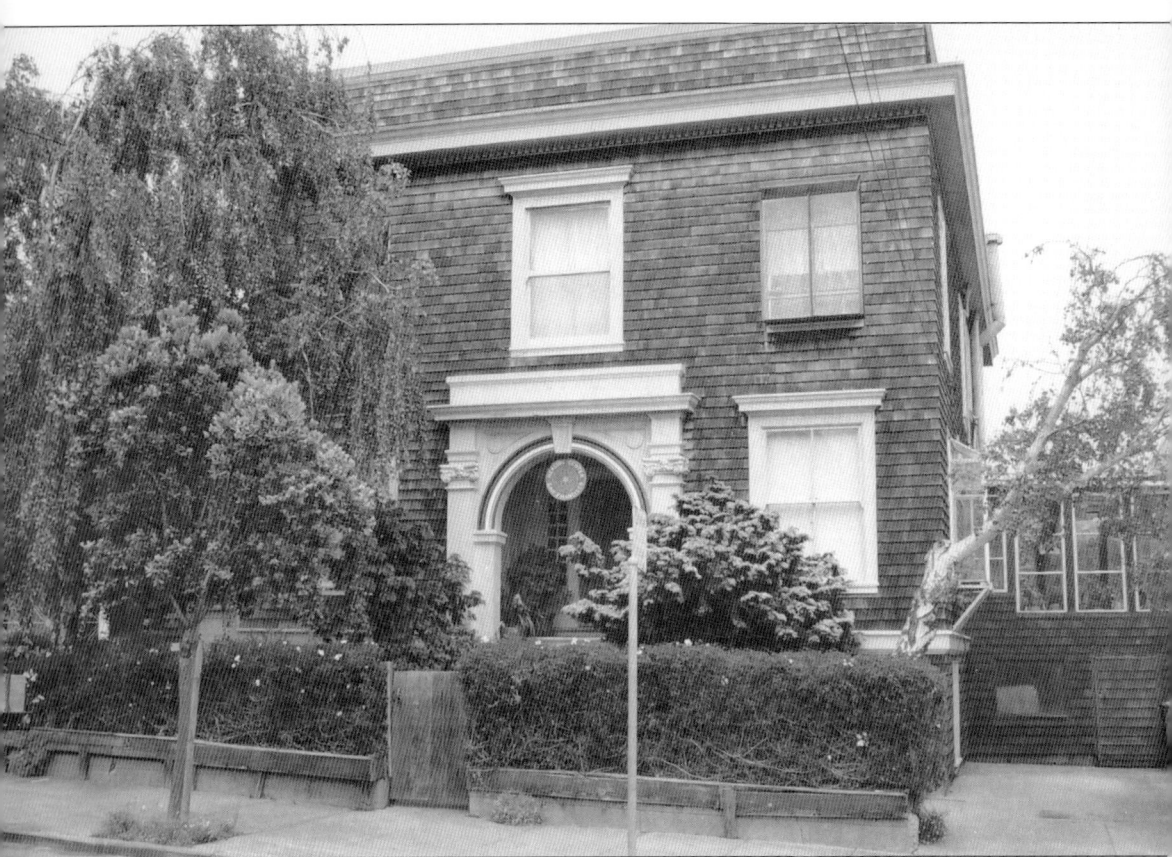
The former site of St. Elizabeth Parish Rectory is now the home to the Healing Center of San Francisco, an establishment for holistic healing. (Courtesy of David R. Mehrwein.)

Three
SAN BRUNO AVENUE

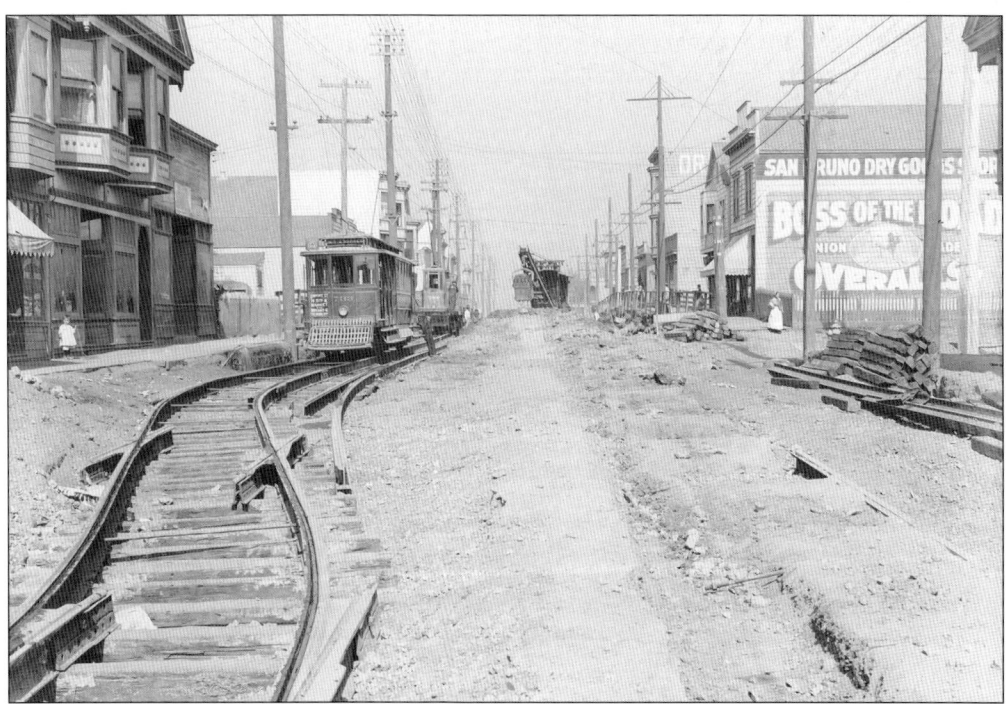

San Bruno Avenue, between Silliman and Felton Streets, is seen in this photograph from October 14, 1912. (Courtesy of the San Francisco History Center, San Francisco Public Library.)

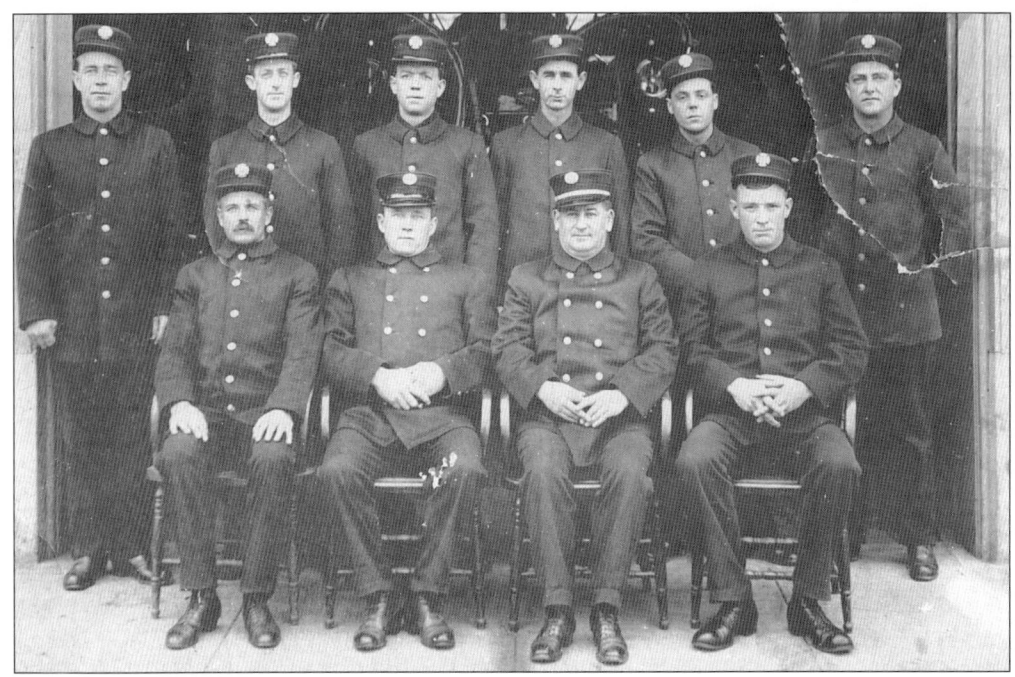

Members of San Francisco Fire Department Engine Company No. 42 pose in front of the fire station at 2430 San Bruno Avenue in 1912. (Courtesy of Leonard Nelson.)

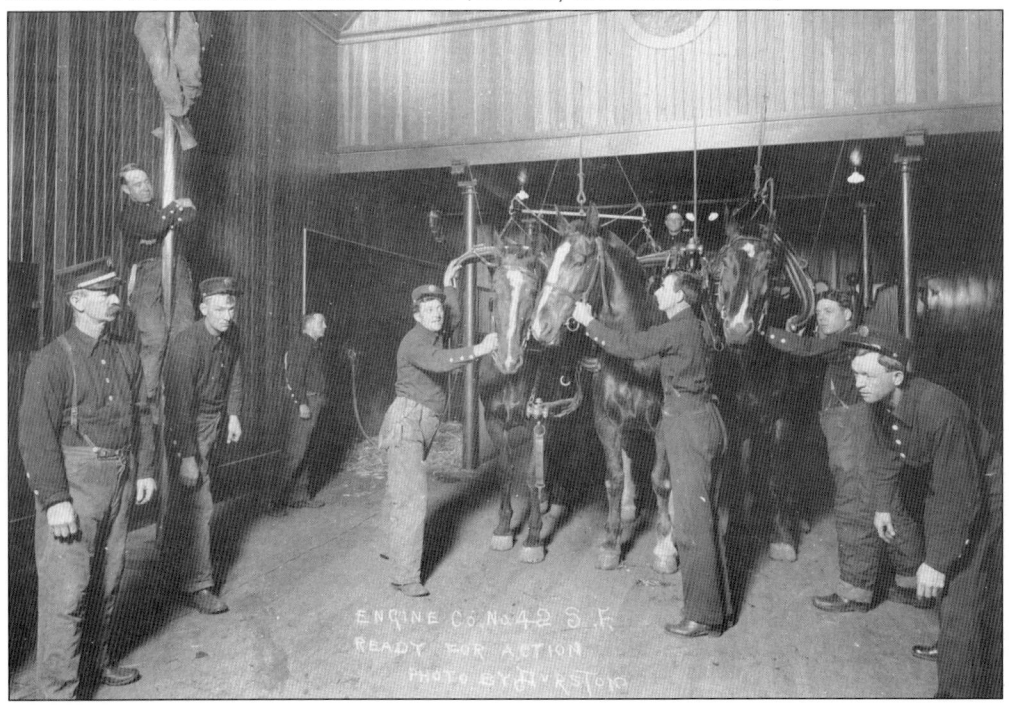

In 1912, members of San Francisco Fire Department Engine Company No. 42 are getting ready for a day's work at the fire station at 2430 San Bruno Avenue. From left to right are Captain Walsh, Lieutenant Lewis (top man on pole), Ernest Nelson (bottom man on pole), Frieland, unidentified, unidentified, unidentified, Lovette, and Gene Mulligan. (Courtesy of Leonard Nelson.)

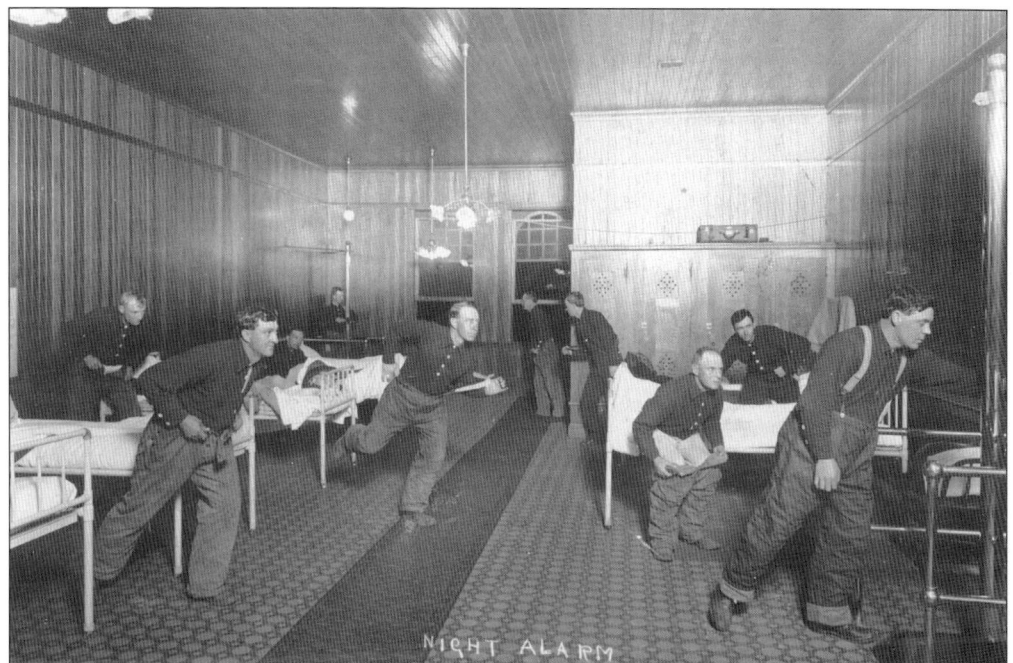

In 1912, members of San Francisco Fire Department Engine Company No. 42 react to the night alarm. (Courtesy of Leonard Nelson.)

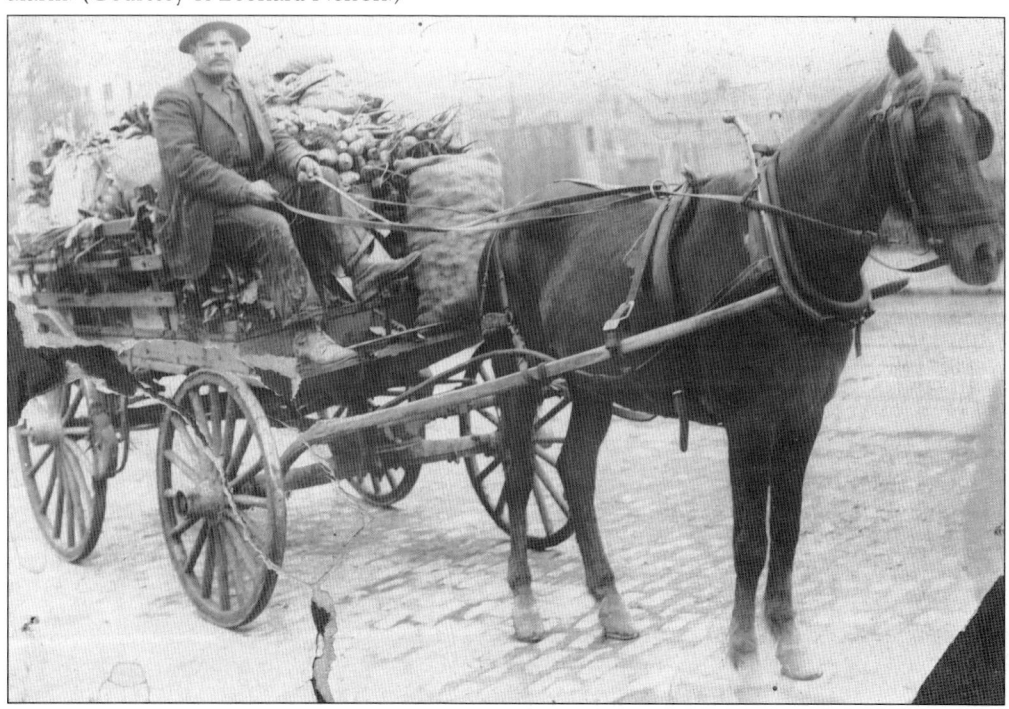

John Fenech and his horse Molly delivered vegetables door to door on Bacon Street in the early 1920s. Fenech bought produce at the produce market at the Embarcadero and then sold it to Portola residents. He later opened a grocery store at the corner of Bacon and Girard Streets. (Courtesy of John Fenech.)

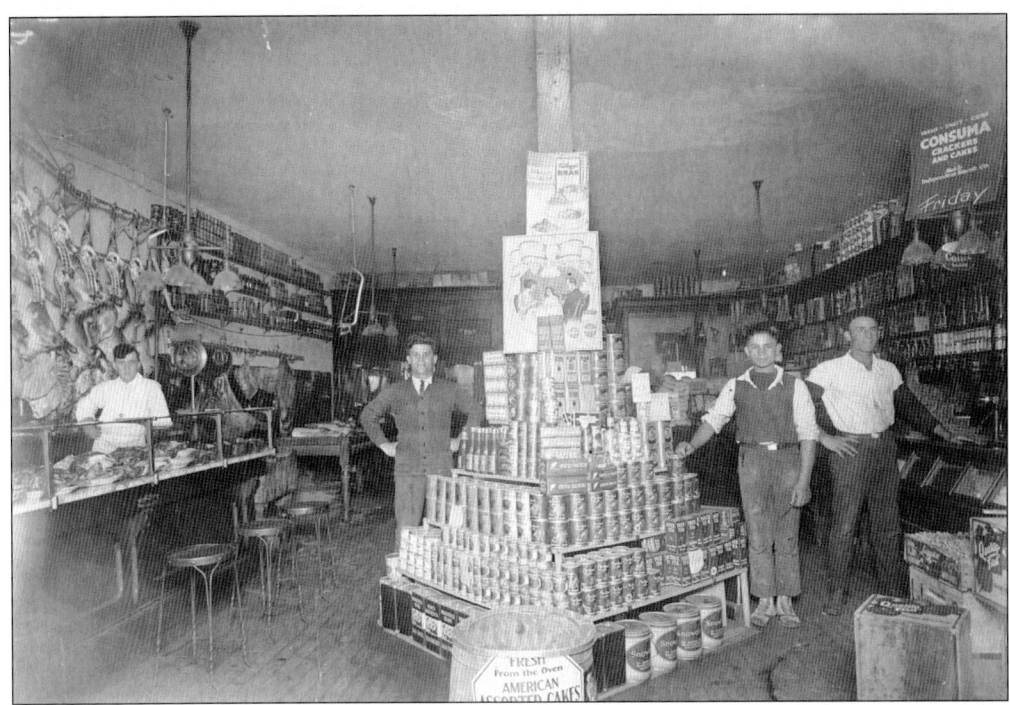

The original Muscat Market is seen here in 1920. Pictured from left to right are unidentified, Joe Muscat, Charlie Muscat, and Jim Muscat. (Courtesy of James Muscat.)

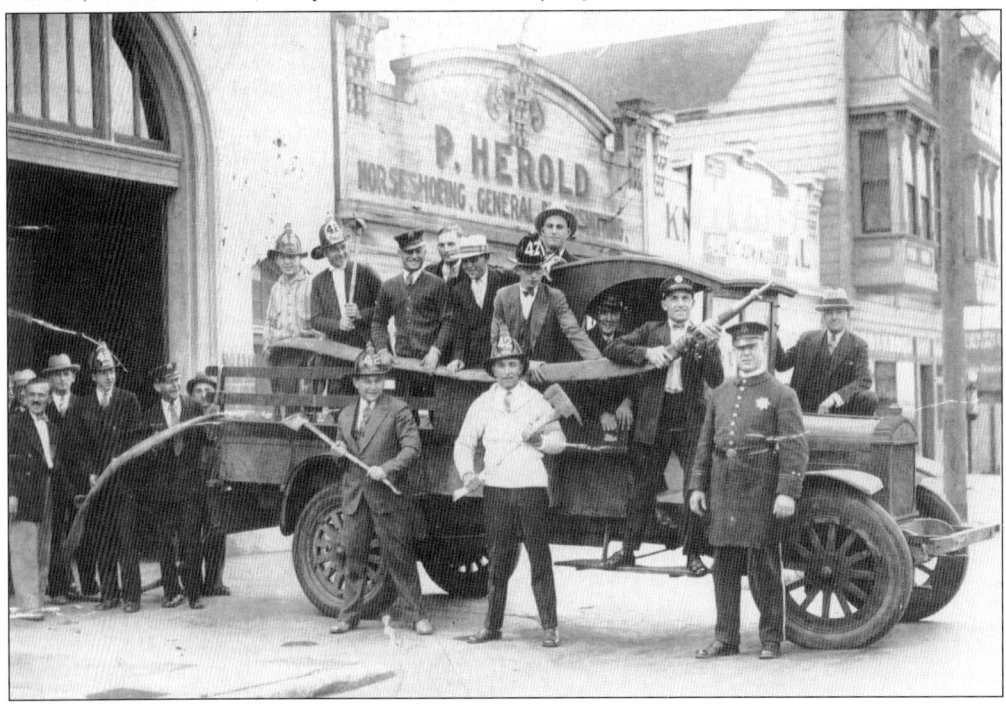

A group of Portola residents poses in front of San Francisco Fire Department Engine Company No. 42 at 2430 San Bruno Avenue in the late 1920s. The establishment beside the fire department is P. (Phillip) Herold Blacksmithing. (Courtesy of Miriam Muscat.)

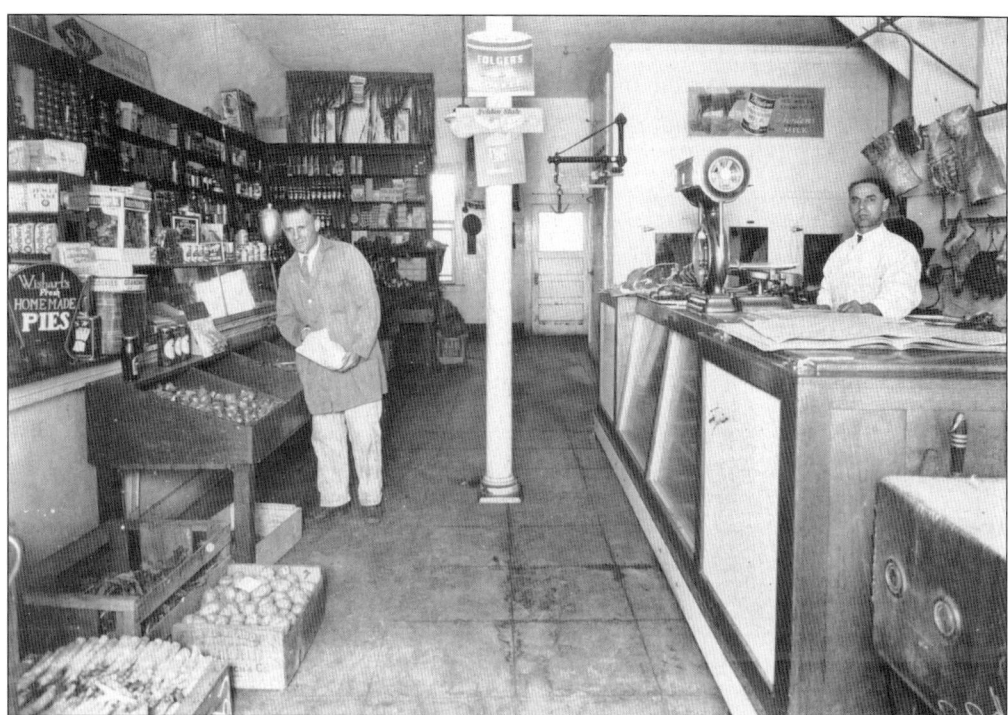

The Thrift Market on San Bruno Avenue was located between Woolsey and Bacon Streets. Ted Hoppe ran the grocery store, and Joe Thrift ran the butcher shop. Hoppe owned the store from 1921 to 1939 when he was forced to close because his customers had run up large tabs, and he could no longer pay his suppliers. A longtime Portola resident, Hoppe never refused anyone's pleas for groceries, and his wife collected what money people could afford to pay so the Thrift Market never had to file for bankruptcy. Pictured here are Ted Hoppe (left) and Joe Thrift. (Courtesy of Louann Hoppe Saltel.)

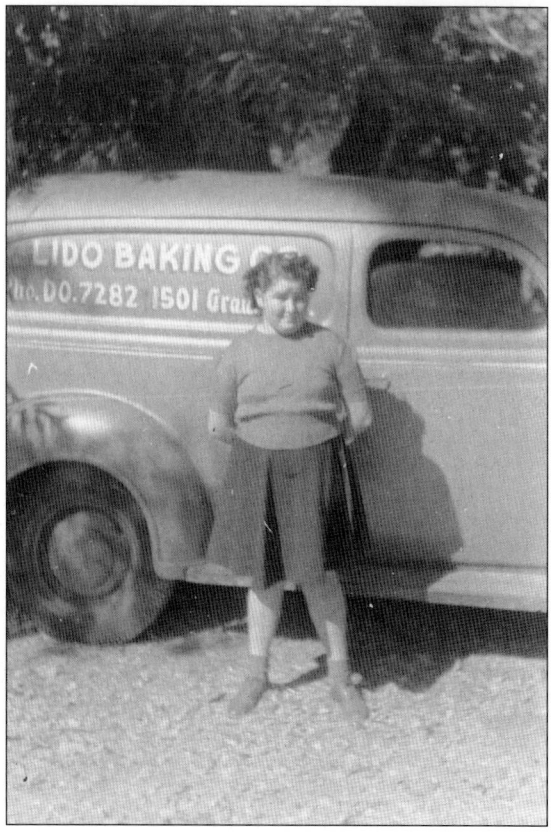

Dorothy Garibaldi stands in front of the Lido Baking delivery truck in the 1940s. (Courtesy of author.)

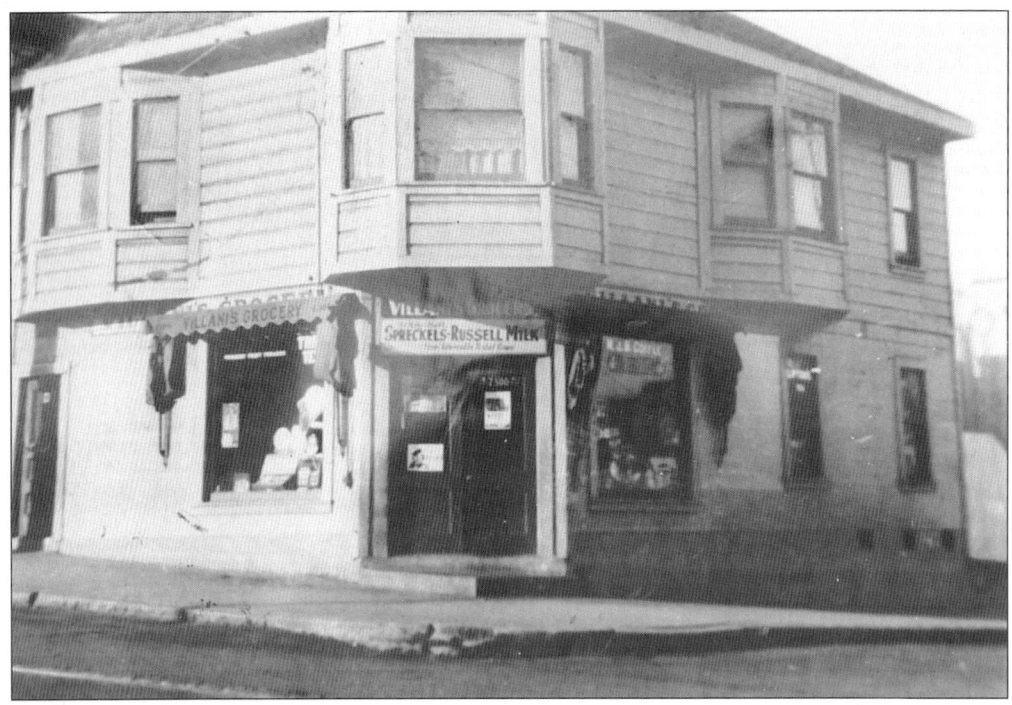

Villani's Grocery Store occupied a space at the corner of San Bruno Avenue and Gaven Street in 1932. (Courtesy of Harry Cohn.)

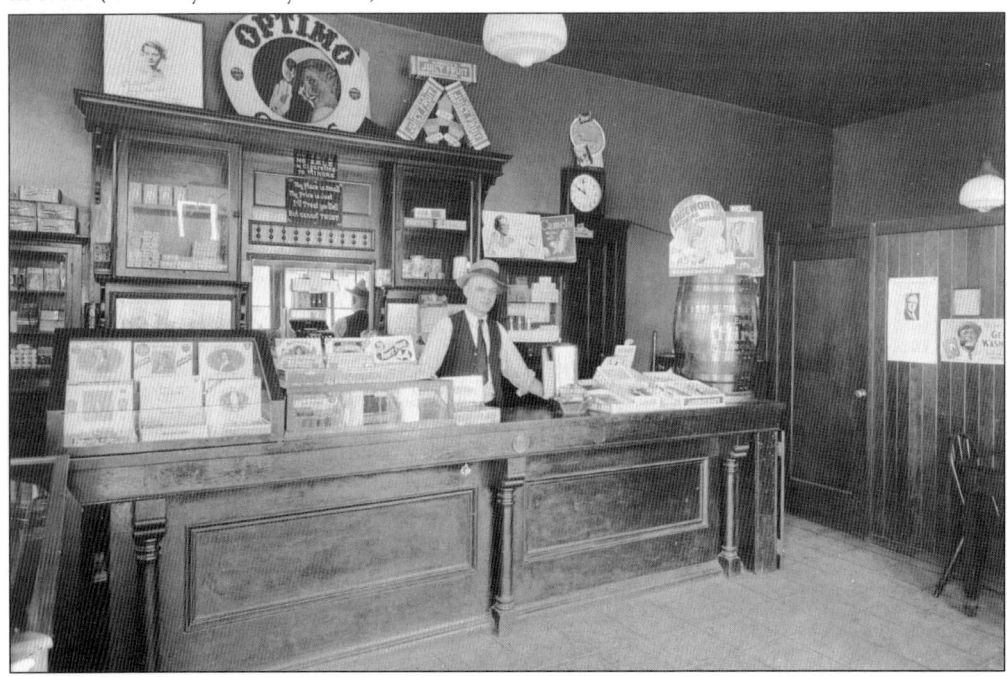

In 1932, during Prohibition, John Camilleri opened a cigar store at 2399 San Bruno Avenue. After Prohibition ended, he reopened the store as the Lucky Lager Tavern in 1934. After the store was remodeled in 1936, the name changed once again to White Palace since it had the same name as a popular beer company. (Courtesy of Joe Camilleri.)

Bernice's Beauty Shop on San Bruno Avenue was located next to the Avenue Sweet Shop. Pictured here are, from left to right, Bernice Waterman and Bernice Garibaldi. (Courtesy of Gerald Garibaldi.)

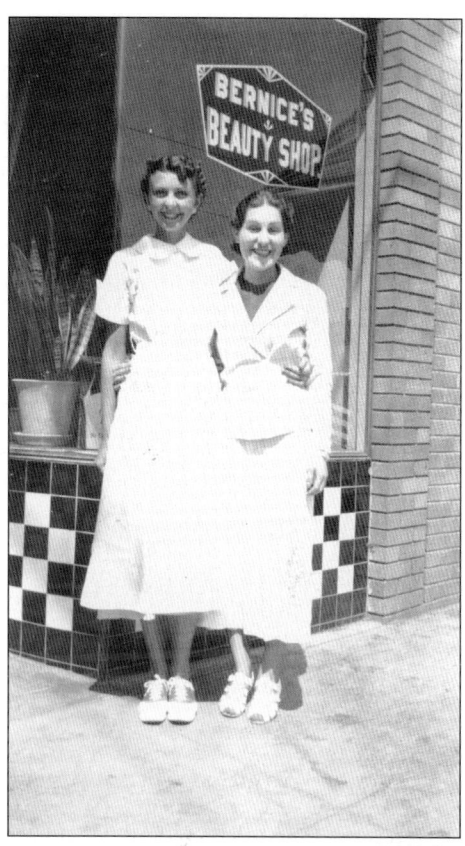

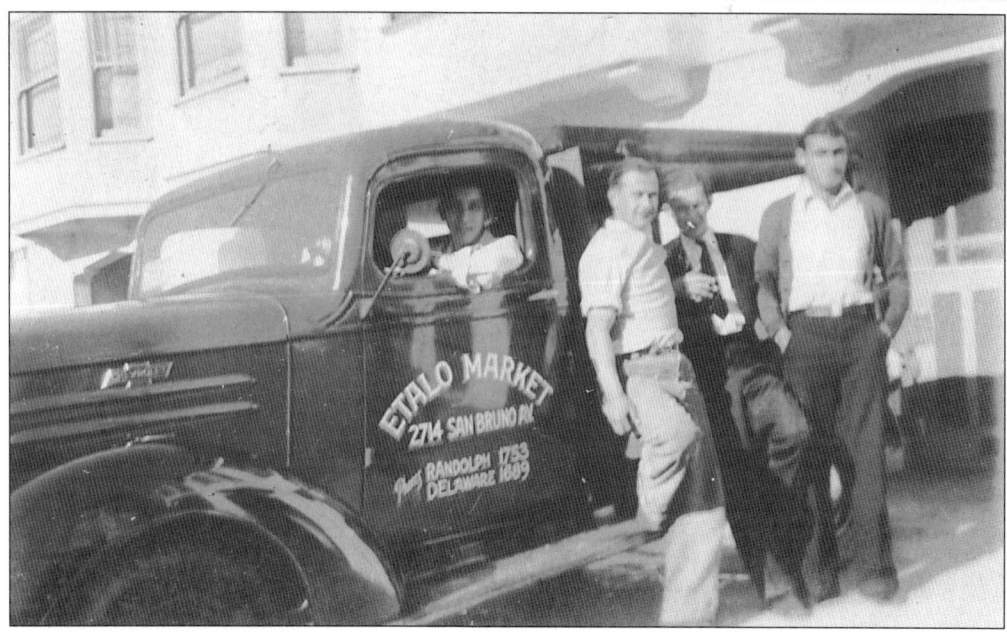

In the driver's seat of the Etalo Market delivery truck is Gus Marinello, who later became the owner of the meat department. Standing in this 1939 photograph are, from left to right, Angelo Parodi, Joe Memmen, and Fred ?. (Courtesy of Jack Parodi.)

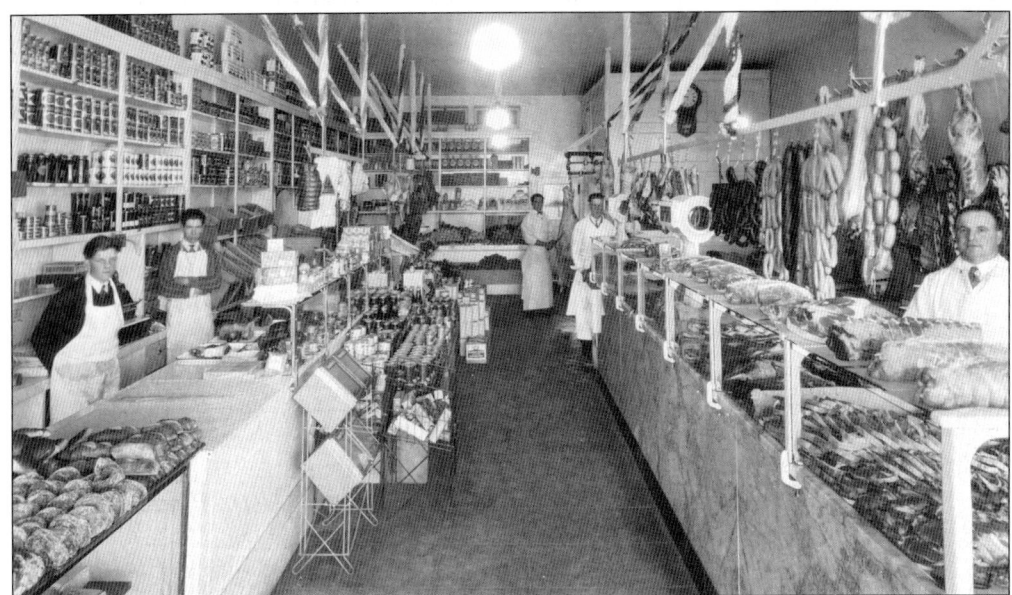

Employees are photographed inside the Etalo Market c. 1924. Unidentified employees are on the left side of the photograph. On the right side of the photograph, starting from the front, are Etalo Giacomelli, Harold Gasta (who opened his own meat market next door to the deli), and Ray Bersi. (Courtesy of Jack Parodi.)

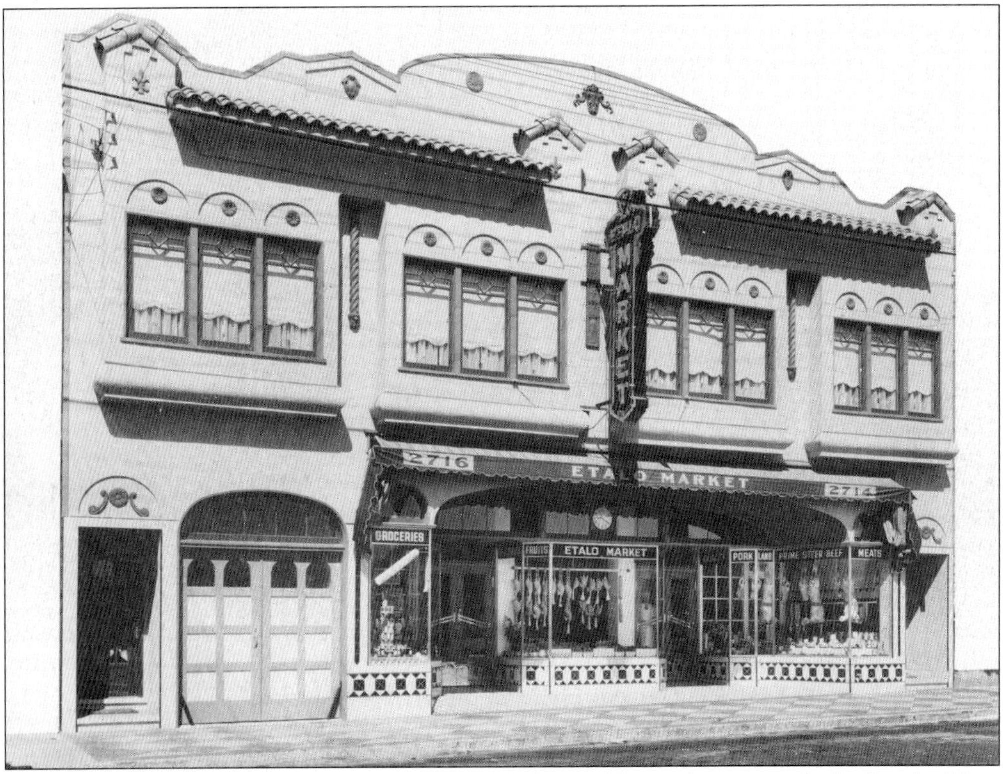

In 1927, owner Etalo Giacomelli added a second half to Etalo Market to match the first building at 2714 San Bruno Avenue. (Courtesy of Jack Parodi.)

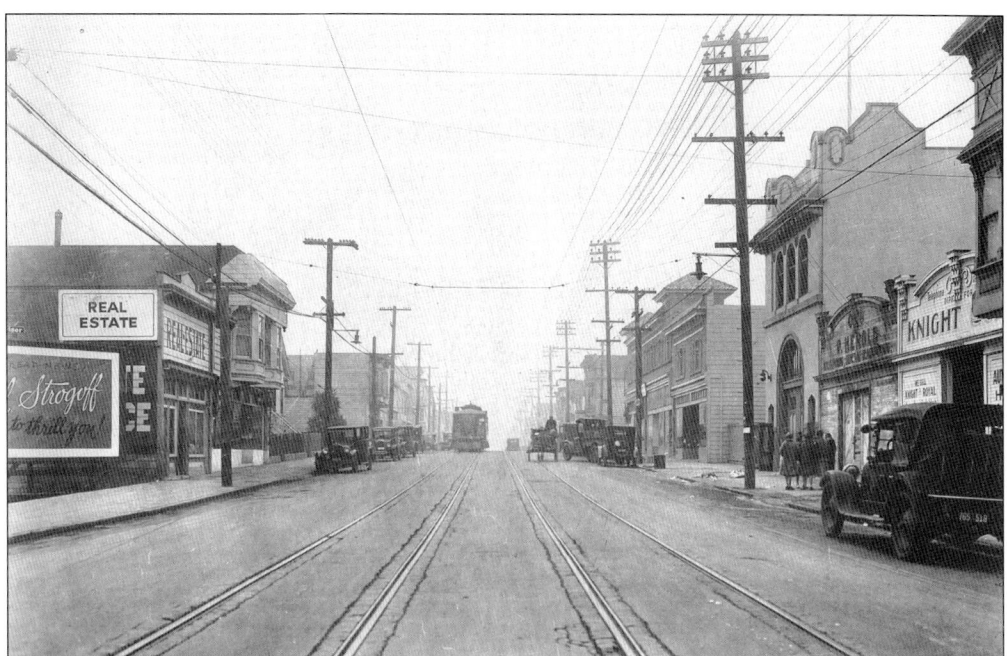

San Bruno and Silver Avenues are depicted in this photograph around 1927. To the right of the photograph is San Francisco Fire Department Engine Company No. 42 and P. (Phillip) Herold Blacksmithing. (Courtesy of the San Francisco History Center, San Francisco Public Library.)

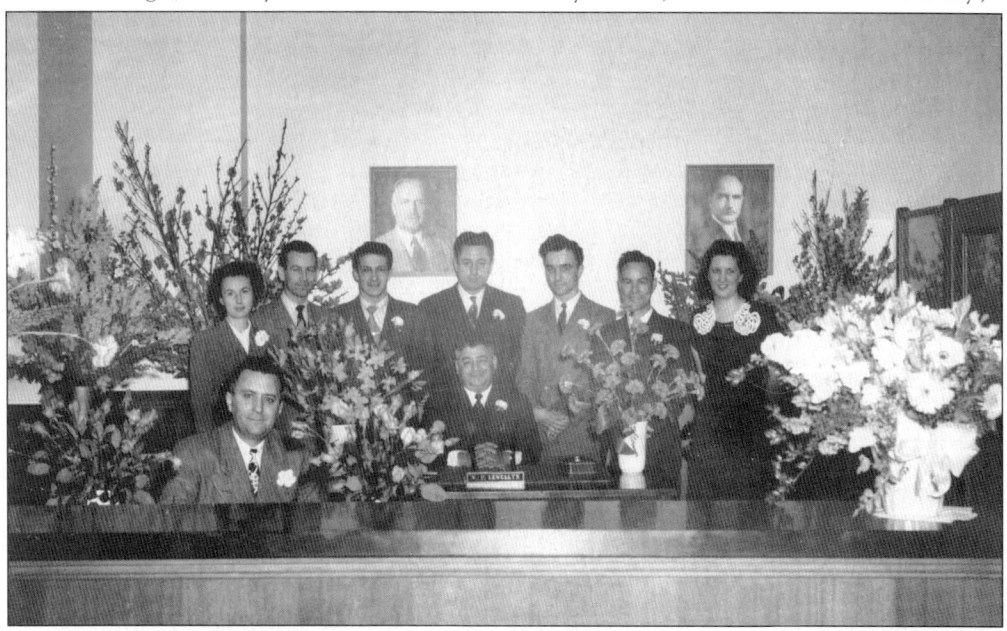

This photograph documents the grand opening of the Portola branch of the Bank of America at 2485 San Bruno Avenue. W. P. (Bill) Lewellyn is seated in the middle surrounded by Mario Giampaoli, assistant manger, and branch employees. Lewellyn, a longtime Portola resident, was a catcher for the San Francisco Seals from 1918 to 1919 and was optioned to play with the New York Yankees but chose to remain in San Francisco. He managed the Portola branch of the Bank of America from 1937 until his retirement in 1957. (Courtesy of the Lewellyn family.)

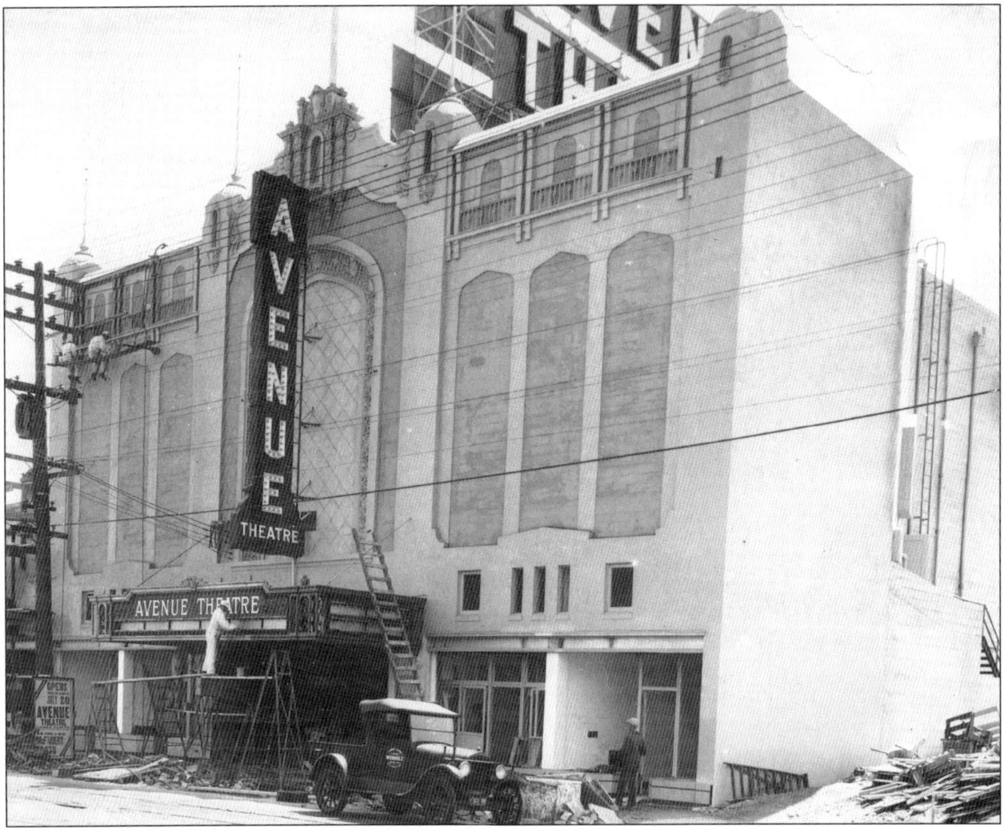

On July 15, 1927, the Avenue Theatre at 2650 San Bruno Avenue prepares for its opening day. This theatre was owned by the four Levin brothers—H. S., Ben, Jesse, and Manuel, who also managed other theatres in San Francisco and was in business from July 20, 1937, until December 22, 1984. The Avenue showed popular movies of the day, and one could also collect dinnerware pieces in weekly promotions. In its later years, the theatre showed revivals of silent movies. (Courtesy of the San Francisco History Center, San Francisco Public Library.)

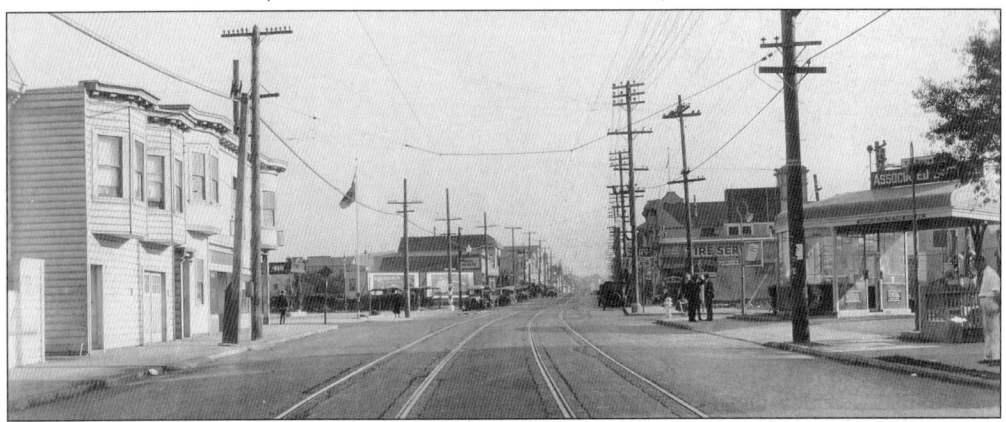

This early photograph depicts San Bruno Avenue at Silver Avenue in 1929. To the left of the photograph is John Camilleri's cigar store at 2399 San Bruno Avenue, which later became the White Palace Tavern. To the right of the photograph is the Associated Gas Station. (Courtesy of the San Francisco History Center, San Francisco Public Library.)

Corrigan's Lunch at 2819 San Bruno Avenue specialized in breakfast, lunch, and short orders. In this April 10, 1939, photograph are, from left to right, Iva Corrigan Fitzgerald, Vince Fitzgerald, and Minnie Corrigan. (Courtesy of Patricia Semenero.)

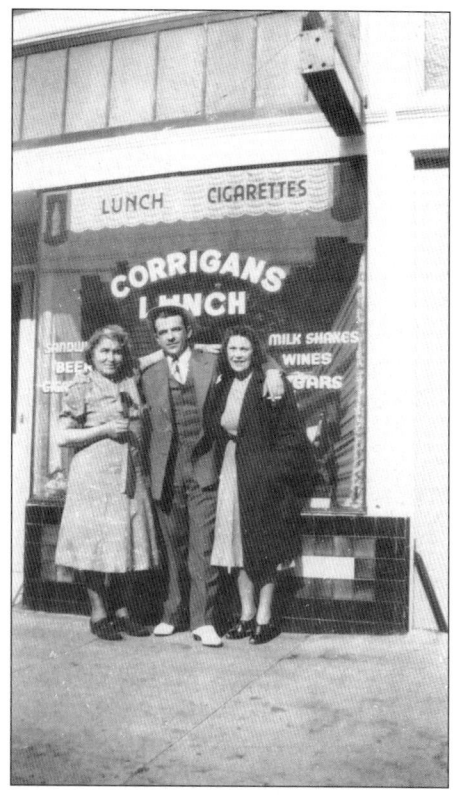

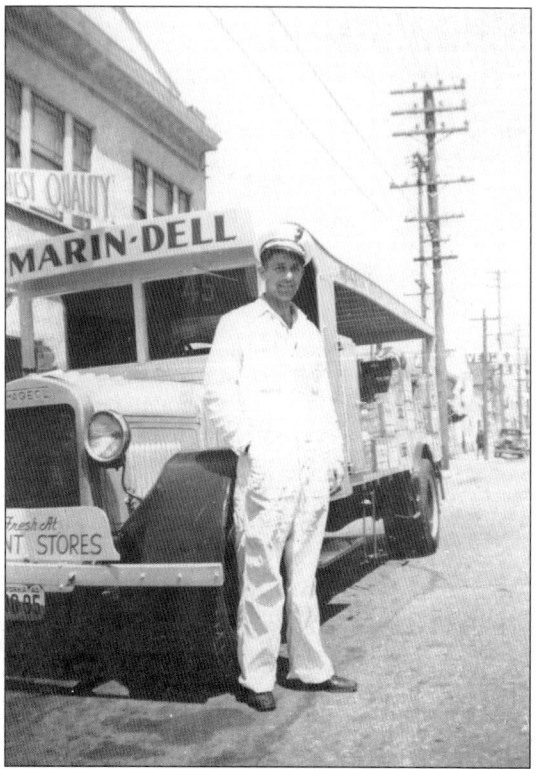

The Marin Dell milkman prepares to make his daily deliveries in the neighborhood. In this photograph from June 10, 1940, he is pictured on San Bruno Avenue and Wayland Street. (Courtesy of Patricia Semenero.)

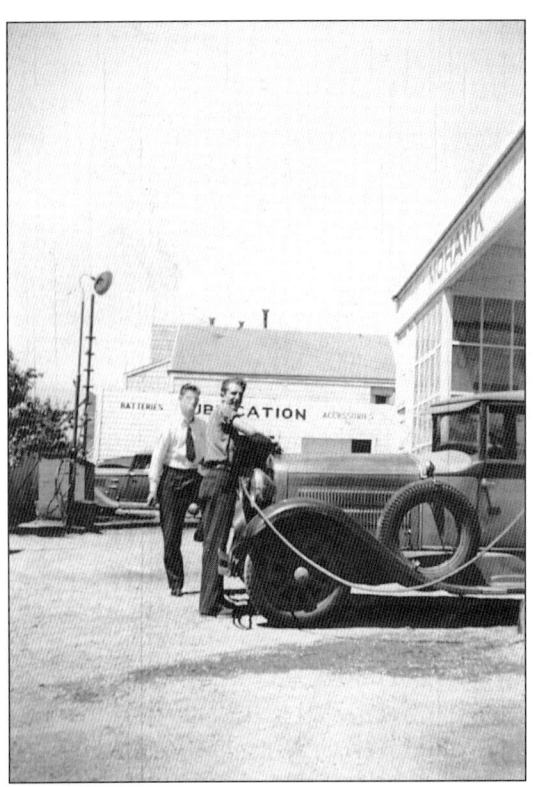

Many Portola residents bought their gasoline from the Mohawk gas station on San Bruno Avenue and Wayland Street. This photograph was taken on June 10, 1940. (Courtesy of Patricia Semenero.)

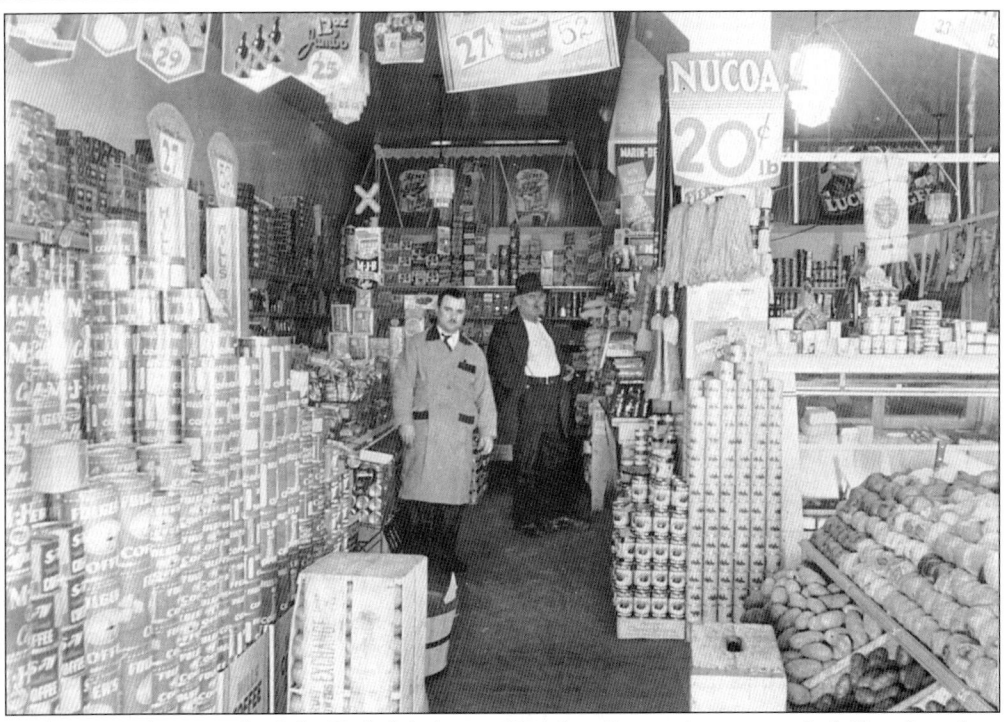

In this 1946 photograph of the Etalo Market at 2714 San Bruno Avenue are Jack Parodi and an unidentified customer. (Courtesy of Jack Parodi.)

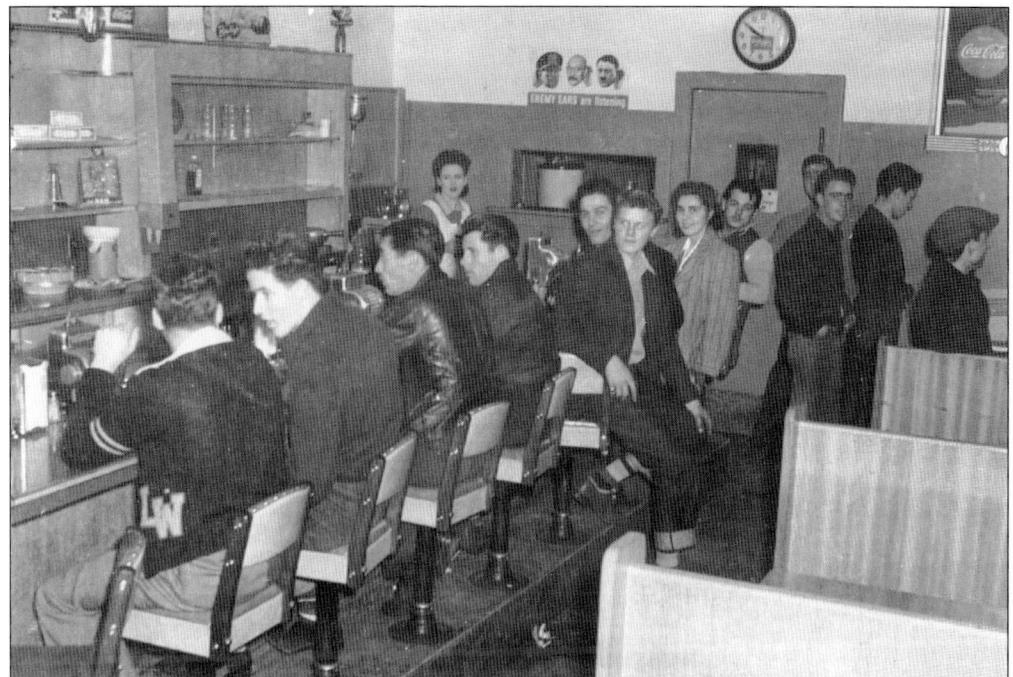

Babe's Creamery at 2680 San Bruno Avenue was a popular place to eat in the 1940s. It would later be known as the Avenue Sweet Shop. Pictured from left to right are three unidentified men, Jack Kelly, Al Nielson, unidentified, Aileen Ragone, two unidentified men, Ed O'Connor, Jack Ross, and unidentified. Adele Didier is behind the counter. Note the poster in the background that depicts Mussolini, Hirohito, and Hitler and states, "Enemy Ears are Listening." (Courtesy of Mr. and Mrs. Victor Garibaldi.)

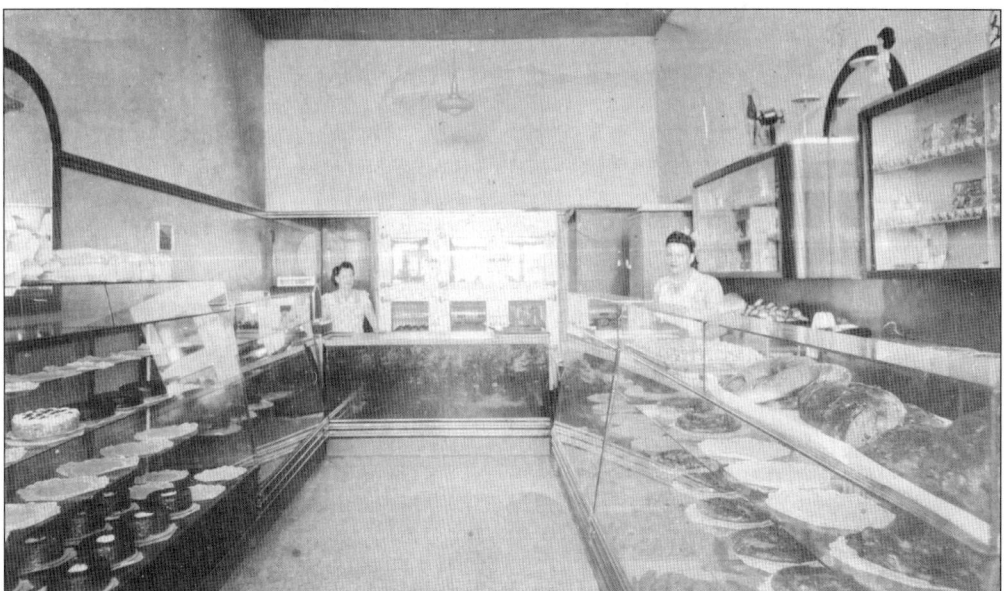

In 1941, Lido Pastry, located at 2684 San Bruno Avenue, was owned by Fritz and Madeline Zahn. The bakery was known for its St. Honore cakes, an Italian tradition. Pictured here are Bruna Lembi (left) and Evelyn "Babe" Bosso. (Courtesy of Margaret Baker.)

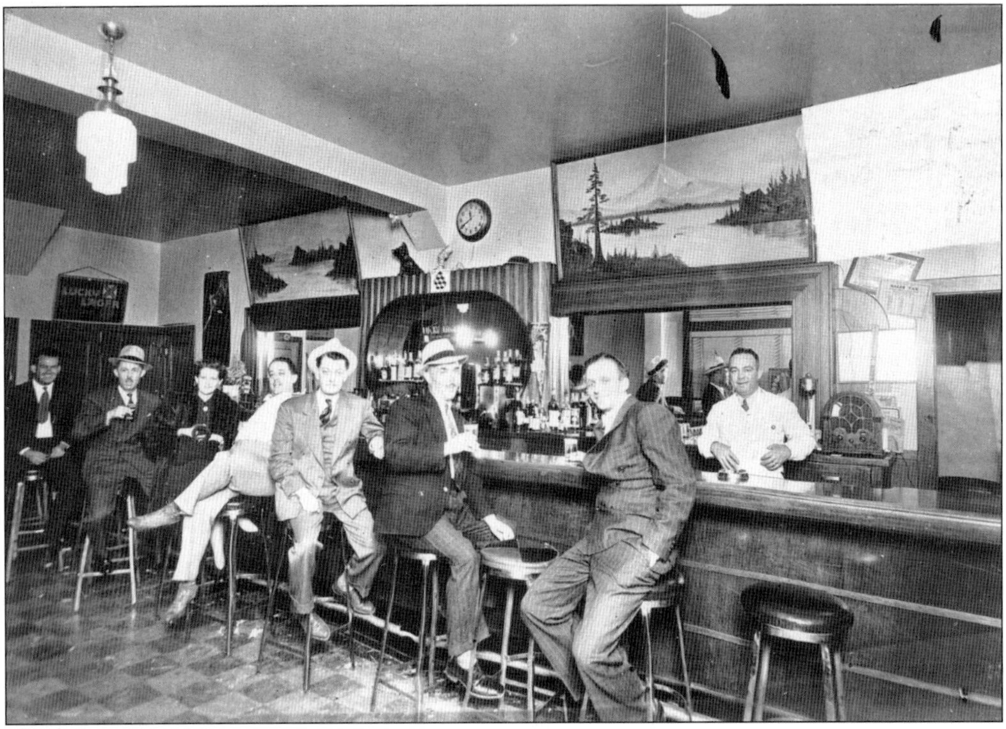

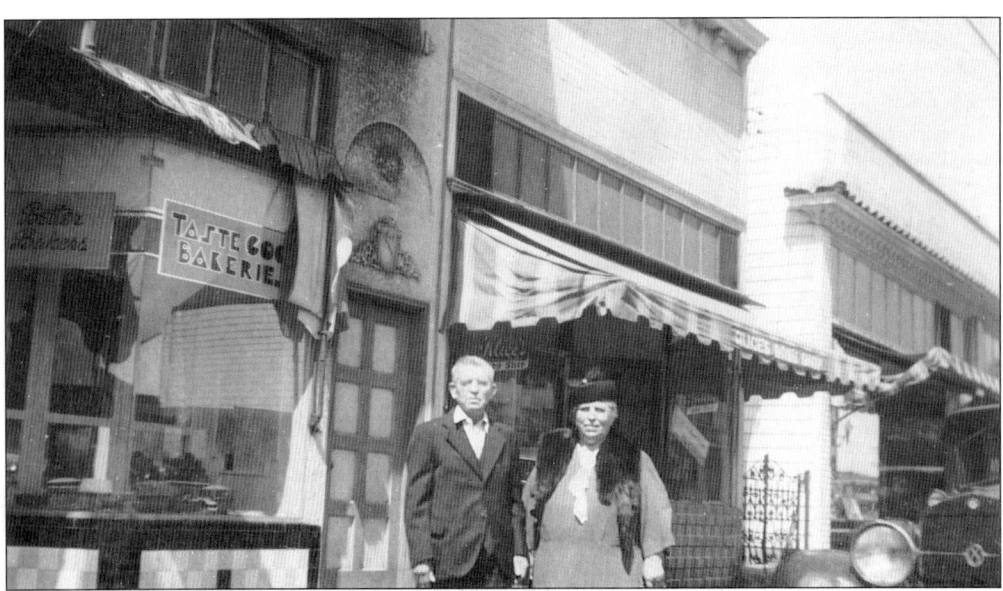

Customers of the White Palace Tavern at Silver and San Bruno Avenues enjoy an evening out c. 1943. The bartender is Thomas "Tommy" Conlon. (Courtesy of the Conlon family.)

A couple poses in front of the Taste Good Bakery at 2520 San Bruno Avenue in this August 1947 photograph. The Taste Good Bakery was a franchise. Goods were baked elsewhere and sold at various locations. This store was managed by Alice Ribero. (Courtesy of Pearl Bottino.)

Around 1948, Bruna Lembi holds little Dan Zahn at the Lido Pastry. In the background, owner Madeline Zahn decorates a cake inside the baking room. (Courtesy of Margaret Baker.)

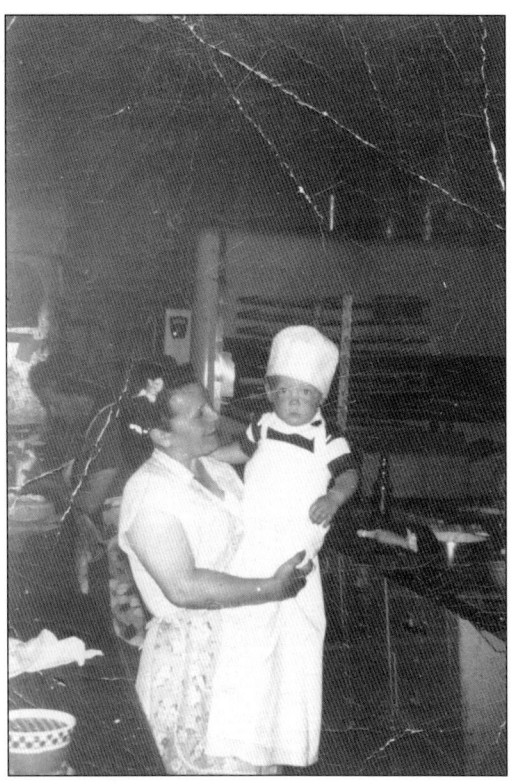

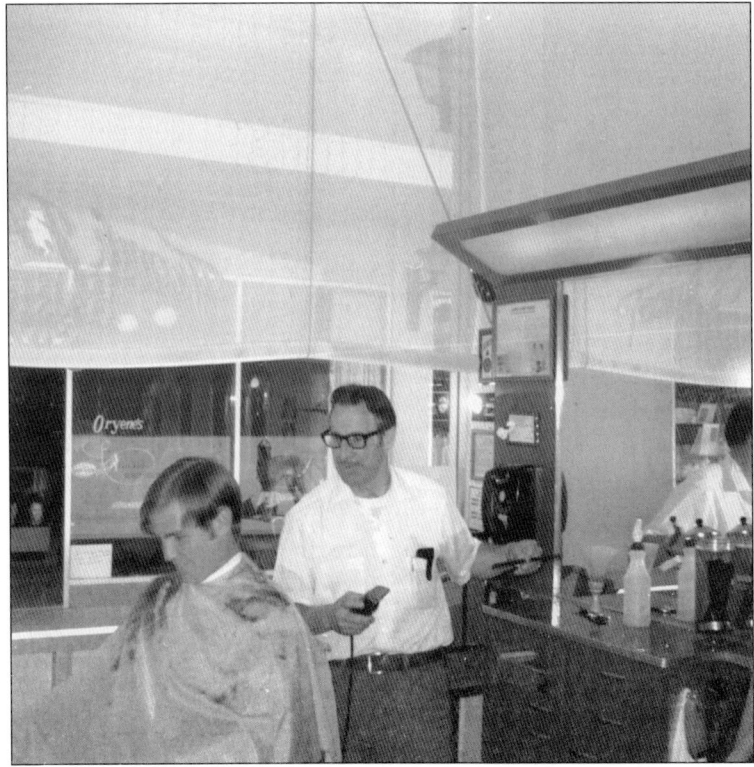

Located at 2466 San Bruno Avenue, Pisa's Barbershop opened in 1948 and was owned by Frank Pisa. Here Frank gives a customer a haircut. (Courtesy of Beverly Pisa Henner.)

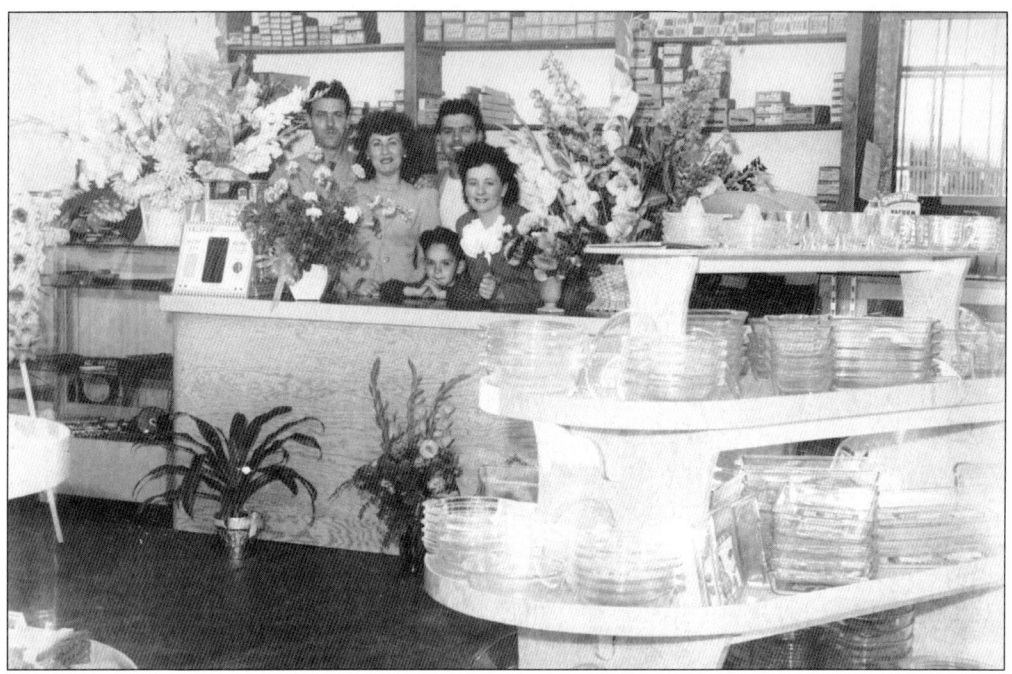

P. V.'s Home Service, a home appliance and washer and dryer company as well as a full hardware store, was located at 2633 San Bruno Avenue. This June 22, 1946, photograph is from the store's opening day. Pictured from left to right are Vincent Ciolino, Juanita Ciolino, Paul Ciolino, Juanita Ciolino, and Ronald Ciolino. The Ciolino brothers both married women named Juanita. (Courtesy of Juanita Ciolino.)

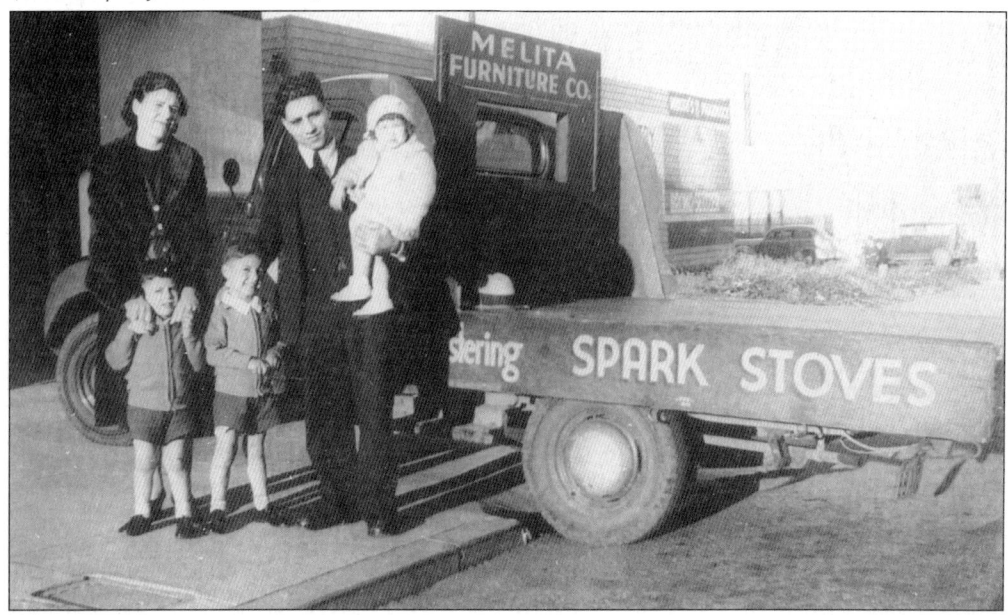

Joe "Melita" Tonna and his wife, Nina, who lived at 124 Bacon Street, are seen here with the Melita Furniture truck in the early 1940s. Joe Tonna was one of the partners in the Melita Furniture Company, which was located at 2660 San Bruno Avenue. Also pictured from left to right are their children Charlie, Jimmie, and Marianne. (Courtesy of the Tonna family.)

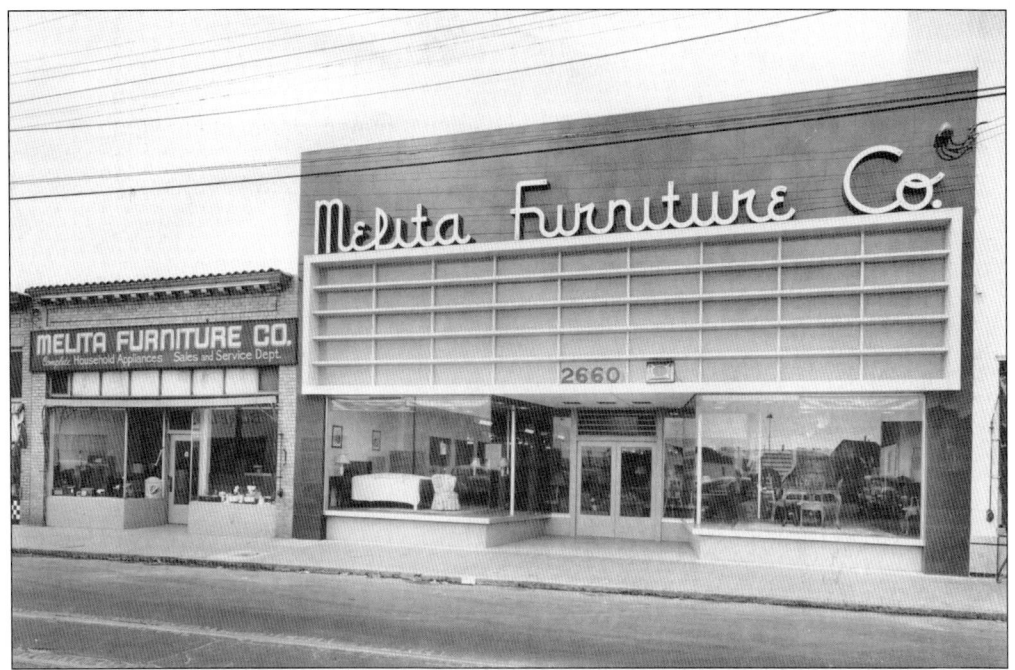

The Melita Furniture Company at 2660 San Bruno Avenue was a partnership of Tom Fenech and Joe "Melita" Tonna. Many Portola residents shopped for sofas, lamps, and other household items here. This photograph was taken on June 7, 1946. (Courtesy of Barbara Fenech.)

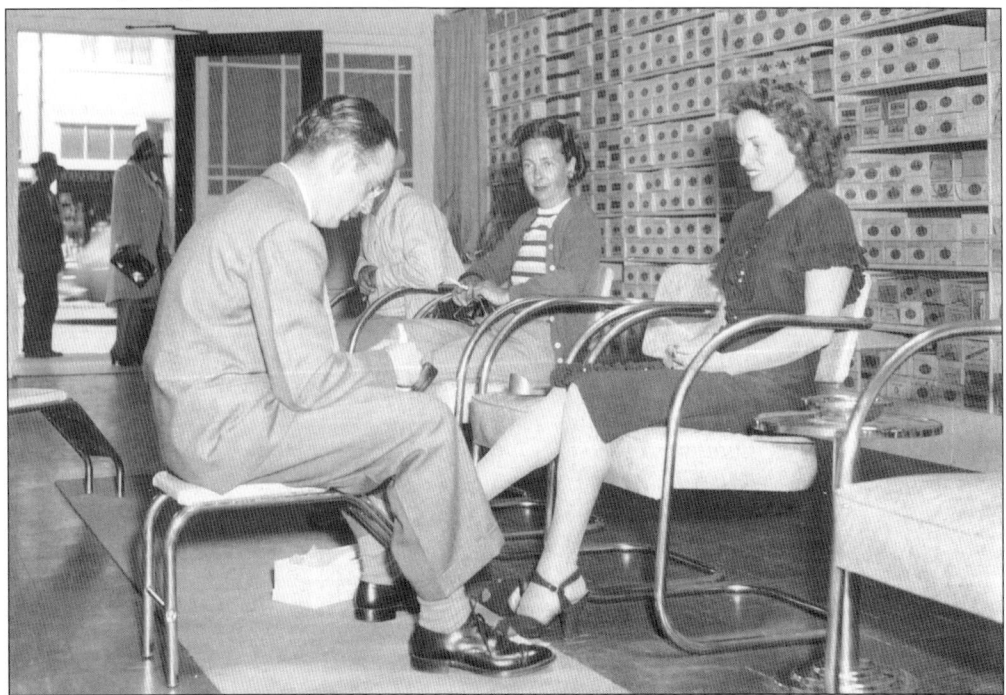

In 1947, Renato Ferrera opened Ferrera Shoe Store at 2601 San Bruno Avenue. Pictured here is owner Renato Ferrera helping his wife, Margaret, try on shoes. Sitting next to Margaret are Ann and Ed Pryal. (Courtesy of Renato Ferrera.)

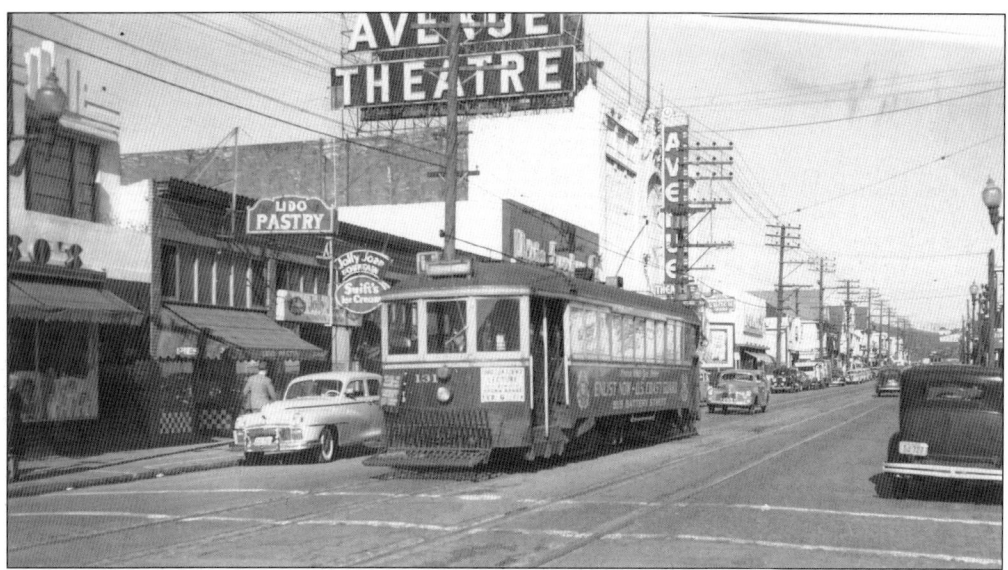

San Bruno Avenue is pictured here around 1947. The 25-streetcar line ran from Fifth and Market Northbound to Wilde Street Southbound and cost 5¢ to ride. Portola resident Ray Gnecco was once a conductor on the line. Lido Pastry and the Avenue Theatre can be seen in the background. (Courtesy of the San Francisco History Center, San Francisco Public Library.)

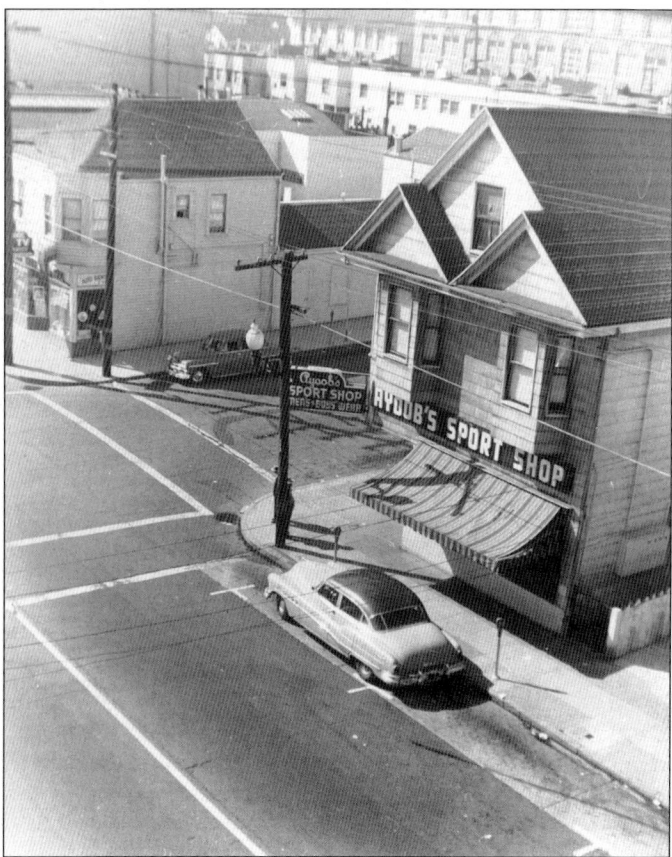

Ayoob Sport Shop at 2598 San Bruno Avenue specialized in men's and boy's clothing and athletic equipment. (Courtesy of Dana Ayoob.)

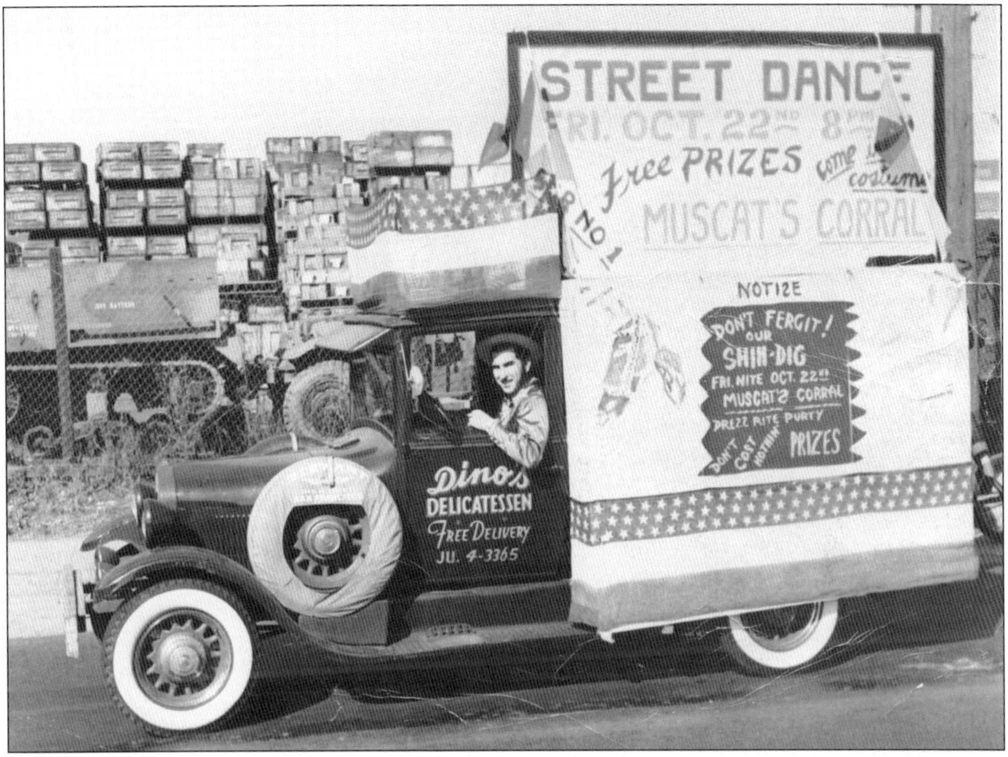

In this October 1948 photograph, Dino Malerbi is pictured in his delivery truck advertising an upcoming street dance to be held at Muscat's Corral. (Courtesy of Beverly Malerbi Casella.)

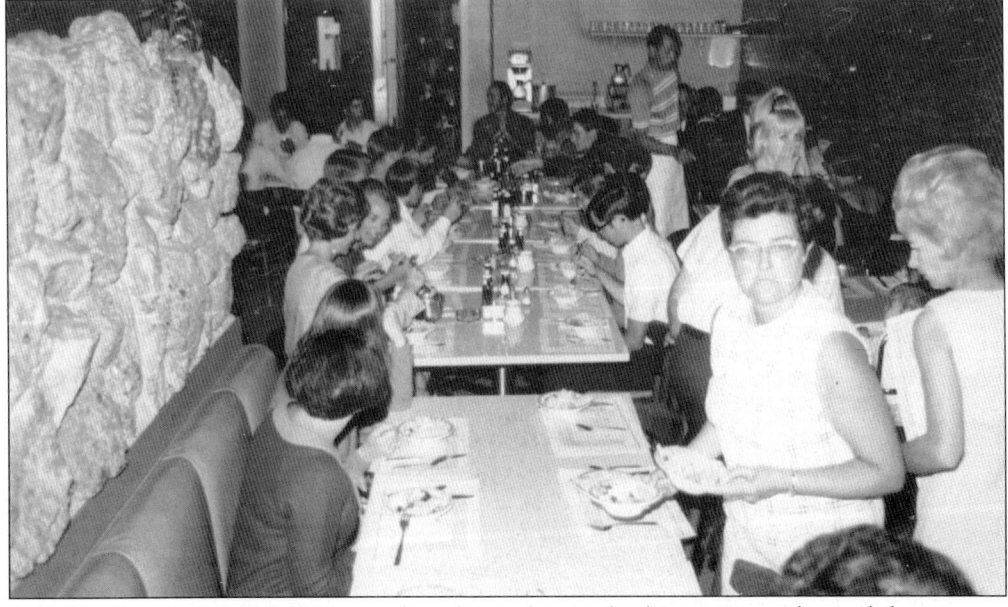

In 1954, Ken and Toni Hoffman purchased Angelo's Seafood Restaurant, changed the name to Ken's Seafood Bowl, and continued to serve customers at that location until they moved into their own location at 2424 San Bruno Avenue. The restaurant remained in business until 1988, when it closed. This photograph was taken in the 1950s. (Courtesy of Toni Hoffman.)

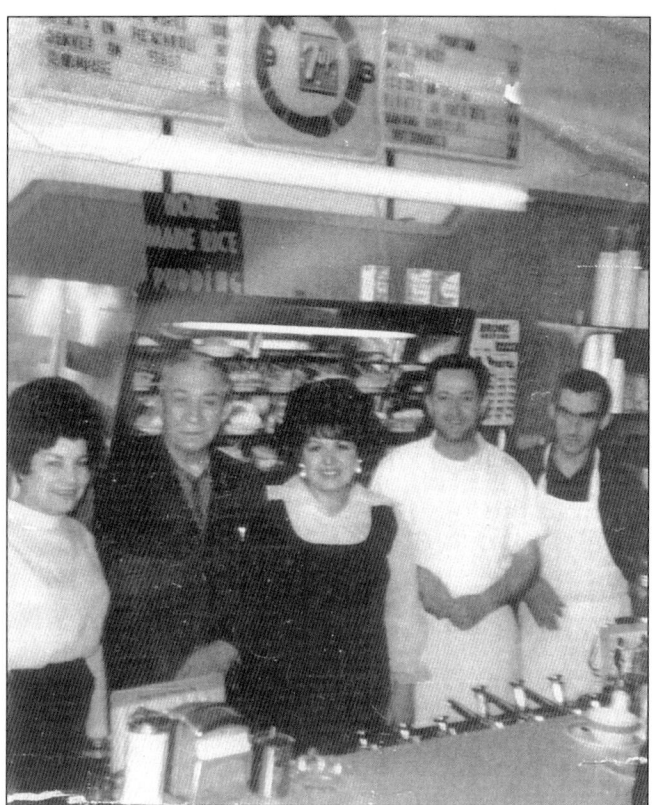

The Avenue Sweet Shop at 2680 San Bruno Avenue has been under the management of different owners over the years. In this undated photograph are, from left to right, Sophie Boyadzis, Gus Boyadzis, Millie ?, Pete ?, and unidentified. (Courtesy of Anthony Boyadzis.)

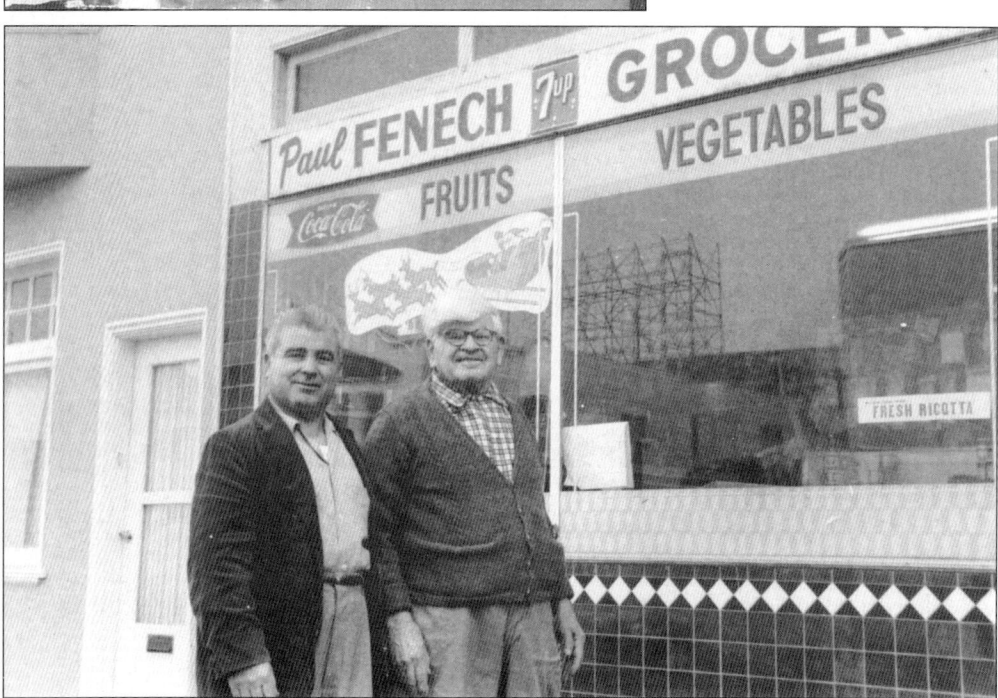

Paul Fenech's grocery store at 153 Bacon Street used to deliver groceries at no charge. Pictured are John and Tom Fenech. (Courtesy of Barbara Fenech.)

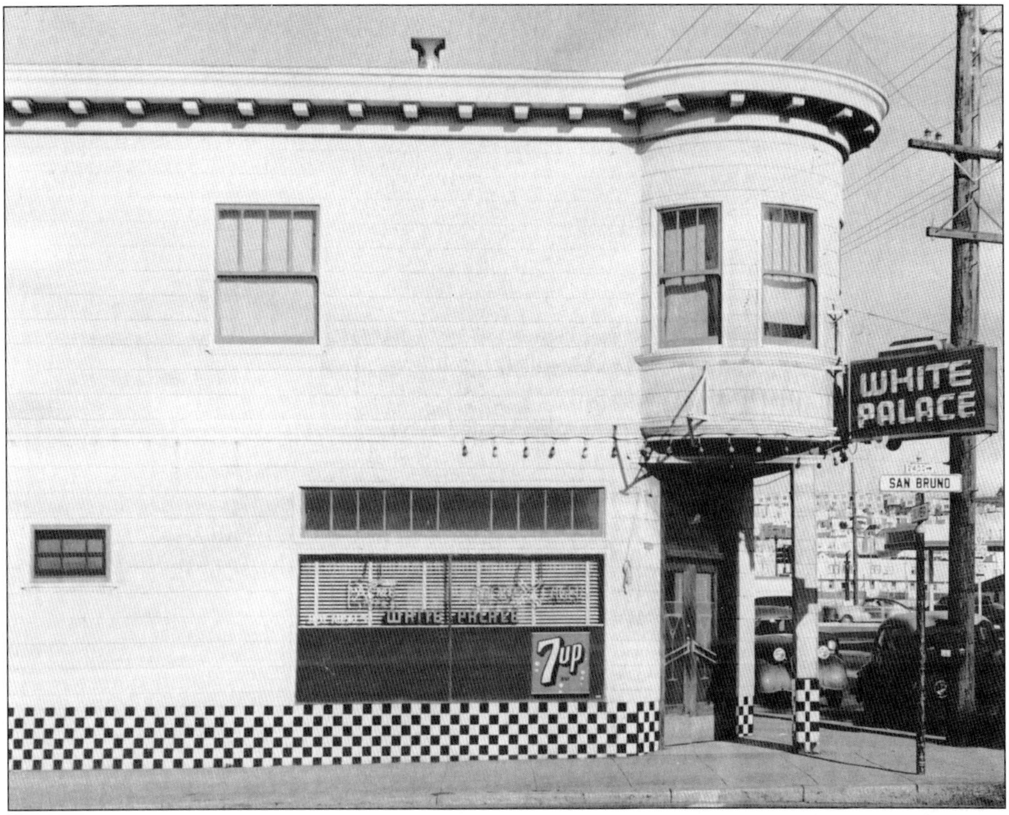

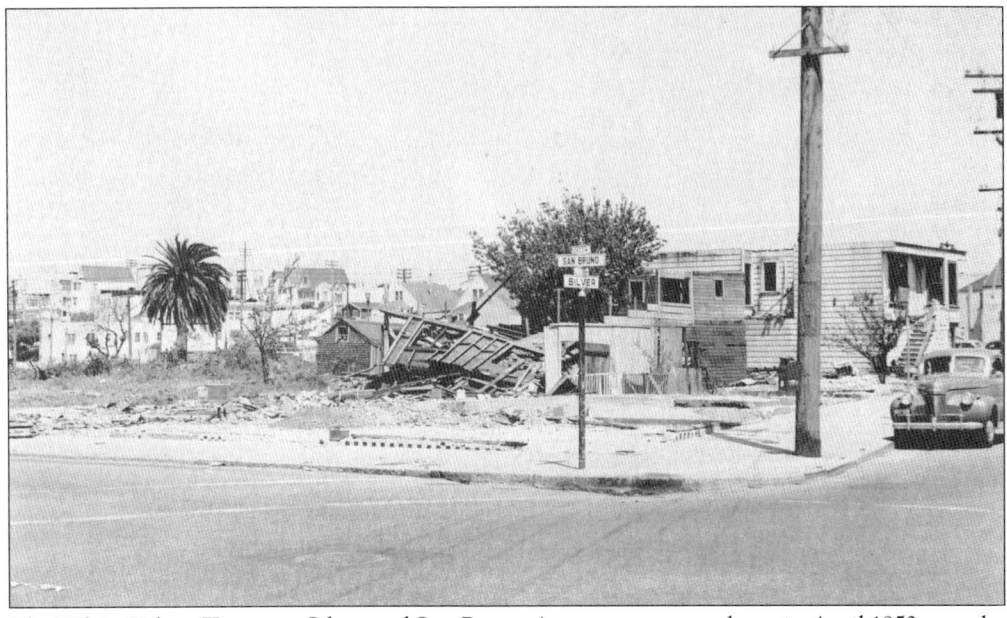

This January 1953 photograph shows the White Palace Tavern at Silver and San Bruno Avenues. (Courtesy of Joe Camilleri.)

The White Palace Tavern at Silver and San Bruno Avenues was torn down in April 1953 to make room for the James Lick Freeway. (Courtesy of Joe Camilleri.)

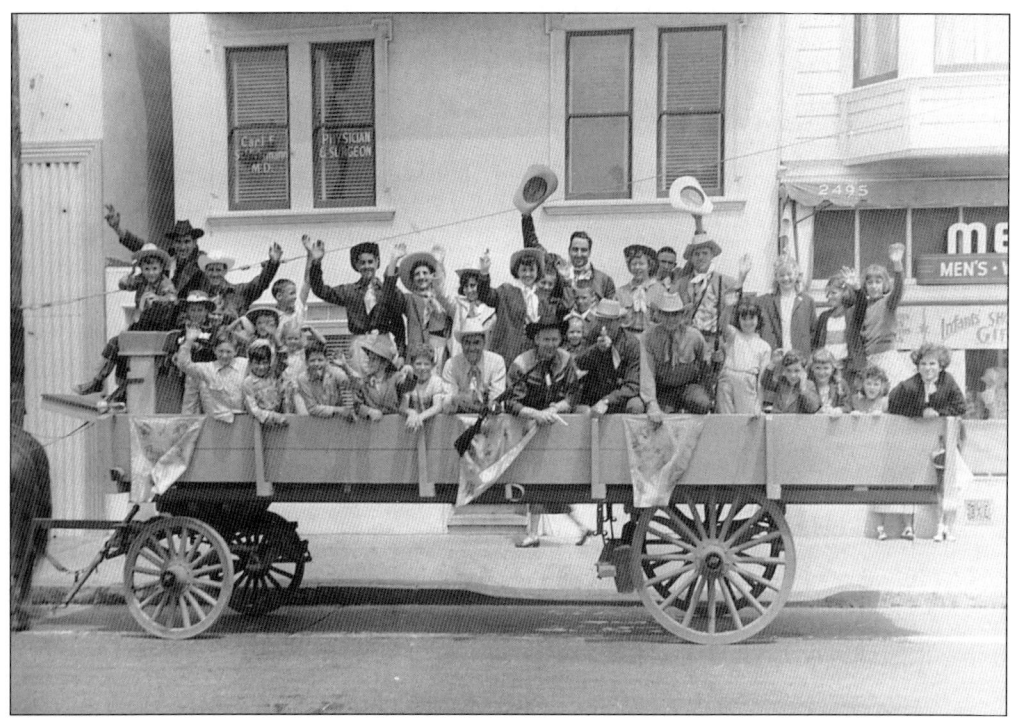

To commemorate the opening of the new Silver Avenue overpass in 1954, Portola merchants and their families celebrated Western Days. Dino's Delicatessen owner, Dino Malerbi, is at the reins as the wagon travels northbound on San Bruno Avenue. (Courtesy of the Armanino family.)

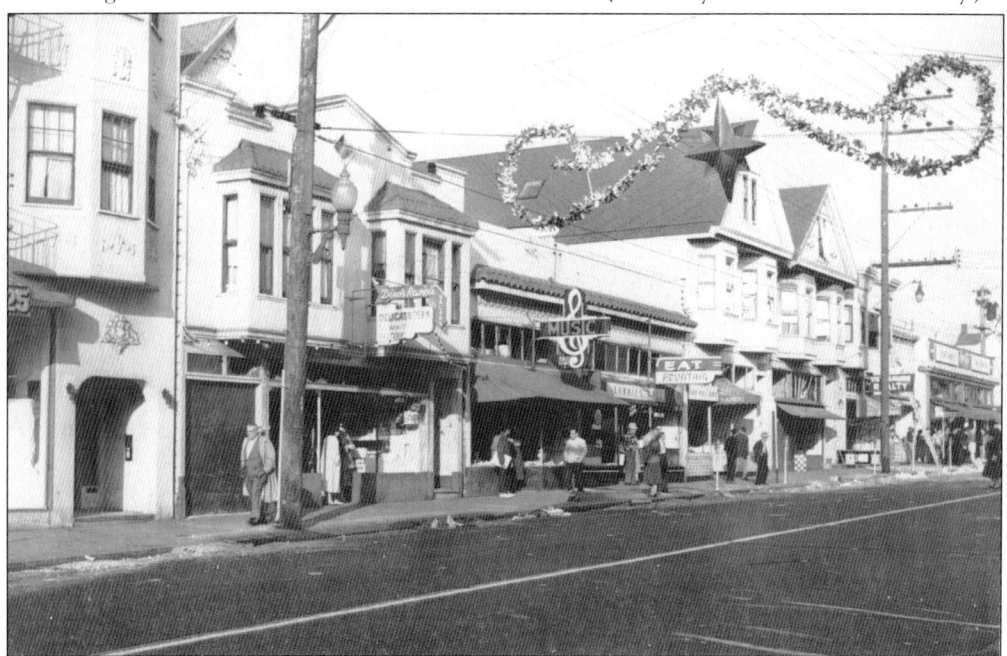

Dino's Delicatessen, a family run business located at 2550 San Bruno Avenue, opened in 1944 and served a variety of Italian specialties. Owner Dino Malerbi was well known for his homemade ravioli. (Courtesy of Beverly Malerbi Casella.)

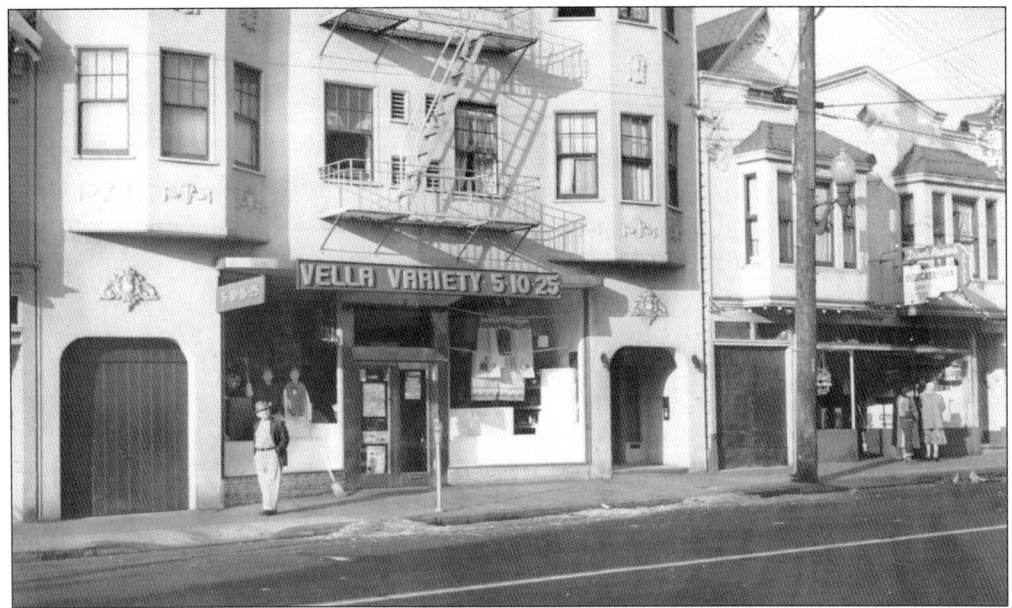

Vella Variety was one of the last five-and-dime stores in the area. (Courtesy of Beverly Malerbi Casella.)

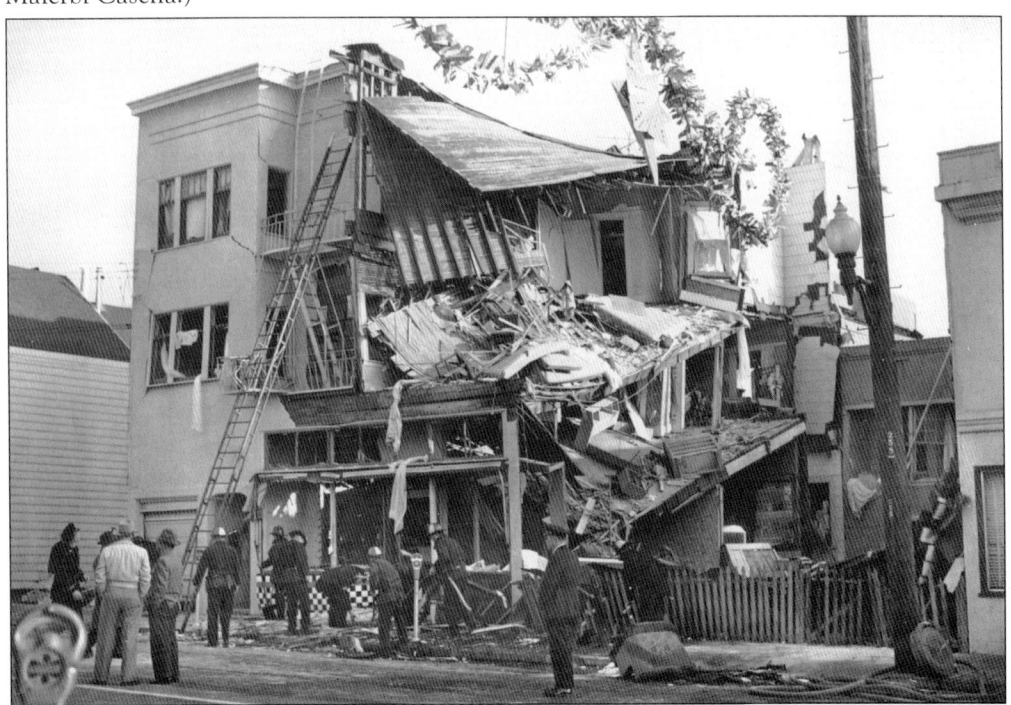

On January 9, 1957, Portola residents were awakened by a large explosion at an apartment house located at 2531 San Bruno Avenue. A resident preparing to paint his apartment disconnected some of the gas appliances while leaving the water heater connected and placed a wooden plug in the gas line. While answering an early morning telephone call, the apartment dweller lit a cigarette causing the fumes from the leaking gas pipe to ignite, demolishing the building. Businesses in the area suffered damage to their establishments. (Courtesy of Beverly Malerbi Casella.)

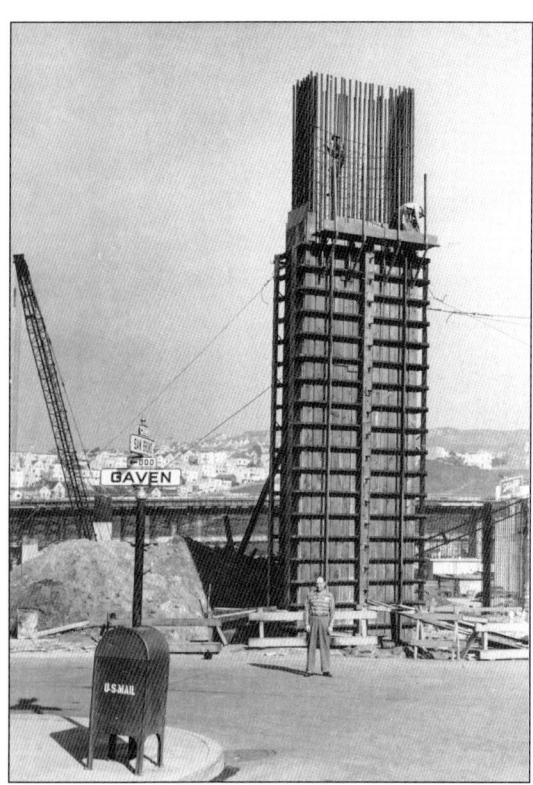

The construction of the James Lick freeway, as seen from the corner of Gaven and San Bruno Avenues, is the subject of this 1959 photograph. (Courtesy of Harry Cohn.)

This view looks north on San Bruno and Paul Avenues in December 1960. An older model Muni bus can be seen on the right of the photograph, and the Foothill Market can been seen to the left. (Courtesy of Pearl Bottino.)

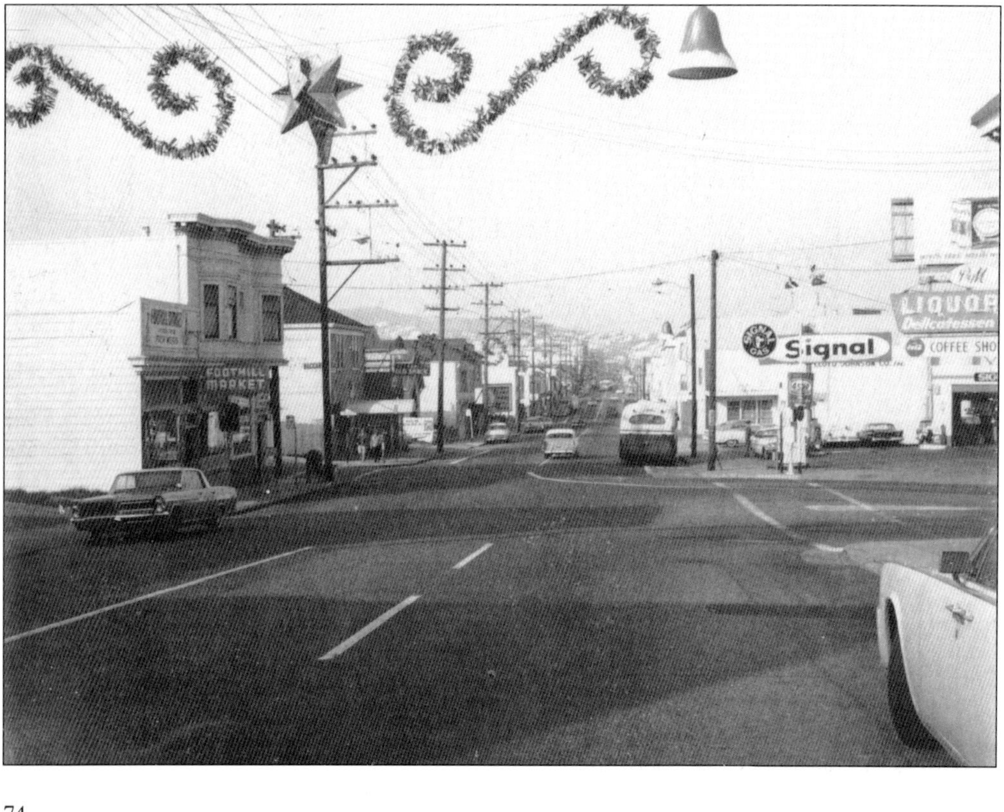

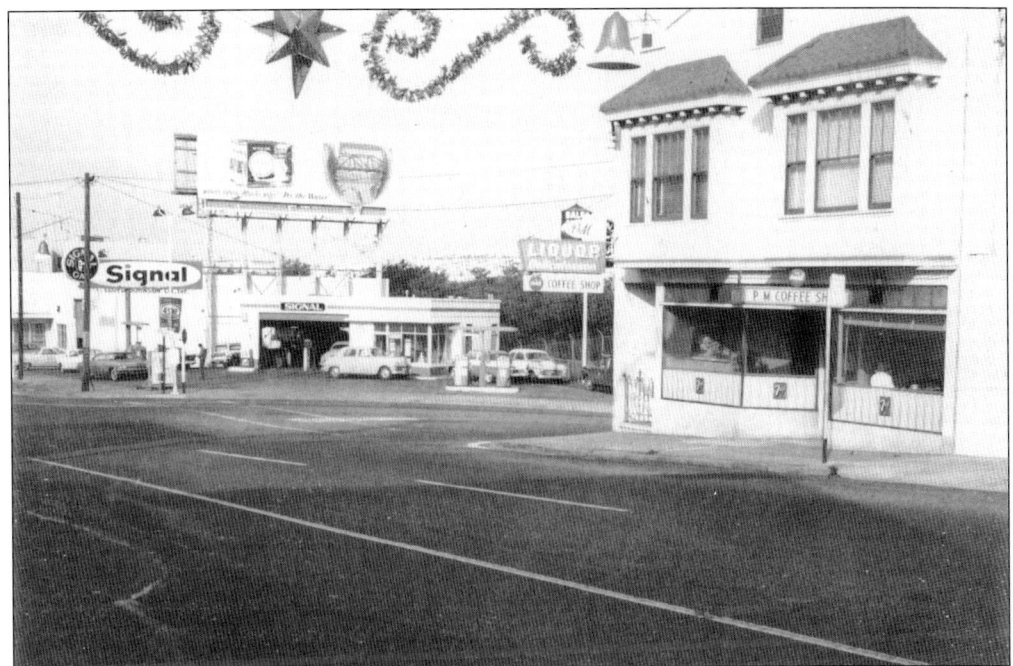

A photograph taken in December 1960 shows P and M Liquors and Café at the corner of San Bruno and Paul Avenues. The Signal gas station is on the opposite corner. (Courtesy of Pearl Bottino.)

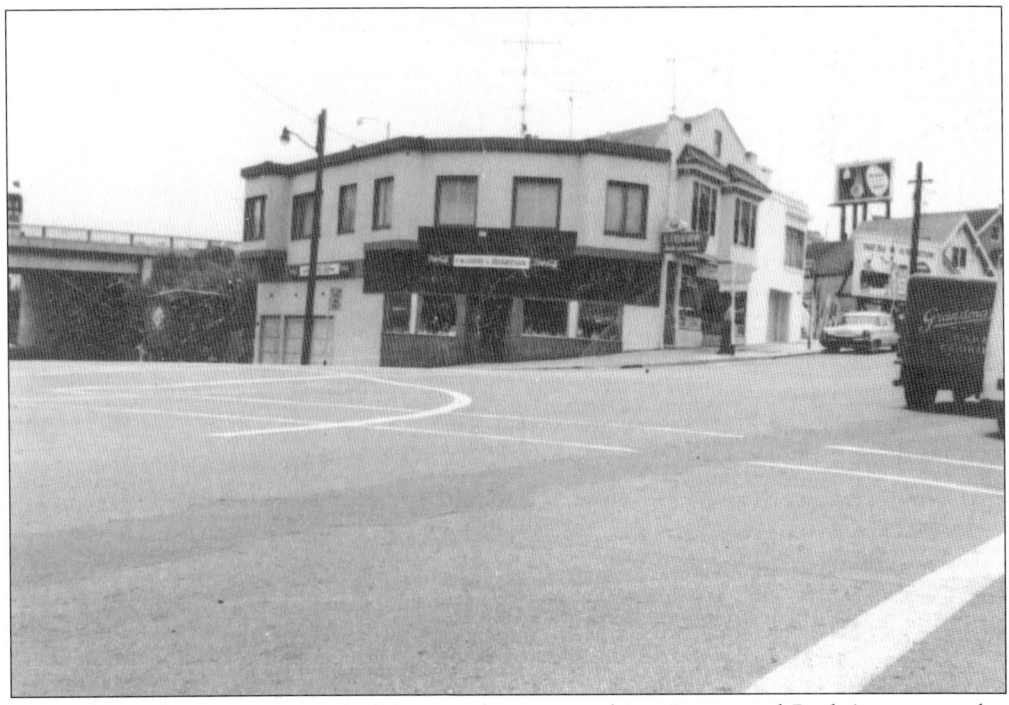

This view of P and M Liquors and Café at the corner of San Bruno and Paul Avenues is also from the 1960s. Original owner Pearl Bottino is the proprietor of the oldest establishment still in business. (Courtesy of Pearl Bottino.)

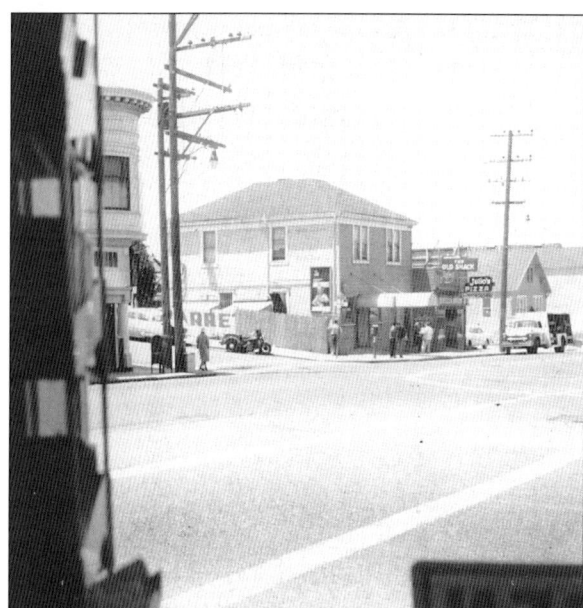

Another angle looks across San Bruno and Paul Avenues towards Dwight Street in this June 13, 1963, photograph. Popular establishments such as The Old Shack and Julio's Pizza can be seen from inside P and M Liquors and Café. (Courtesy of Pearl Bottino.)

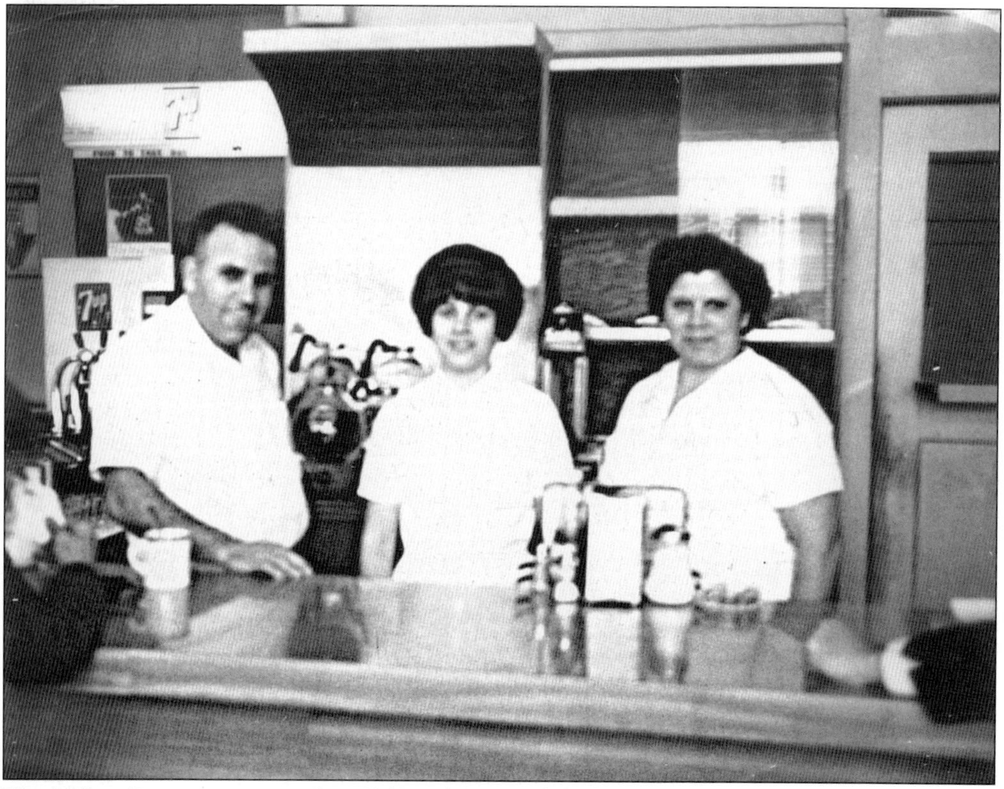

The Valleta Restaurant opened in 1963 and was run by John and Doris Darmanin. Located next to the Avenue Theater, it became a gathering place for the Maltese members of the neighborhood. The restaurant was known for Maltese specialties like pastizzi and timpani as well as the large hamburgers and french fries for 50¢. Pictured from left to right are John Darmanin, Helen Caruana, and Doris Darmanin. (Courtesy of Rita Darmanin Goldberg.)

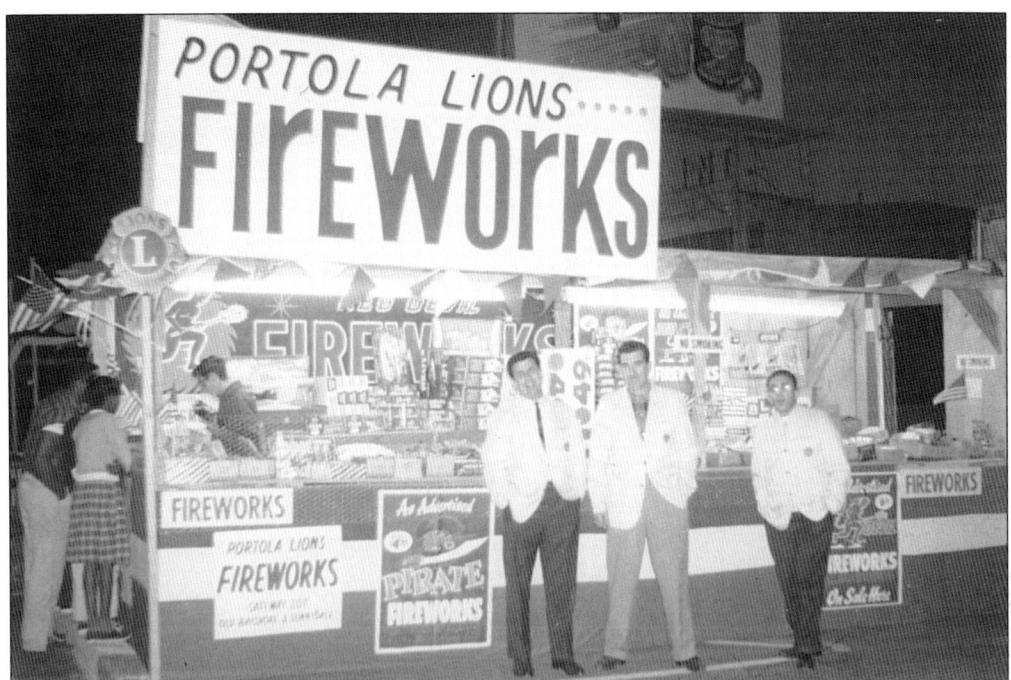

The Portola Lions became the first Lions organization in the neighborhood to sell fireworks, seen here in this July 1963 photograph. The fireworks were sold in a Safeway parking lot on Bayshore Boulevard. In the first week, they made a $5,000 profit. (Courtesy of Renato Ferrera.)

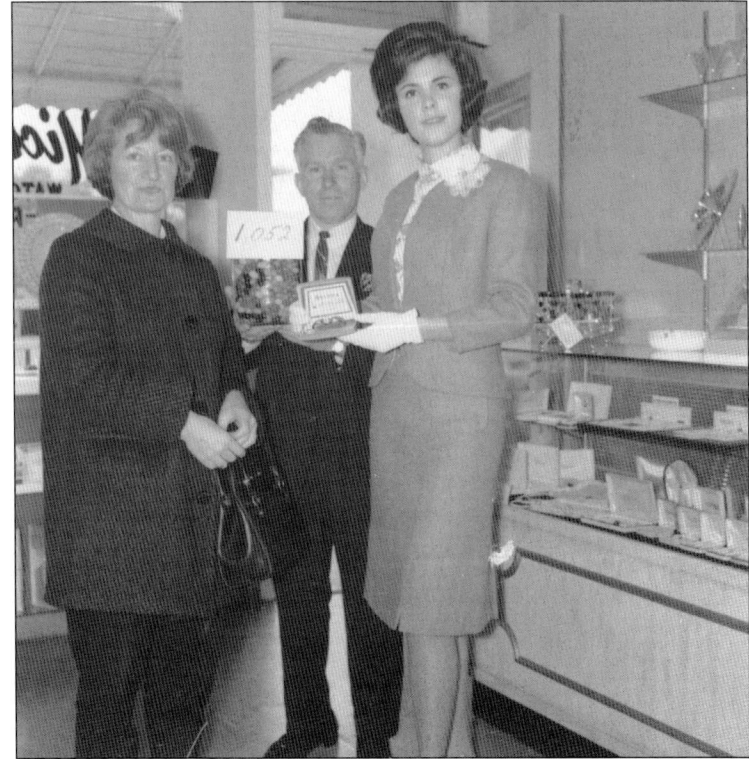

Michael's Jewelers opened at 2708 San Bruno Avenue. A jellybean-counting contest was held in 1963, and the grand prize was a Bulova watch. Pictured with the winning customer is owner Michael San Filippo Sr. and Miss San Francisco 1963, Jeri Sturdevant, a Portola resident. (Courtesy of Michael San Filippo.)

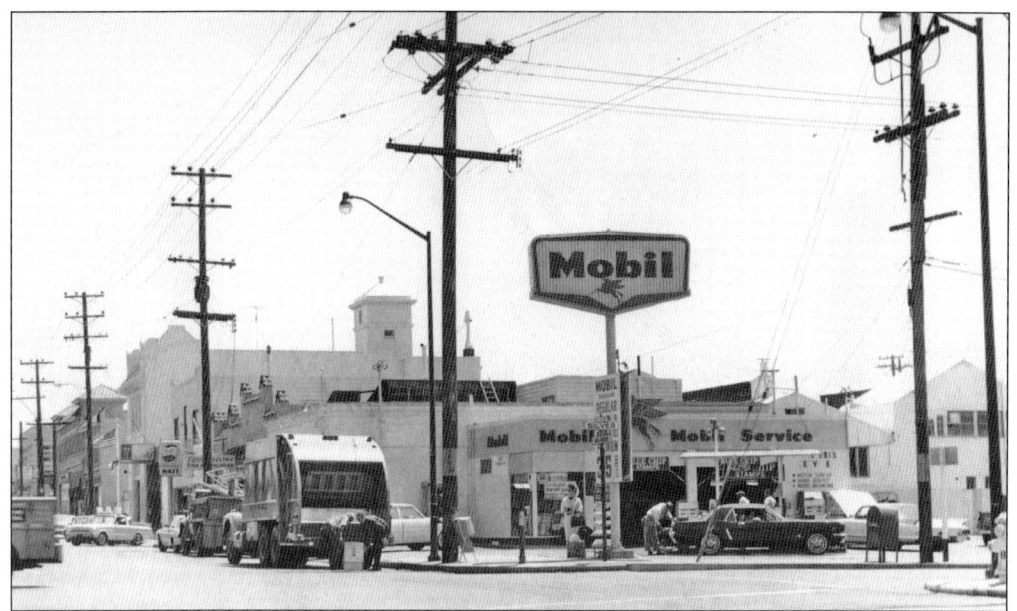

In 1967, the premium gasoline price at the Mobile gas station on the corner of Silver and San Bruno Avenues was 35¢ a gallon. (Courtesy of Mary Jane Camilleri Bragagnolo.)

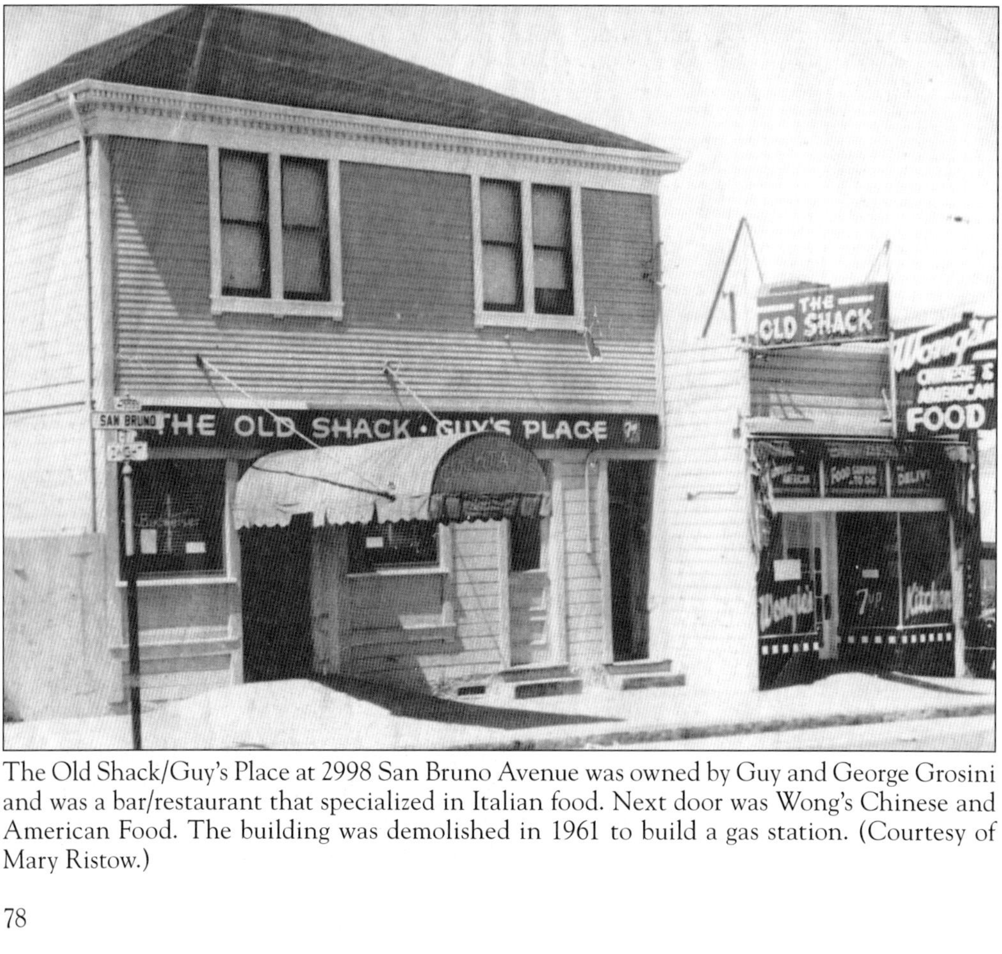

The Old Shack/Guy's Place at 2998 San Bruno Avenue was owned by Guy and George Grosini and was a bar/restaurant that specialized in Italian food. Next door was Wong's Chinese and American Food. The building was demolished in 1961 to build a gas station. (Courtesy of Mary Ristow.)

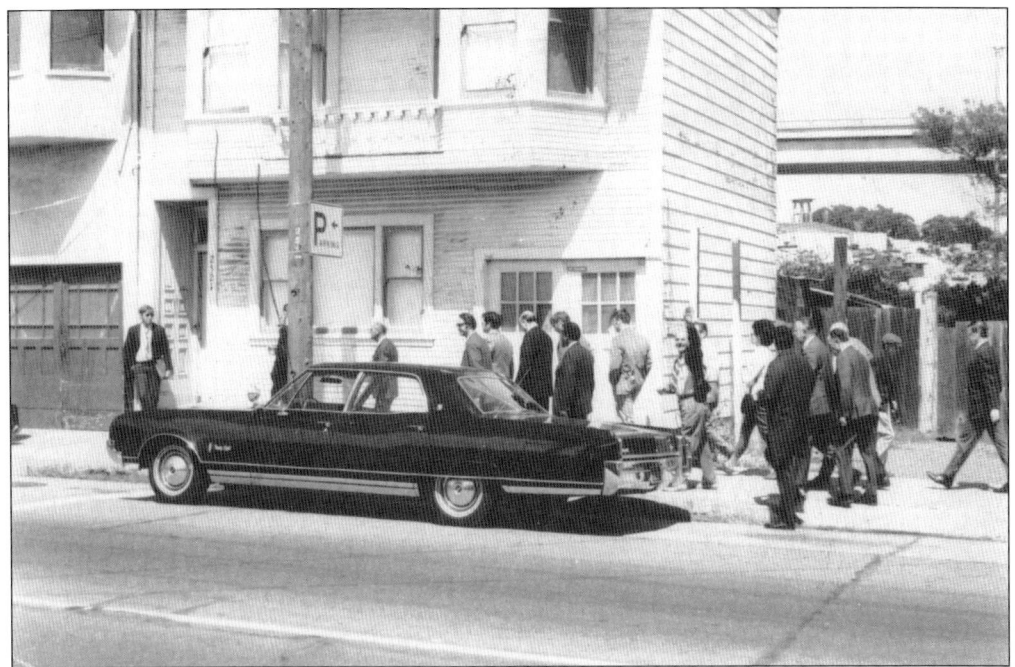

Mayor Joseph Alioto, sixth from the left, tours San Bruno Avenue in May 1969. He is seen walking towards 2521 San Bruno Avenue, which would become the future site of First Federal Savings and Loan Association of San Rafael. Joseph Alioto was inaugurated on January 8, 1968, and was reelected in 1971. (Courtesy of First Federal Savings and Loan Association of San Rafael.)

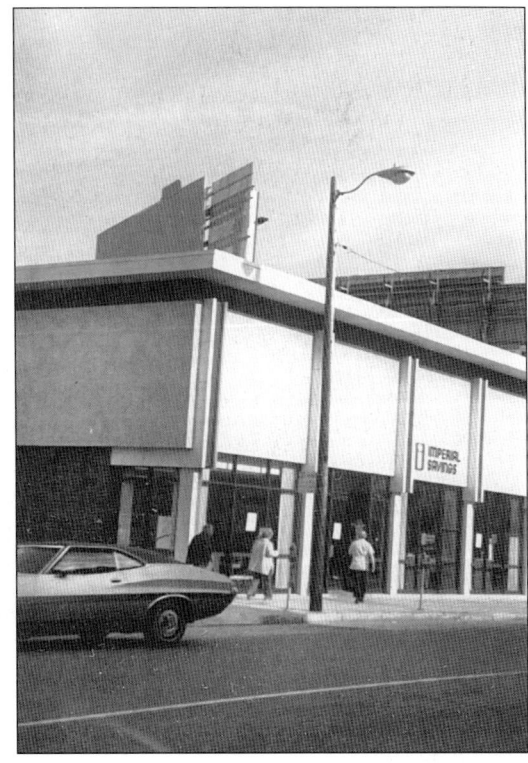

The Imperial Savings and Loan Association at 2675 San Bruno Avenue originally began as Columbus Savings and Loan. The institution changed its name to Imperial Savings in 1972. It was changed once again in 1992 to its current name of Bank of the West. (Courtesy of Bank of the West.)

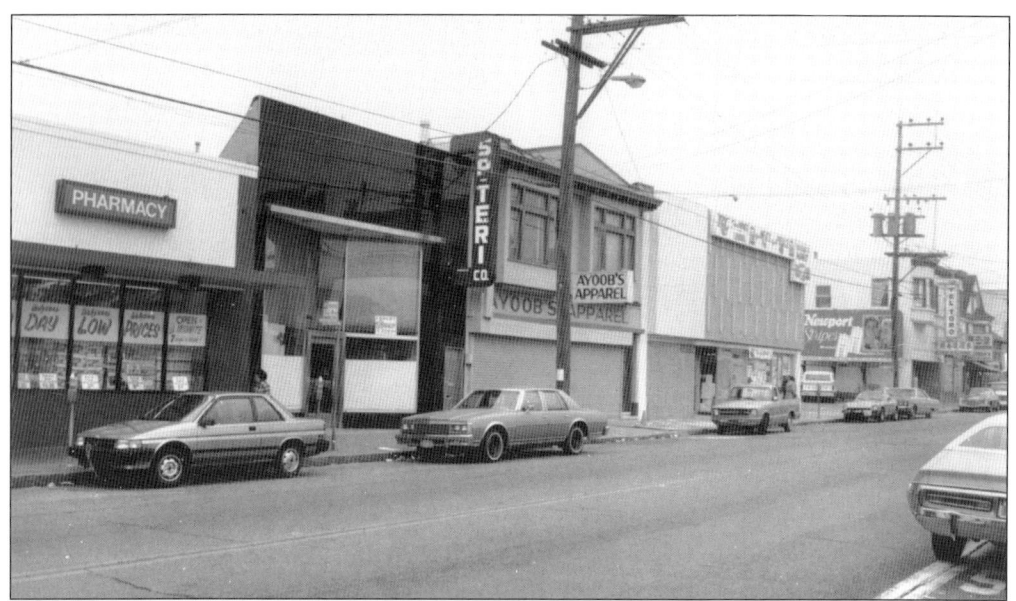

The SP-Teri Company at 2490 San Bruno Avenue was the manufacturing site for the SP-Teri Ice and Roller Skating Boots Company, which moved into the Portola in 1974. The company was owned by longtime Portola residents Joseph Spiteri, Frank Spiteri, Emanuel Spiteri, and Emanuel Falzon. SP-Teri shipped skating boots all over the world and also supplied them to national, world, and Olympic champions from the United States, England, Germany, China, Japan, Canada, and the Soviet Union. In 1989, the company moved to South San Francisco, still shipping boots to world championship–level skaters. (Courtesy of the Spiteri family.)

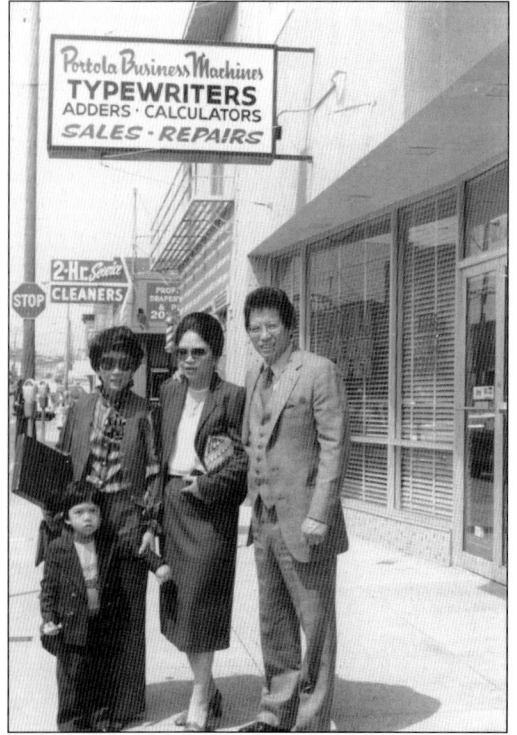

Portola Business Machines, owned and operated by Conrad Bulos, opened in the summer of 1979 at 2713 San Bruno Avenue. A sales, service, and repair shop of typewriters, calculators, adding machines, and cash registers, the store eventually closed in 1994. Pictured from left to right are Myrna Bulos, Jonathan Bulos, and Dulce and Edward Pangelinan. (Courtesy of the Bulos family.)

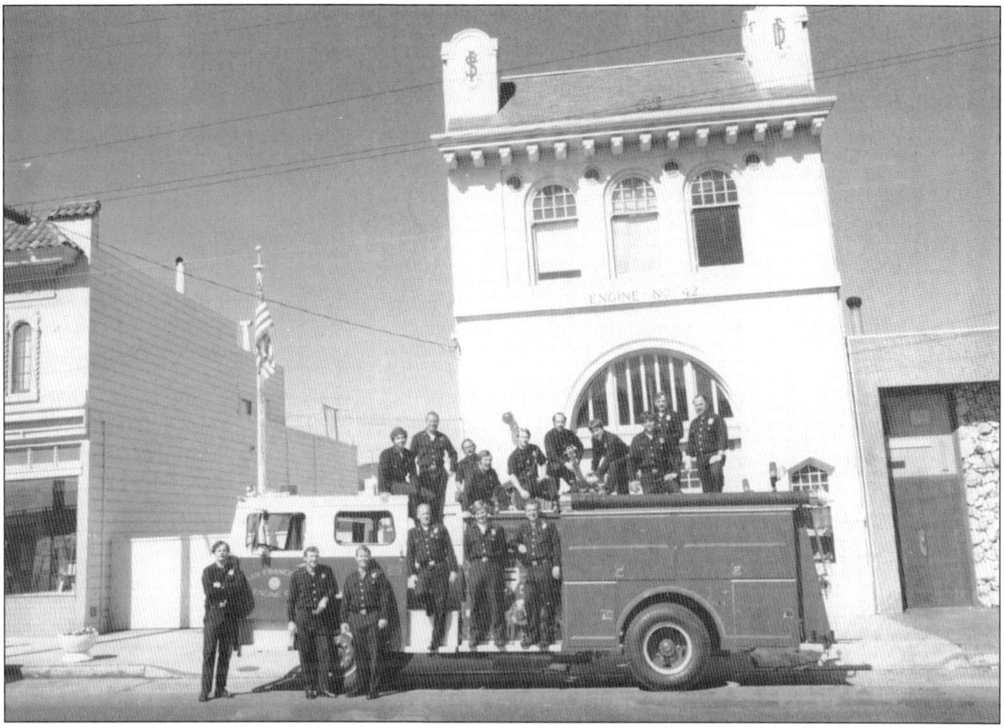

Members of San Francisco Fire Department Engine Company No. 42 take a group photograph in front of the fire station at 2430 San Bruno Avenue in the early 1970s. (Courtesy of Greg Owyang and Engine Company No. 42.)

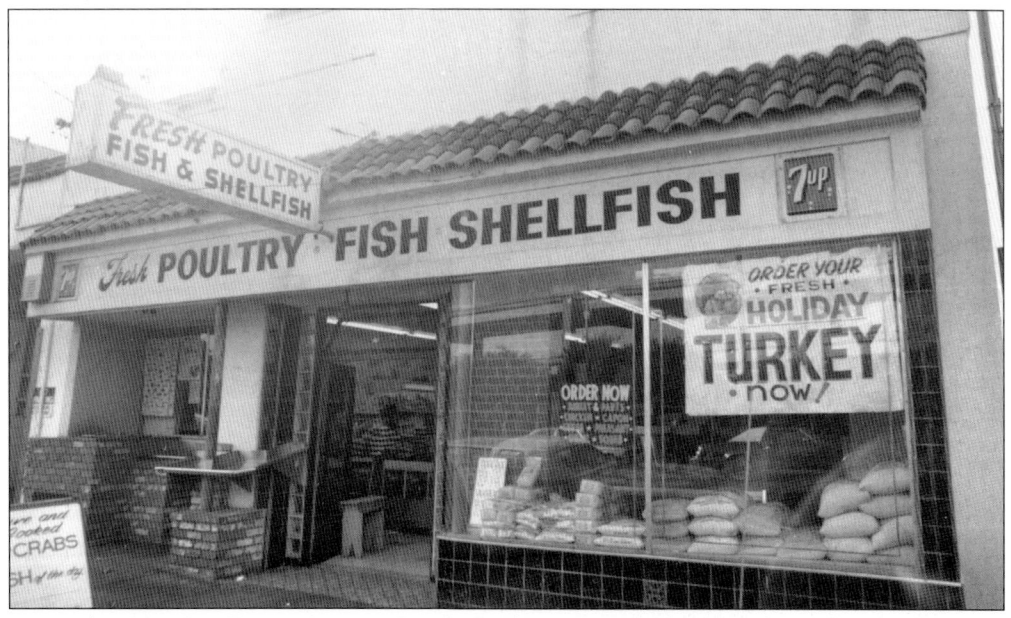

Located at 2414 San Bruno Avenue, Pacific Poultry was a wholesale and retail poultry business owned by Marco Bianchi since 1983. The store was originally a dairy, and the warehouse in the back was used as a chicken processing plant. Eventually Pacific Poultry began selling fish. (Courtesy of Elizabeth Bianchi.)

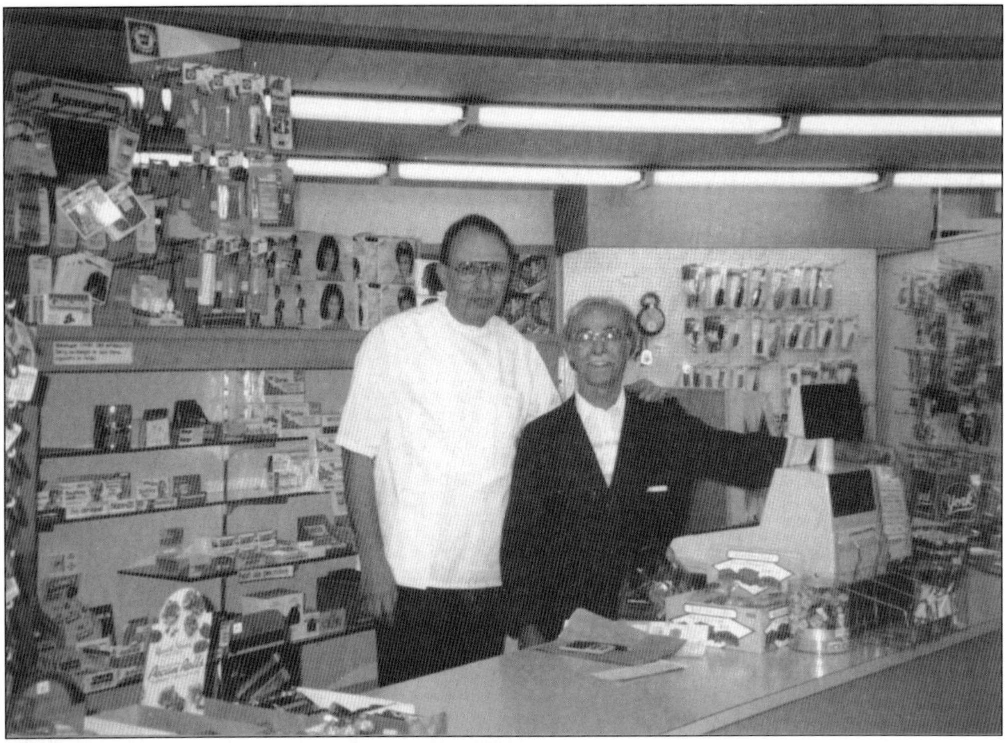

Golden State Pharmacy, located at 2450 San Bruno Avenue, was in business from 1956 to 1994. In 1995, the site became home to the Portola branch of the San Francisco Public Library. Pictured here in 1982 are pharmacist and owner Andrew Giordano and employee Vince Ronco. (Courtesy of the Giordano family.)

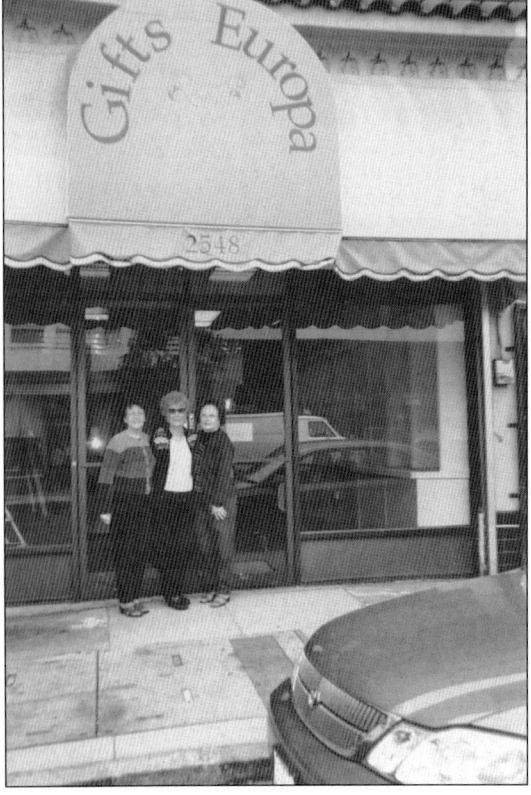

Gifts Europa, a direct importer of European giftware that also specialized in favors for weddings, christenings, and first communions, was located at 2548 San Bruno Avenue. It was in business from September 1985 until its closing in July 2003. Pictured from left to right are Liliana Capitelli, Lola Furlani, and Pia Moro. (Courtesy of Pia Moro.)

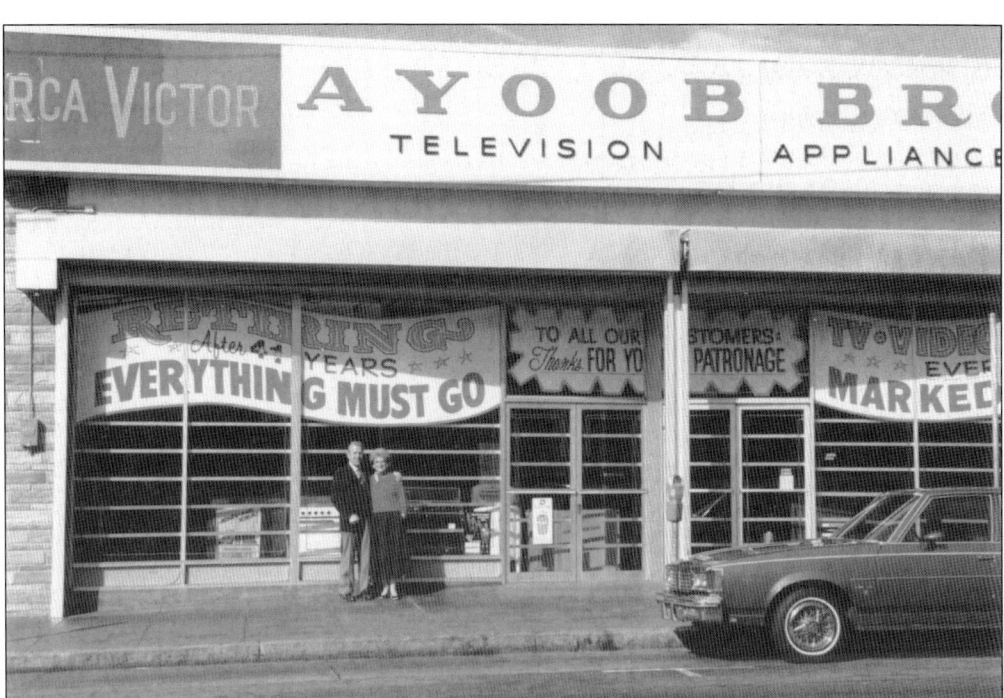

Ayoob Appliance opened its first store in 1946 at 2726 San Bruno Avenue before relocating to 2500 San Bruno Avenue. Pictured here is owner Tom Ayoob and his wife, Diane, at their "Going Out of Business" sale in July 1988. The site is currently the home of Kragen Auto Parts. (Courtesy of Thomas Ayoob.)

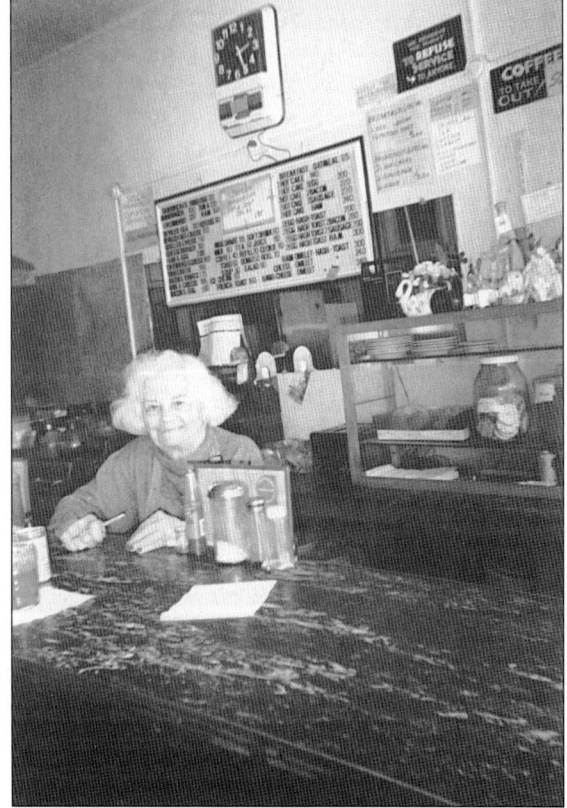

P and M Liquors and Café, at the corner of San Bruno and Paul Avenues, has operated under the same ownership since 1948, when the liquor store opened. In 1954, the café opened alongside it. P and M gets its name from the owners, Pearl, pictured here, and Matt Bottino. (Courtesy of Barbara Fenech.)

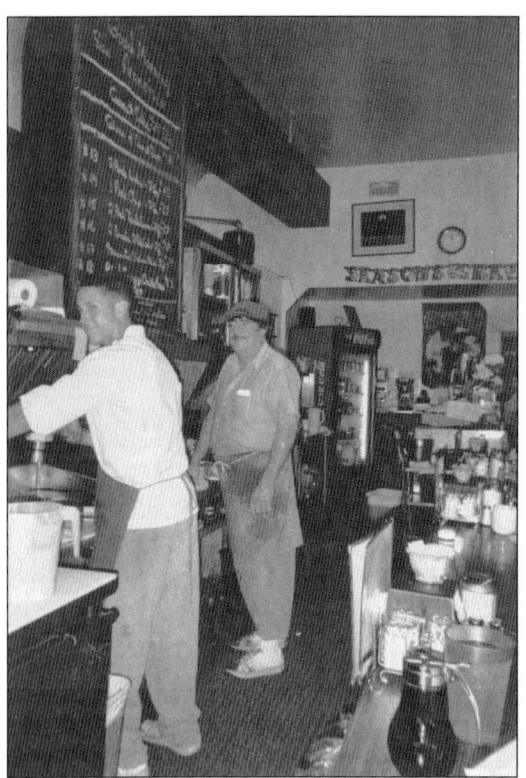

Breakfast at Tiffany's, a Portola dining establishment for 27 years, is located at 2499 San Bruno Avenue. Pictured from left to right are Robbie Adan and Gerald Adan. (Courtesy of author.)

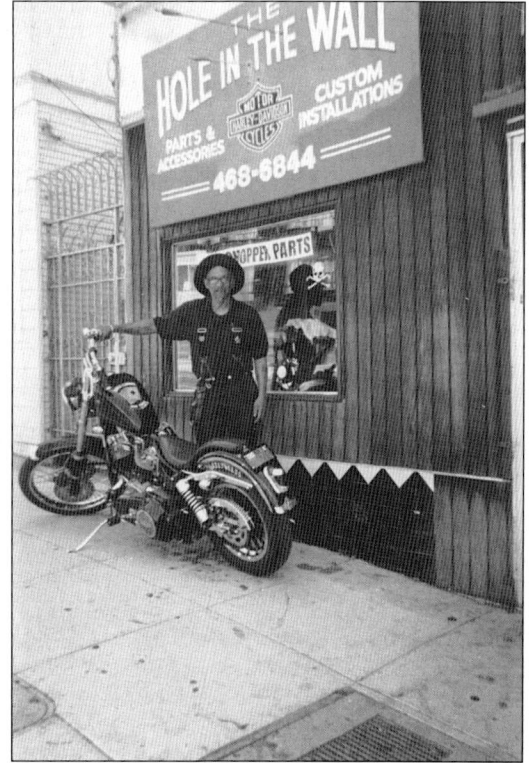

The Hole in the Wall Harley Davidson motorcycle shop has been a fixture at 3030 San Bruno Avenue for 23 years. Pictured is owner George Bennett Jr. (Courtesy of Barbara Fenech.)

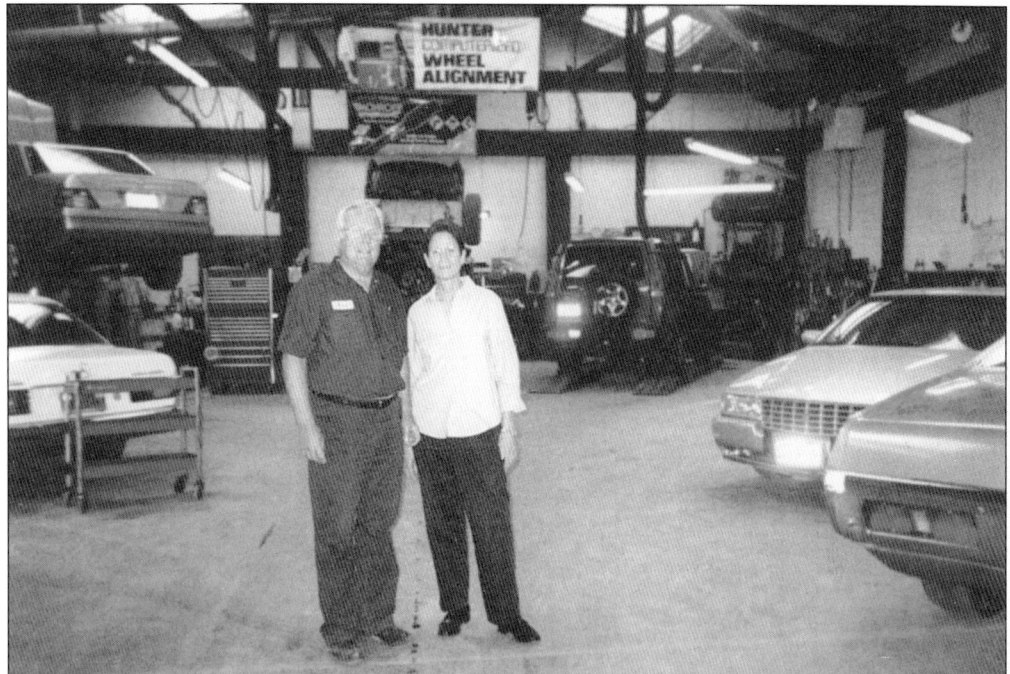

The Portola Auto Service at 2780 San Bruno Avenue has been repairing automobiles in the Portola since its early days. Pictured here are longtime Portola residents Paul and Lorraine Giannini, who have operated the business for 35 years. (Courtesy of author.)

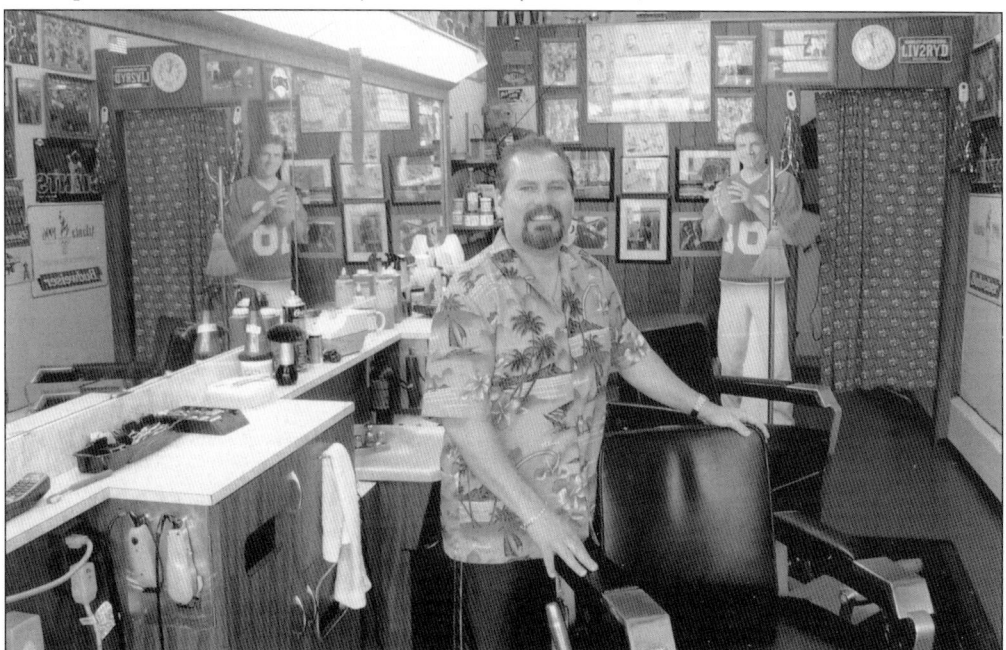

Giannini's Barbershop at 2732 San Bruno Avenue is the last men's barbershop to be found on San Bruno Avenue. Much of the equipment in this establishment was brought over from the old shop at 2656 San Bruno Avenue, which was located next to the Avenue Theatre and owned by Gino Columbano. Pictured is owner Terry Giannini. (Courtesy of David R. Mehrwein.)

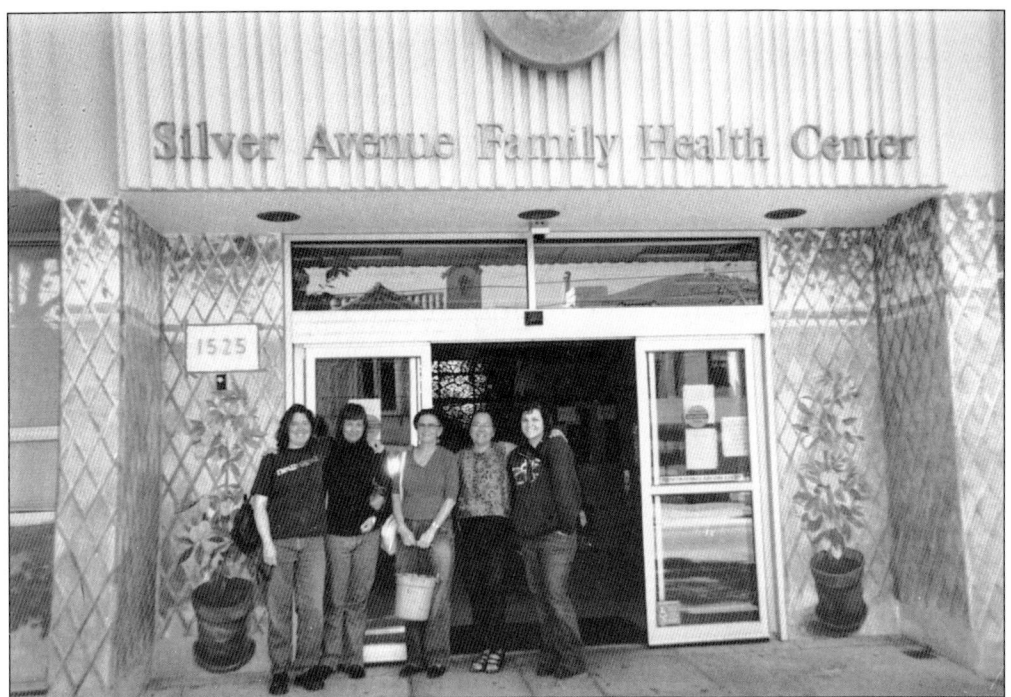

The Silver Avenue Family Health Center at 1525 Silver Avenue provides for the health needs of Portola residents. Pictured are, from left to right, Ginny Bowen and Melinda May, the muralists who painted the outside mural; Susan Cervantes; Marie Palazuelos, M.D.; and Meghan Earley. (Courtesy of Barbara Fenech.)

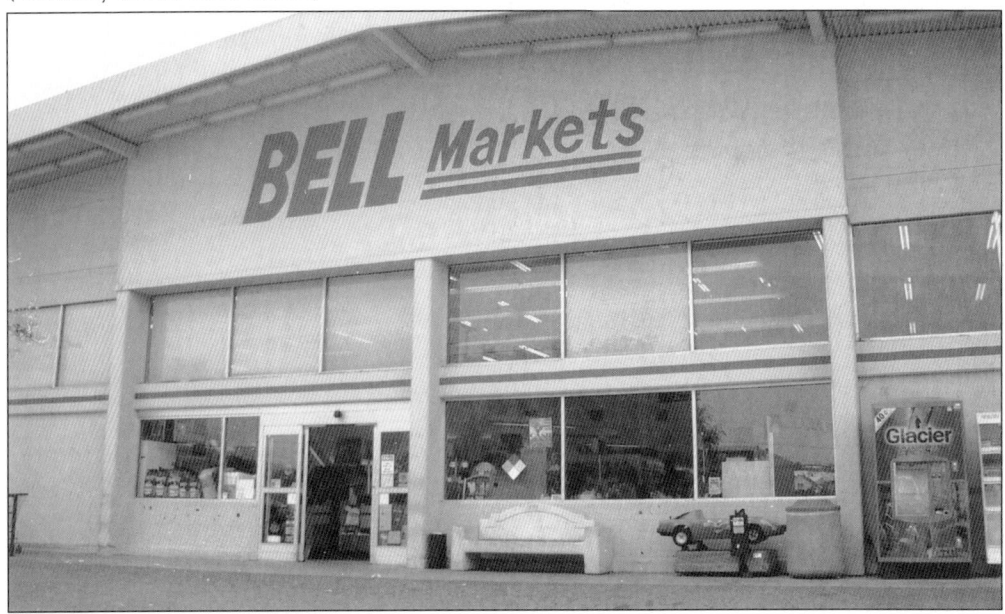

Located at 1390 Silver Avenue, Bell Market, a Portola district establishment since 1964, was owned by Dominic Tintori, Harry Misthos, and Sergio Pardini. The grocery store received its name because the building owner was named Angelo Campana. In Italian, *campana* means "bell." (Courtesy of David R. Mehrwein.)

Owned by Jean Harrell (seen here), Ruth's Children Shoppe, at 2469 San Bruno Avenue, has been at the same location since 1980. The building withstood the 1906 earthquake and much later became the last building left intact to accommodate the 101 South Freeway entrance. In 1970, the site was considered for the future home of Bay View Federal Savings and Loan. (Courtesy of Barbara Fenech.)

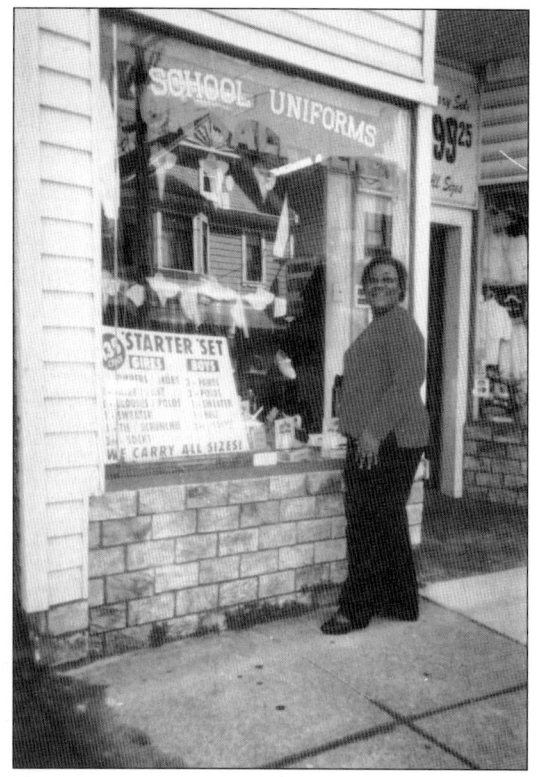

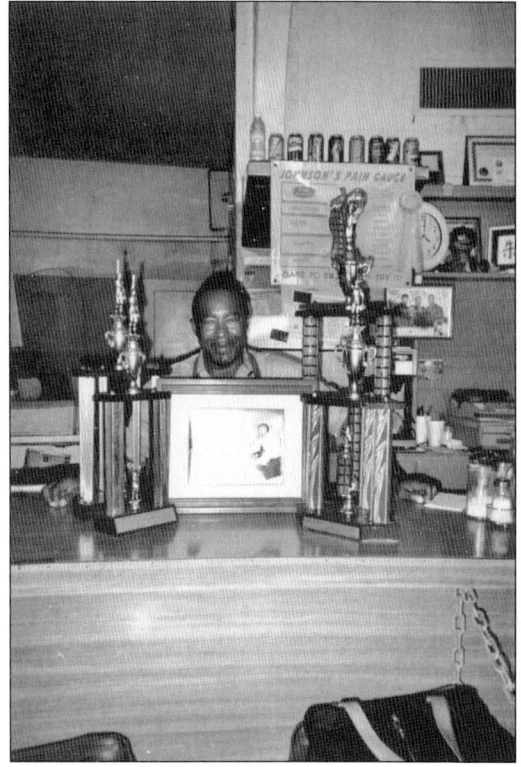

Johnson's Bar-B-Que has been at 2648 San Bruno Avenue for the past 12 years. Owner/operator Joe Johnson poses with some of his trophies from the American Barbeque Association, winning awards in 1991 and 1992 for Best Ribs, Pork, and Sauce in America. Johnson's is home to the "thermal nuclear sauce" invented by Joe's father. Here Joe holds a photograph of himself and Mayor Willie Brown. (Courtesy of author.)

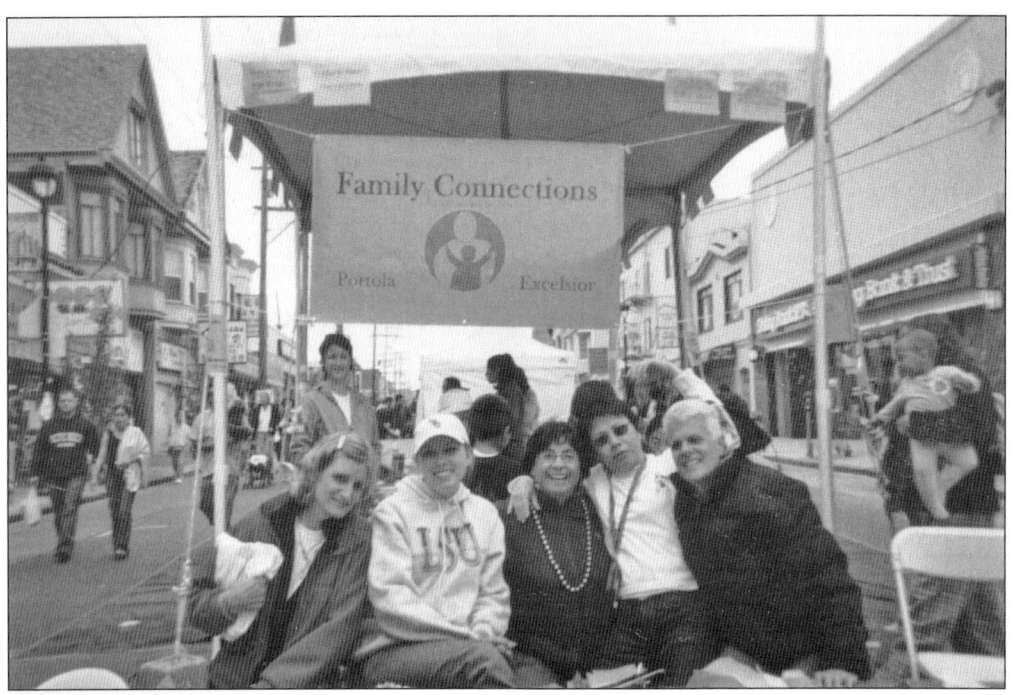

Family Connections, located at 2565 San Bruno Avenue, is a neighborhood-based family resource center that has been providing services to the Portola community since 1993. Pictured from left to right are Maryann Fleming, executive director; Elizabeth Longman; Linda Mastrangelo; Mimi Bui; and Linda DeMartini. Pictured in the back is Gina Mendicino. (Courtesy of Barbara Fenech.)

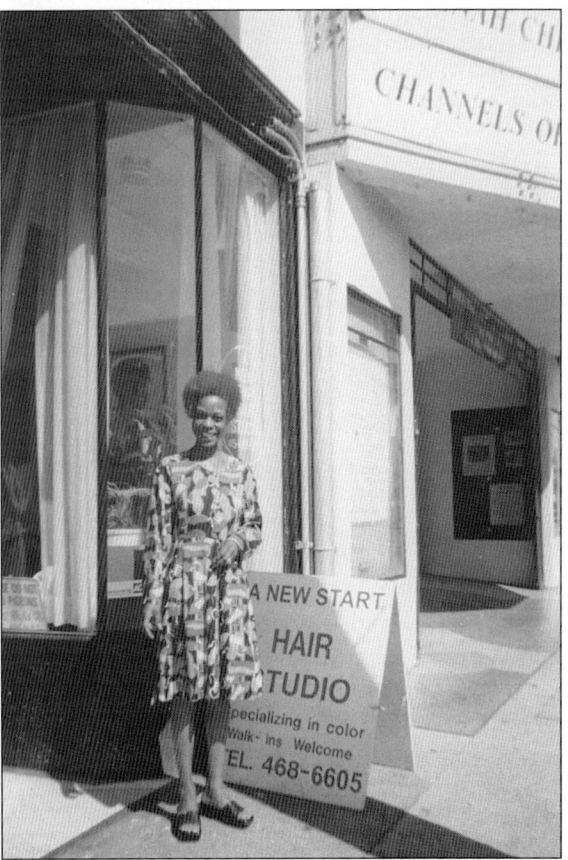

Avonette Walker, the owner of the New Start Hair Studio at 2656 San Bruno Avenue, has been at her current location for eight years. The site was once occupied by a barbershop. (Courtesy of Barbara Fenech.)

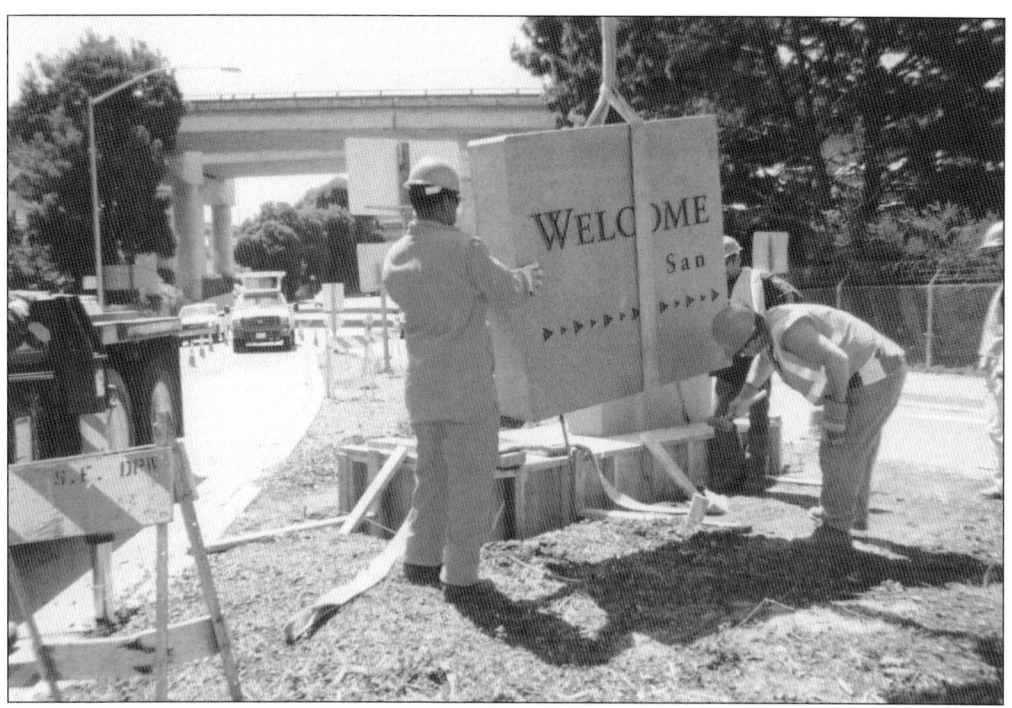

The "Welcome to Portola" monument was installed on February 28, 2000, at San Bruno Avenue and Alemany Boulevard. These pictures show the two-part monument being set up. (Courtesy of Barbara Fenech.)

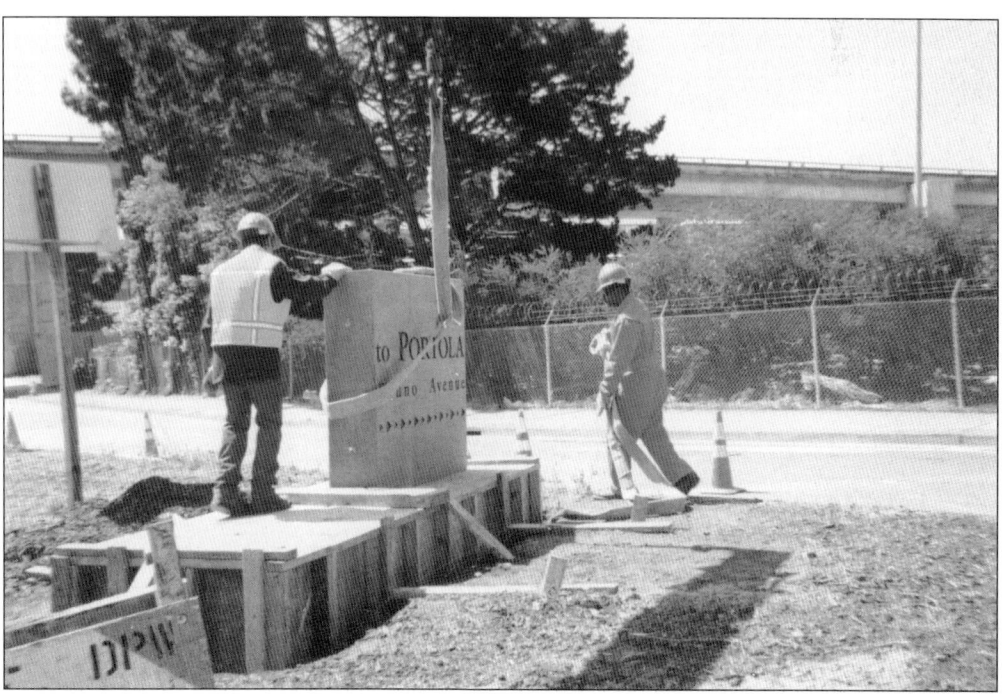

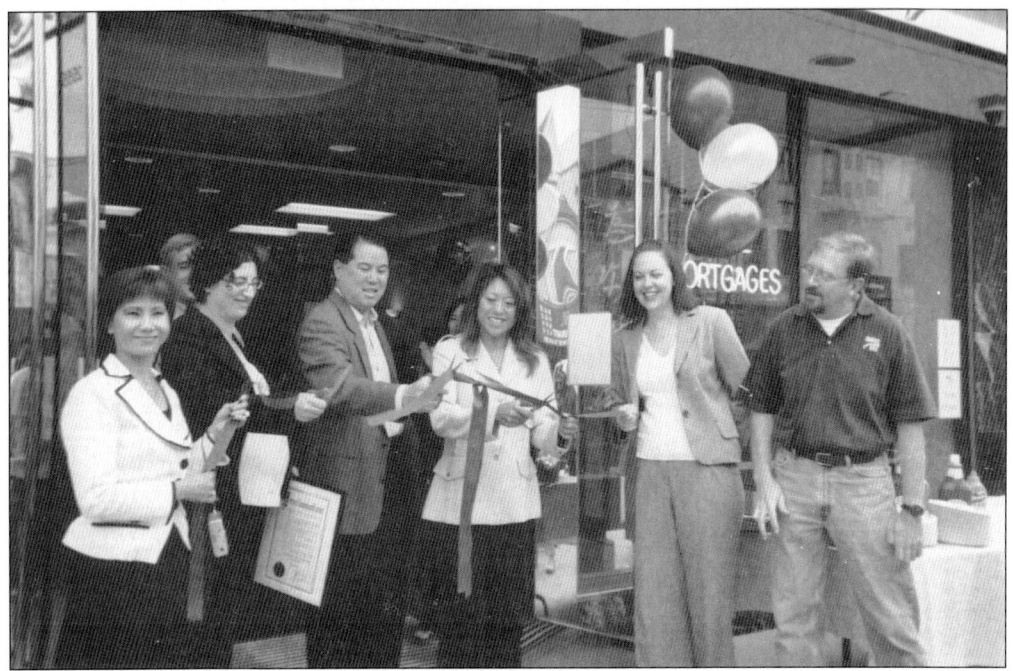

The grand opening of the Sterling Bank and Trust at 2555 San Bruno Avenue was held on August 19, 2006. The bank building was a former Safeway store, once located on Bayshore Boulevard and transported to its current location in the 1930s. Pictured from left to right are Linda Su, Sterling Bank and Trust California assistant regional manager; Amy Cohen, mayor's representative; unidentified; Fiona Ma, District 4 supervisor; Anita Wilson, Sterling Bank and Trust operations assistant; and Stephen Adams, Sterling Bank and Trust managing director, Western Division. (Courtesy of author.)

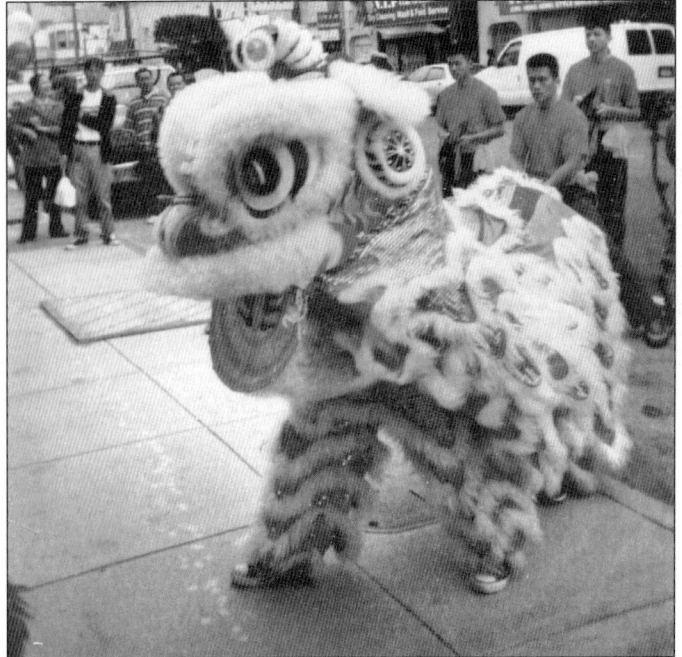

Members of the Cherng Loong Lion Dance Troupe bring good fortune to the grand opening of Sterling Bank and Trust. Lion dances are used to scare away demons and evil spirits and to bring good luck to new businesses. The Cherng Loong Lion Dance Troupe has been in the Bay Area since 2001. (Courtesy of author.)

The fourth annual San Bruno Avenue Street Fair was held on October 1, 2006, and featured booths with arts, crafts, and ethnic foods as well as live entertainment and a children's area. (Courtesy of author.)

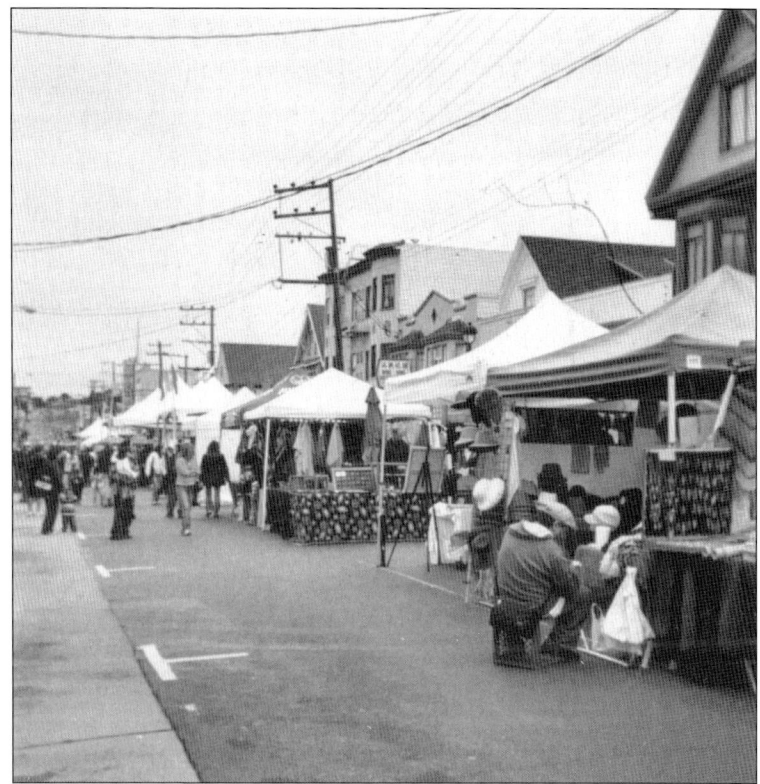

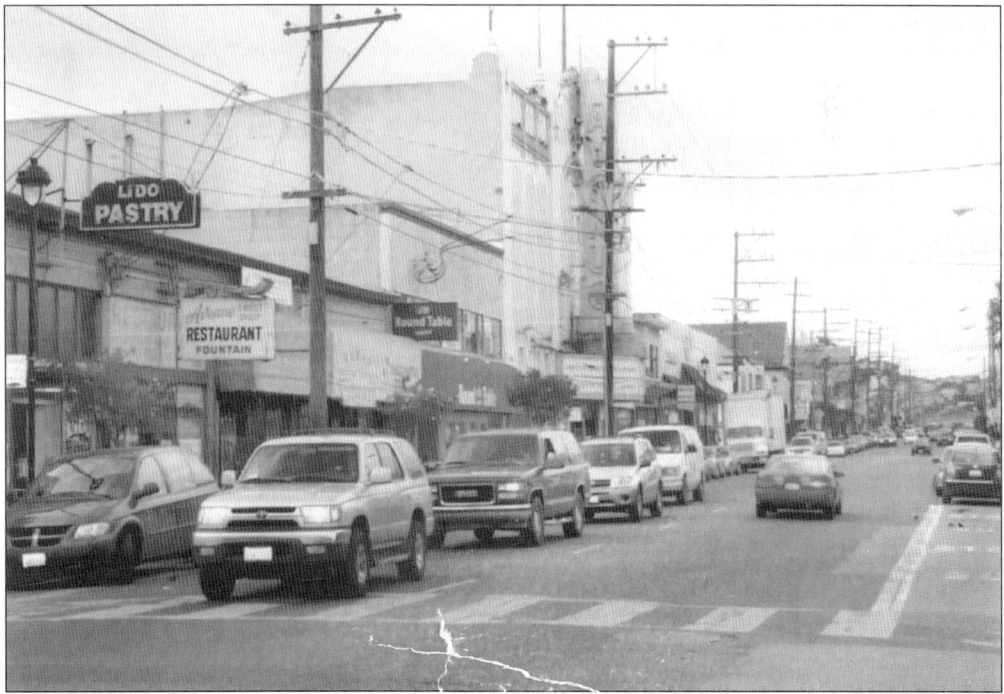

This 2006 photograph shows San Bruno Avenue looking north from Bacon Street. (Courtesy of Dwayne and Terezinha Jusino.)

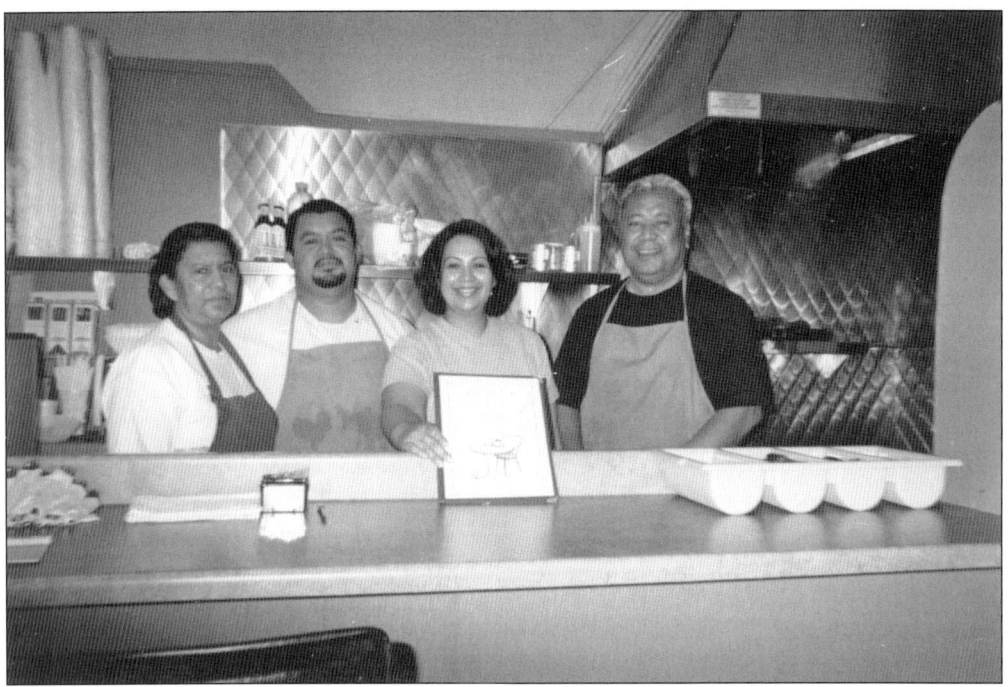

In July 2006, Iriana's Restaurant replaced the Avenue Sweet Shop at 2680 San Bruno Avenue. The new restaurant specializes is Salvadorian and American cuisine. Pictured from left to right are Berta Lopez, Junior Lopez, Mercy Lopez, and Amataga Amataga. (Courtesy of Barbara Fenech.)

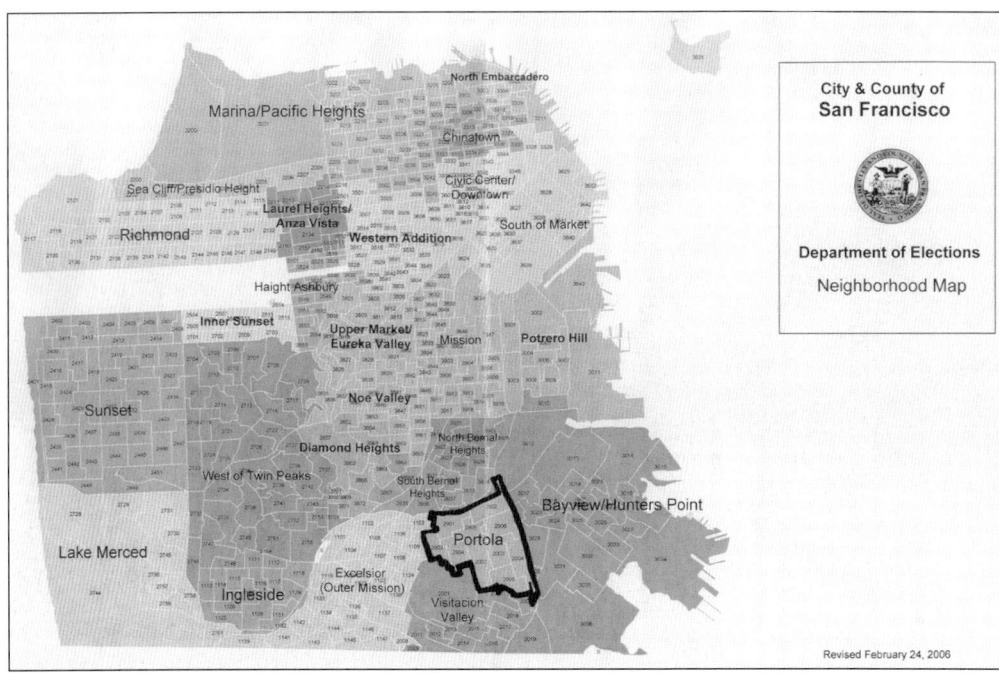

This map shows the Portola's current boundaries. (Courtesy of the City and County of San Francisco, Department of Elections.)

Four
PEOPLE

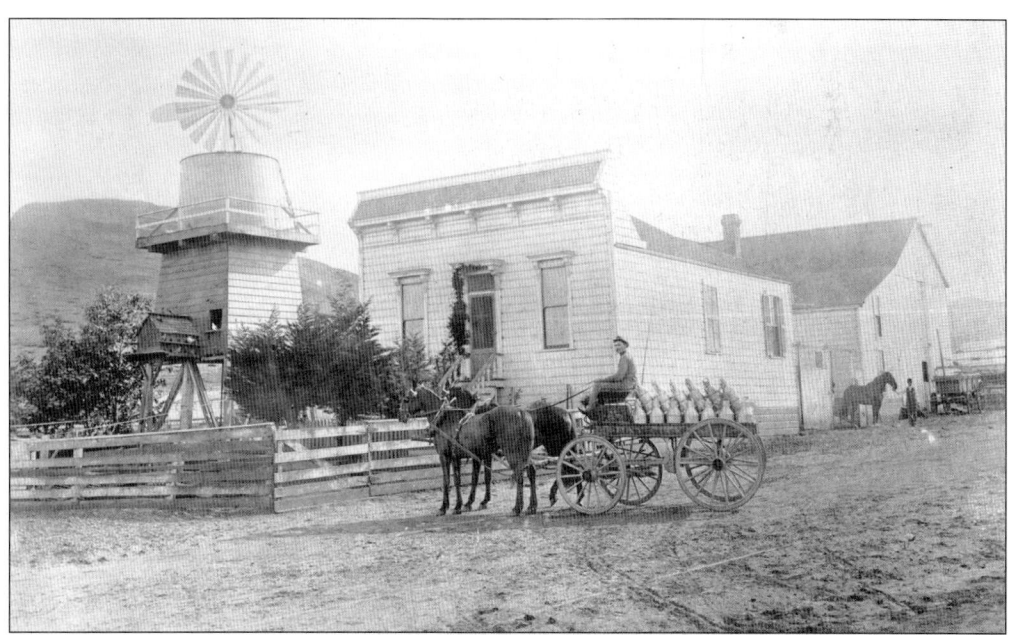

Felix Perini is pictured in his milk delivery wagon in 1882 at 500 Brussels Street at Wayland. The house, which was built in 1867, survived the 1906 earthquake, and San Francisco residents used to come and marvel at the house that endured the disaster. The house, as well as the windmill in the background, is still standing today (see page 114). (Courtesy of St. Elizabeth Church.)

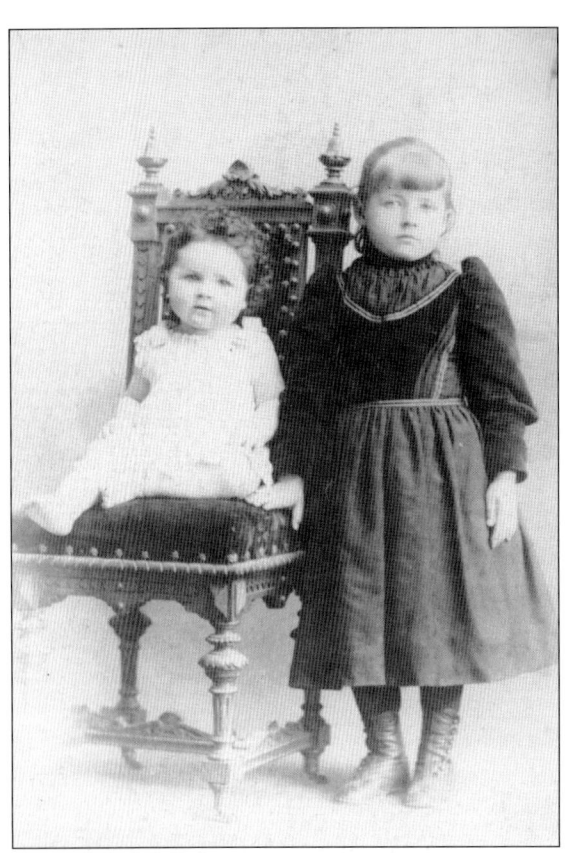

Portola residents Annie Baumann (1892–1968) and her sister Mary (1888–1930) pose for this 1894 photograph. (Courtesy of June Blut Conlon.)

The horse-and-buggy was a common method of transportation in 1909. This photograph depicts Portola resident Bernard Conlon (left) and a friend out for a ride. (Courtesy of June Blut Conlon.)

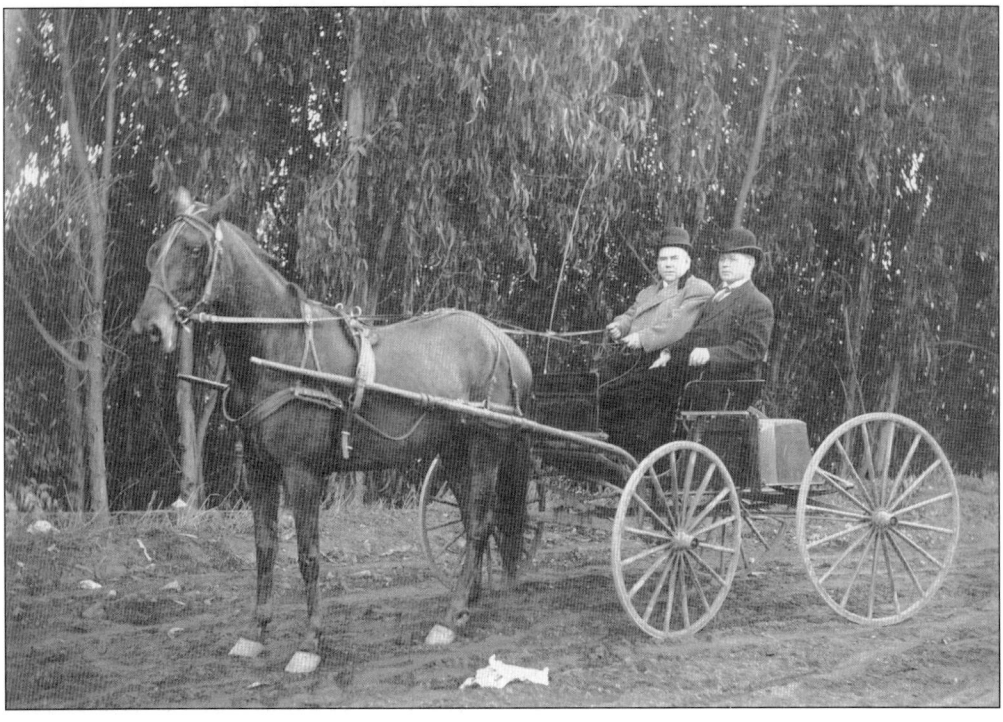

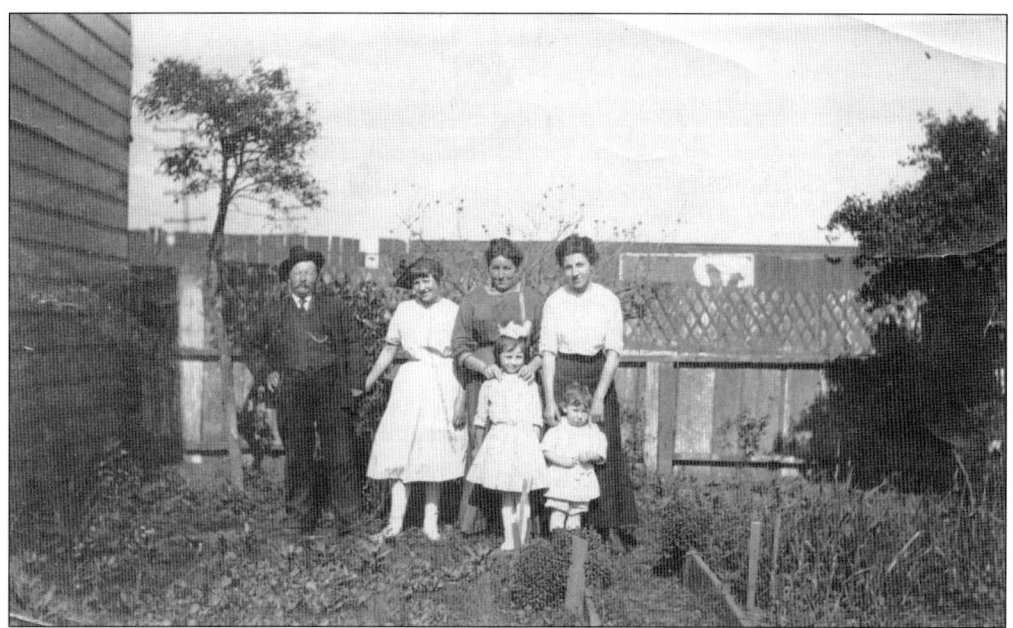

The Baumann family poses for a photograph in the backyard of their home on Somerset Street in 1910. (Courtesy of June Blut Conlon.)

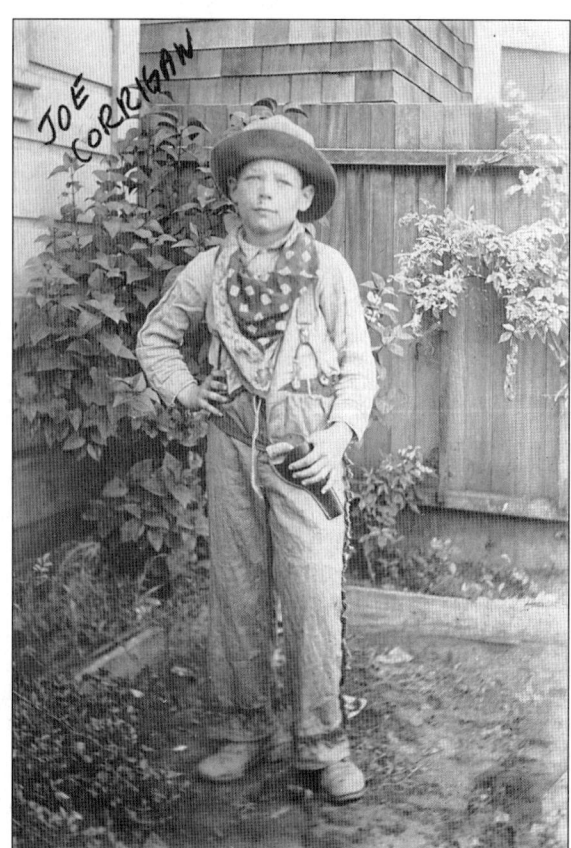

In his cowboy attire, Joseph Corrigan poses for this postcard photograph outside his home at 1128 Bowdoin Street in 1910. (Courtesy of Patricia Semenero.)

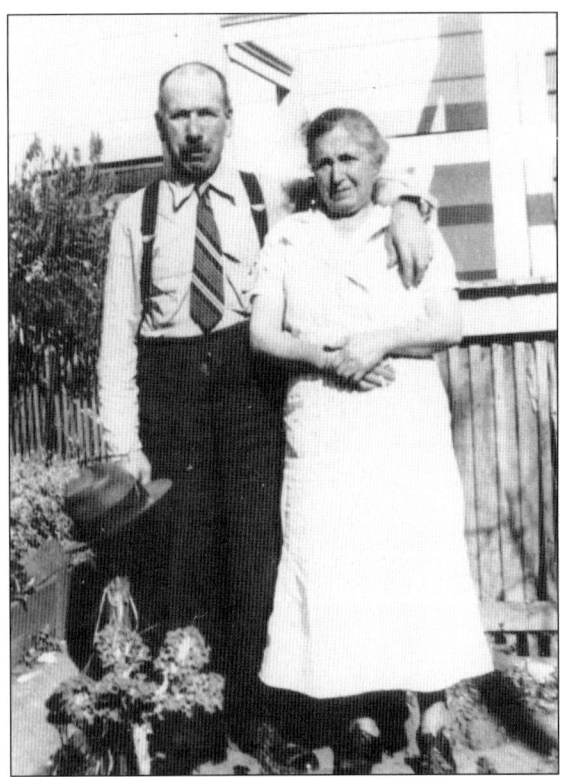

Giacomo and Luisa Parodi settled in the Portola after arriving from Italy. Giacomo immigrated in 1910 and was followed two years later by his wife and four children. He and his wife lived in the house he built for them on San Bruno Avenue until their deaths. (Courtesy of Irene Crescio.)

Therese Hoppe stands at the top of the stairs of her family's home at 628 Girard Street, purchased just before the earthquake and fire of 1906. They were able to watch the city burn from their house. (Courtesy of Louann Hoppe Saltel.)

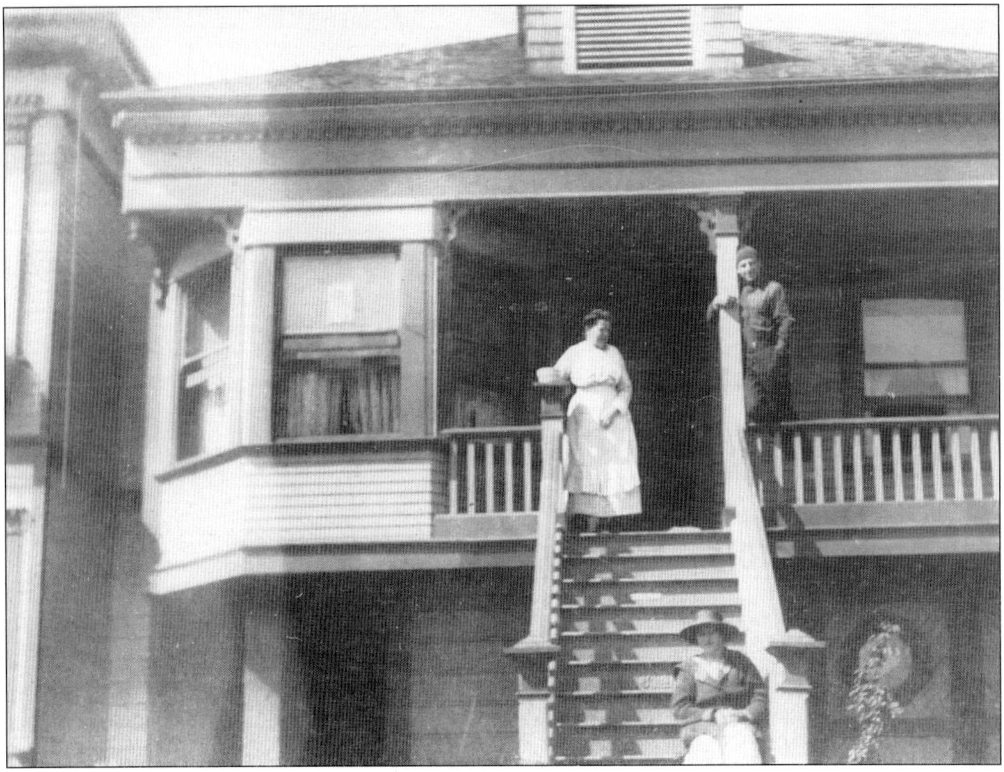

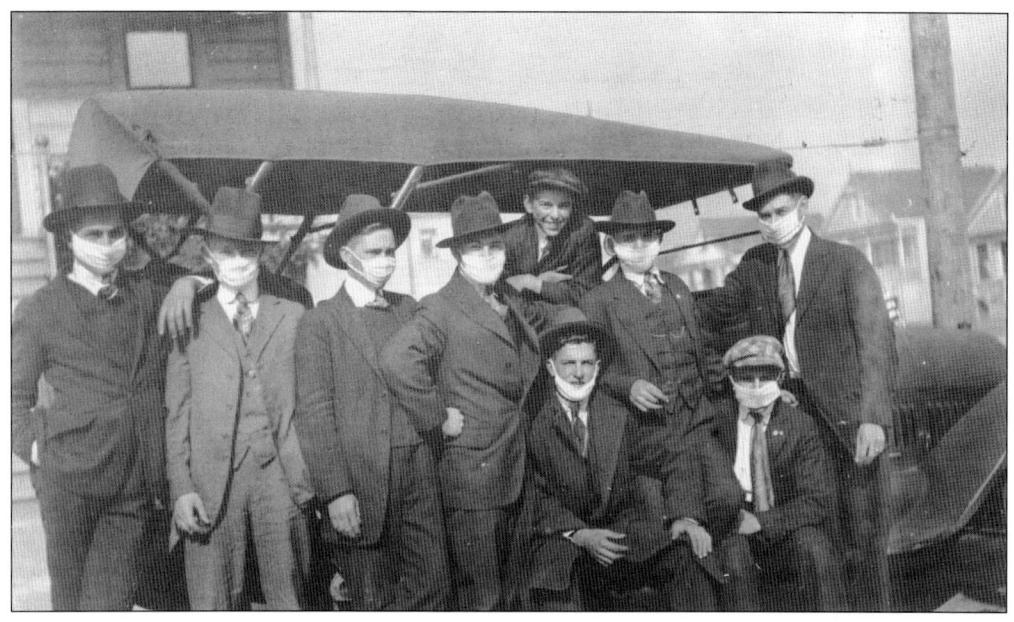

Portola residents wear flu masks in these 1918 photographs taken in front of 628 Girard Street. In the years 1918 and 1919, the influenza pandemic killed between 20 and 40 million people worldwide, infecting 28 percent of all Americans. World War I brought the virus into the United States and it spread quickly throughout the country. In October 1918, it killed more than 200,000 people. People lucky enough to avoid the virus had to obey public health ordinances to help stop the spread of the disease. Public health departments issued gauze masks to be worn in public, and people who ignored these ordinances had to pay large fines. In 1918, the total number of United States flu deaths was 464,959. (Courtesy of Louann Hoppe Saltel.)

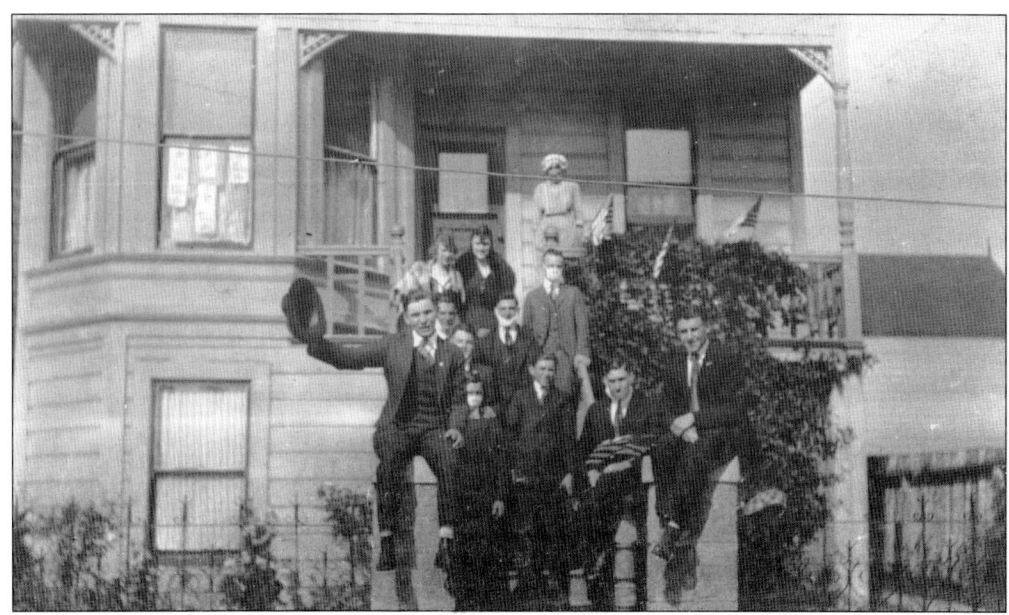

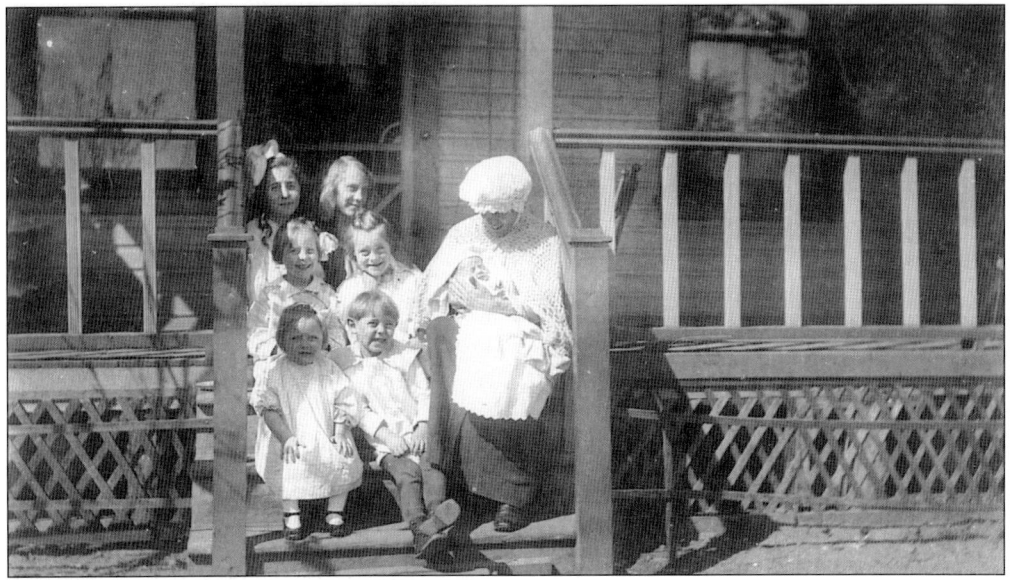

The Gus Coleman family poses in front of their home on 548 Brussels Street in 1917. When automobiles started becoming a popular mode of transportation, Coleman raised the home and built a garage underneath. (Courtesy of June Blut Conlon.)

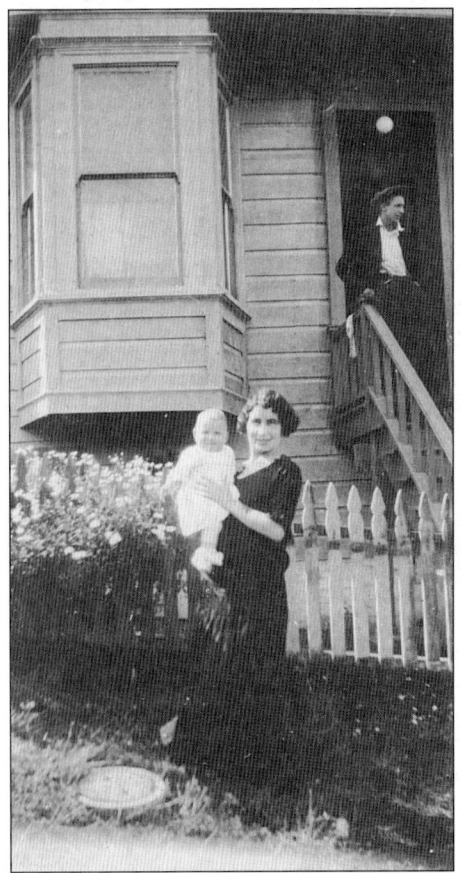

In 1923, the Corrigan family takes a candid photograph in front of 1128 Bowdoin Street. Pictured from left to right are Eleanor Corrigan, Minnie Corrigan, and Henry Corrigan. (Courtesy of Patricia Semenero.)

Jim Grady, pictured outside his Somerset Street home, prepares for his First Holy Communion Day in 1926. (Courtesy of Jim Grady.)

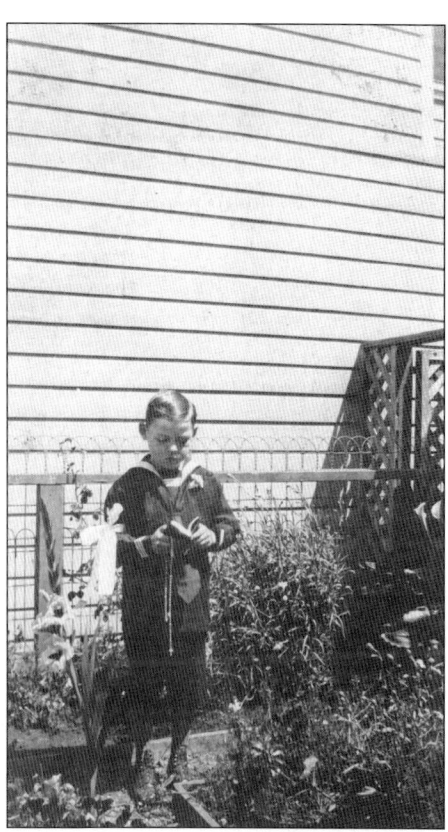

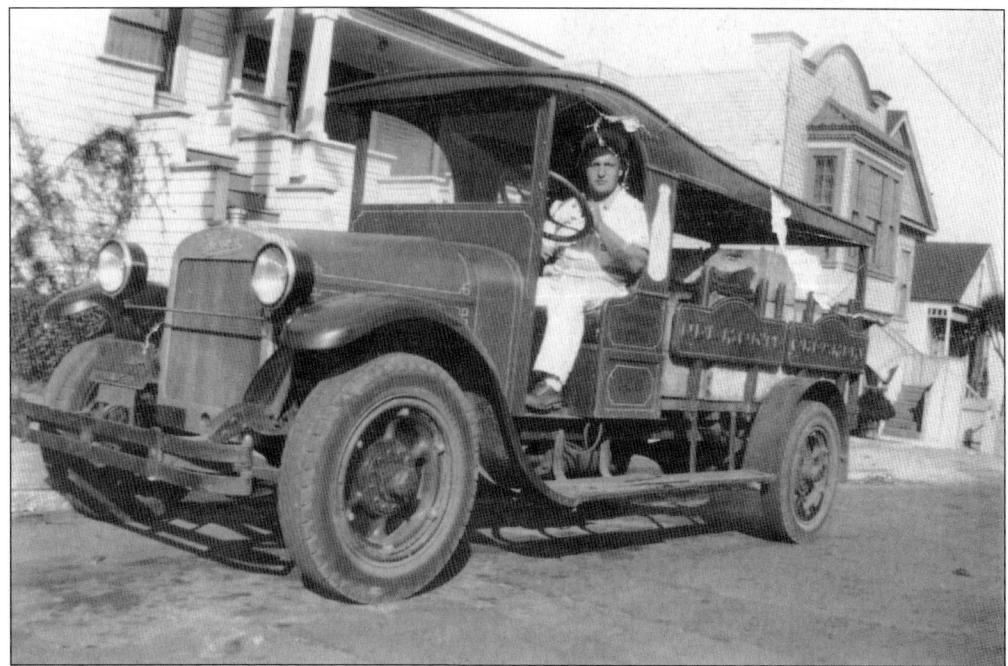

In this 1930s photograph, Martin Fuchs is pictured in his Del Monte Creamery truck at 166 Hale Street. (Courtesy of Leona Kennel.)

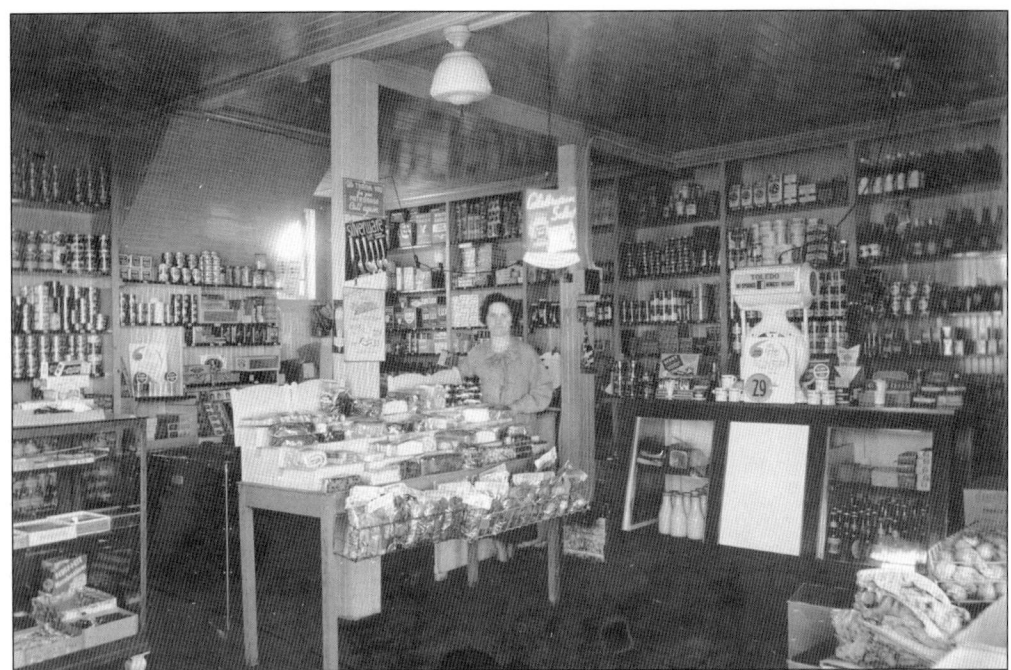

Joseph Baumann was in the process of building a milk depot when he died unexpectedly of a ruptured appendix in 1911. His wife, Mary, opened the store at 200 Somerset Street (at Felton) that same year to sell milk, bread, and school supplies. The business continued to grow until Mary turned it over to Annie Baumann Carroll, pictured here in the grocery store on November 30, 1935. (Courtesy of June Blut Conlon.)

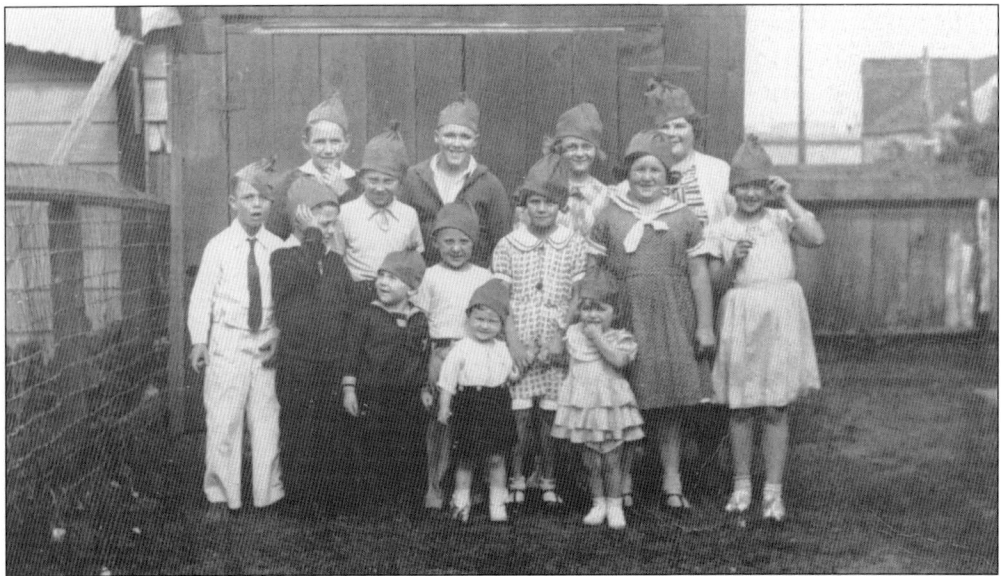

Portola children celebrate Tom Conlon's second birthday on September 2, 1935. The photograph was taken in the backyard of 405 Brussels Street. Pictured from left to right are (first row) Jerry Schroff, Jerry Cahill, Tom Conlon, and Marilyn Keating; (second row) Ed O'Connor, Jack Cahill, Jim Cahill, Gloria Keating, Pat Keating, and Shirley Schroff; (third row) Bill Keating, Barney Schroff, Rita O'Connor, and Lillian Keating. (Courtesy of June Blut Conlon.)

Joseph and Assunta Sant smile for the camera in the backyard of their home at 136 Hamilton Street on October 12, 1934. (Courtesy of the Sant family.)

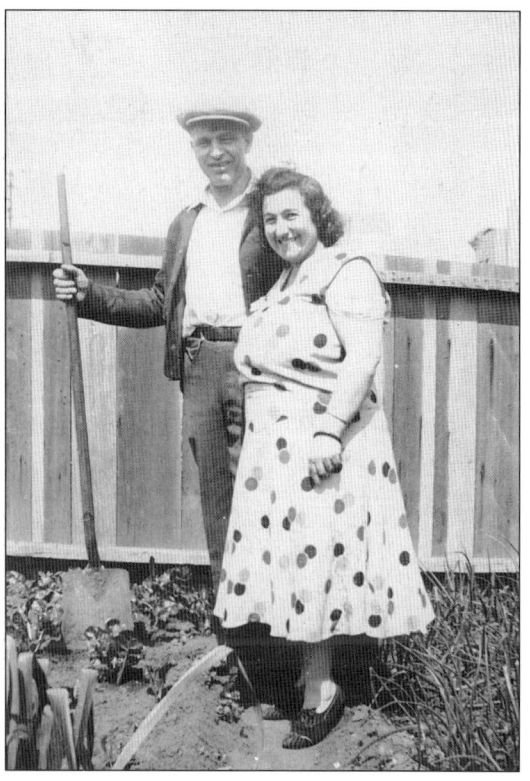

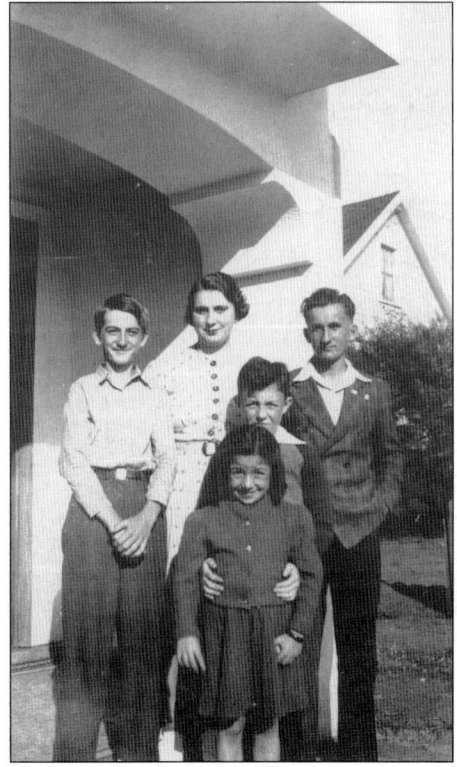

Seen in this late 1930s photograph, taken in front of the Parodi home on San Bruno Avenue, from left to right are Peter Balich, Marie Balich, Steve Balich, George Crescio, and Irene Crescio. (Courtesy of Irene Crescio.)

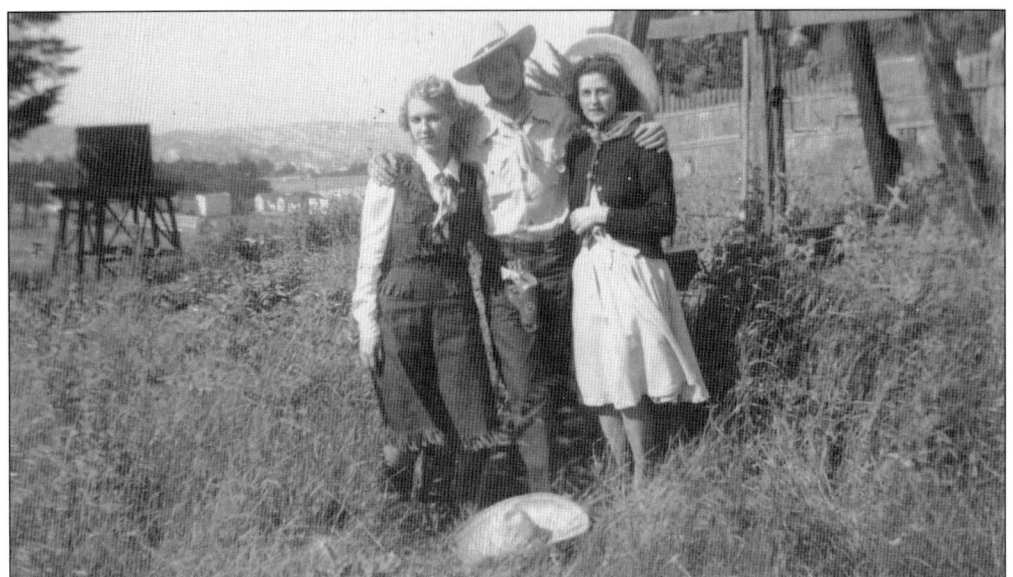

In 1939, the city of San Francisco celebrated Fiesta Week and the Golden Gate International Exposition on Treasure Island. Pictured here in 1939 behind Brussels Street are, from left to right, Marie Tovaraz, Emil Hauman, and Evelyn Mortola. (Courtesy of Carol A. Strach.)

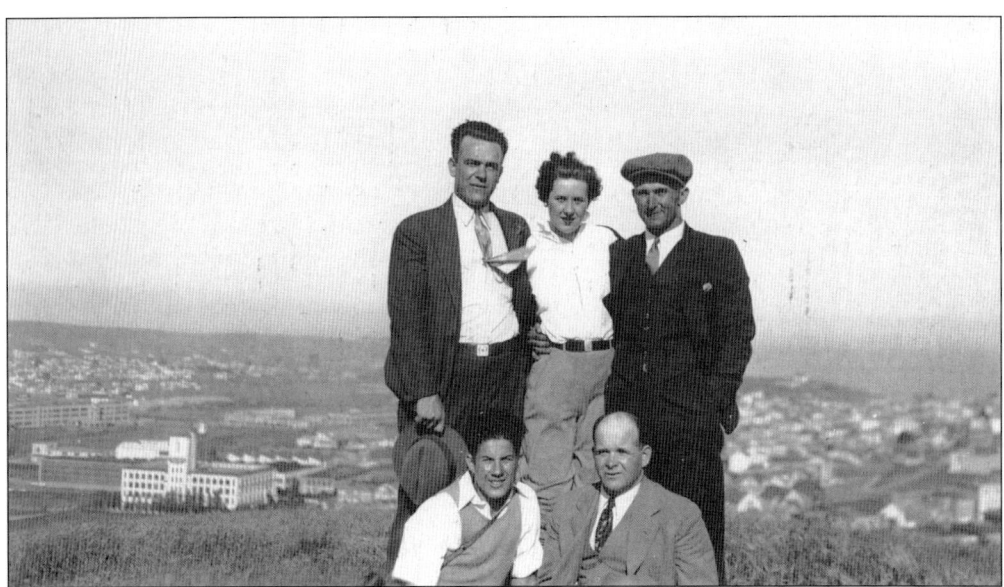

Pictured here in this 1935 taken on the hills behind Brussels Street are, from left to right, John Jakovina, John Lepri, Milan Gasparovich, Mathea Jakovina, and Ljubo Kulisich. The Ferry Morse Seed Company, which sold packaged flower and vegetable seed to gardeners, is the building in the left of the photograph. (Courtesy of Carol A. Strach.)

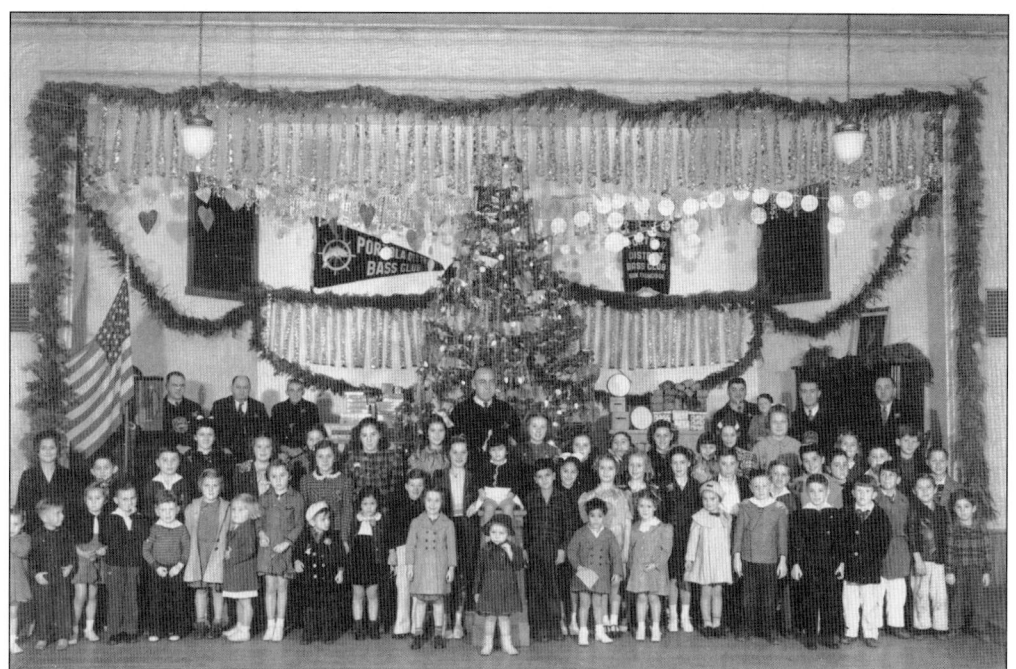

The Portola District Bass Club was a fishing club for men started by William Schwabe, Anton Bin, and Peter Ratto in 1933. Membership was limited to 100, and many men were put on a waiting list until a spot became available. In this December 20, 1939, photograph, children of the members pose for a Christmas photograph. The Bass Club closed in 1983. (Courtesy of Mary Jane Bragagnolo Camilleri.)

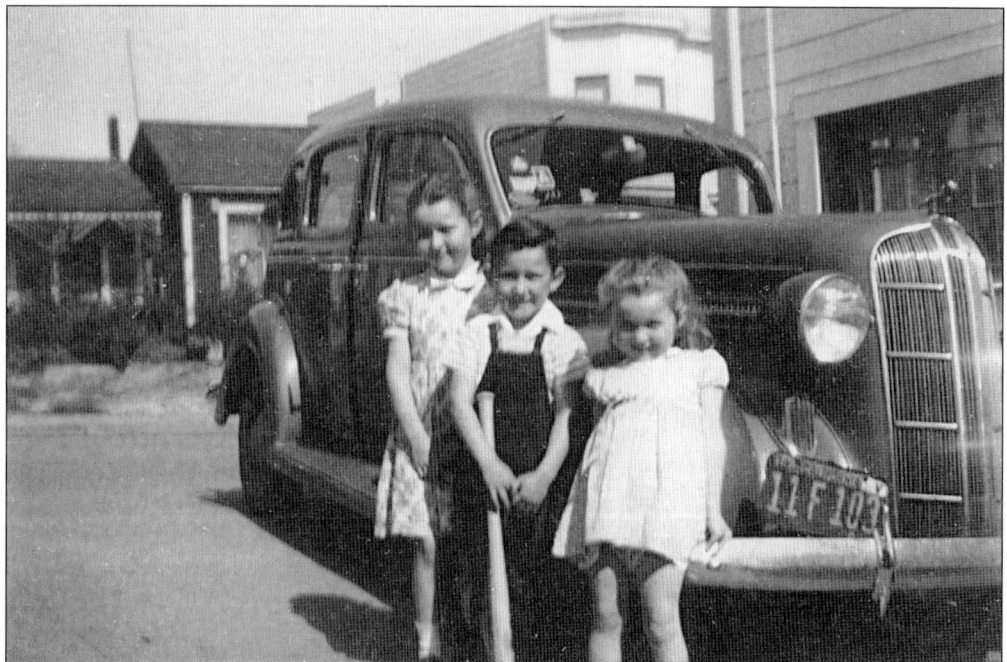

The Gregoire children are pictured in front of the family's Dodge automobile in the 1940s. Pictured from left to right are Lois, Jerry, and Joanie. (Courtesy of the Gregoire family.)

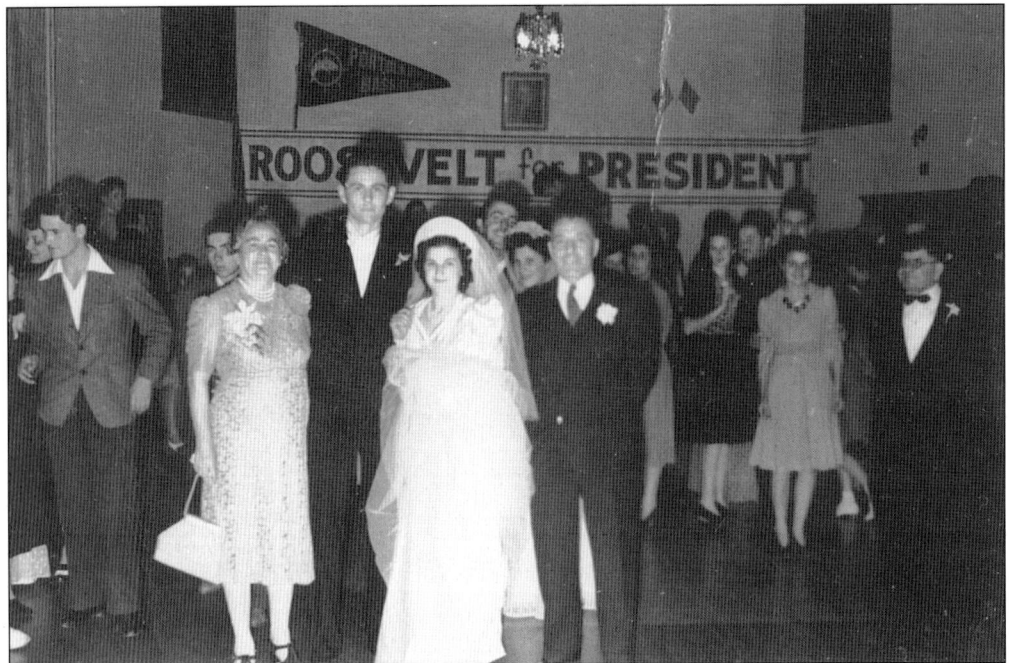

The wedding reception of Angela Fenech and Charles Cappai at Portola Hall on San Bruno Avenue is seen in this 1940 photograph. A "Roosevelt for President" banner is in the background. (Courtesy of Angela Cappai.)

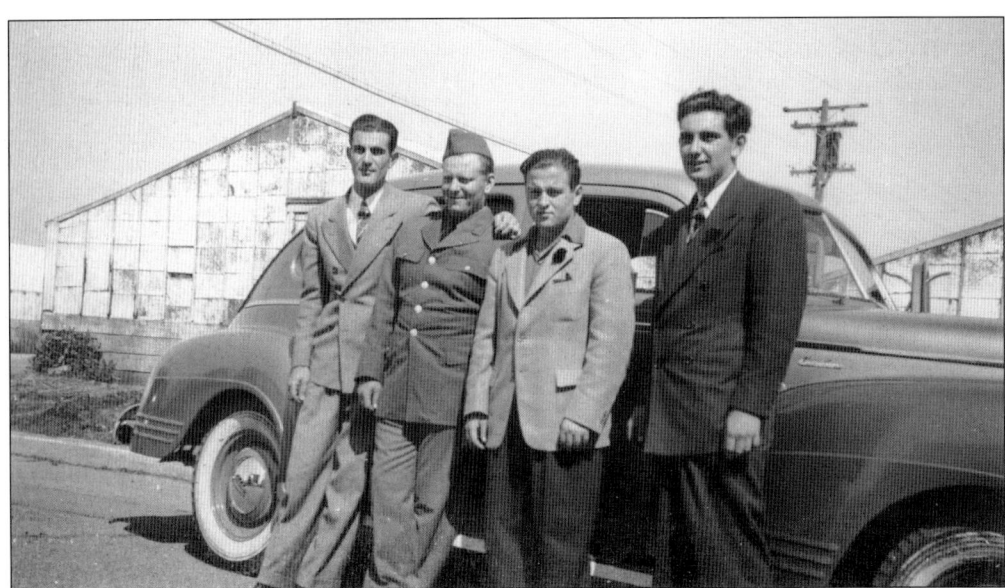

Back from the war in 1940 are Romeo Granara, Ernest Garibaldi, Raymond Garibaldi, and Martin Hauman. Romeo Granara, Ernest Garibaldi, Raymond Garibaldi went to work for their families' nurseries after the war. Martin Hauman went to work for the post office. They lived in the Portola all their lives. (Courtesy of author.)

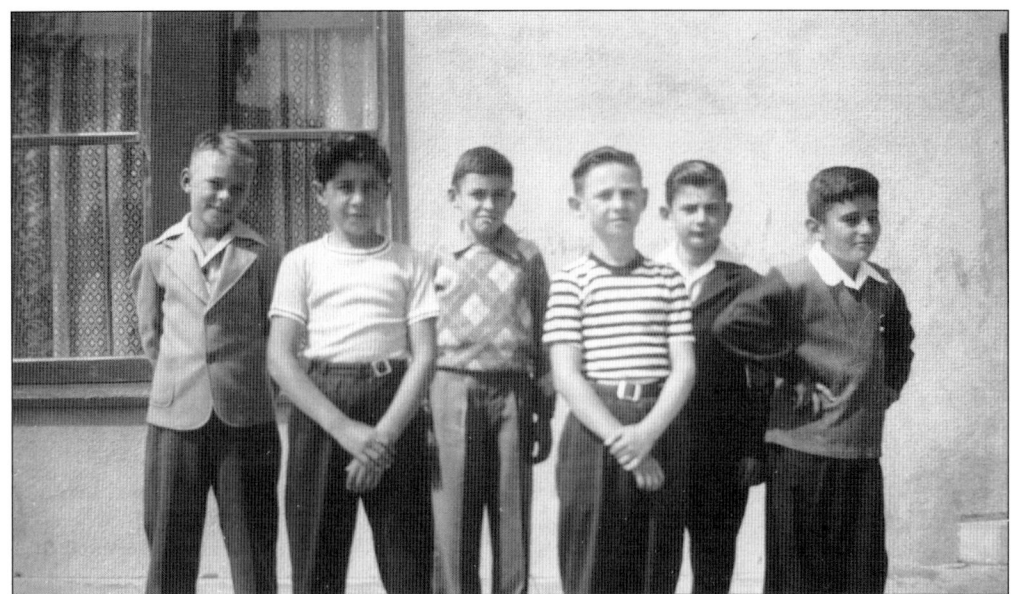

Portola neighborhood boys pose for a photograph in 1941. From left to right are Dick Kalor, Frank Cosentino, Bob Pratt, Tom Conlon, Alex Petropulos, and unidentified. (Courtesy of June Blut Conlon.)

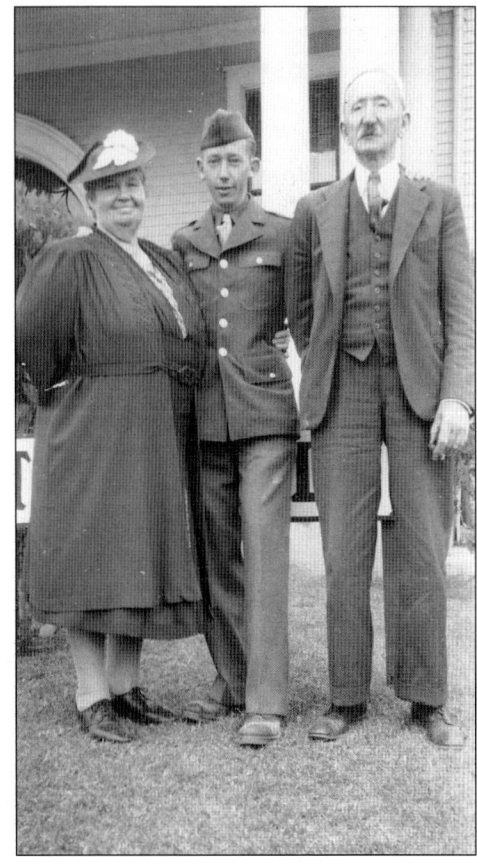

Irma Champion Gregoire, Paul George Gregoire, and Joseph Gregoire accompany Paul to his induction into the United States Army in 1942. (Courtesy of the Gregoire family.)

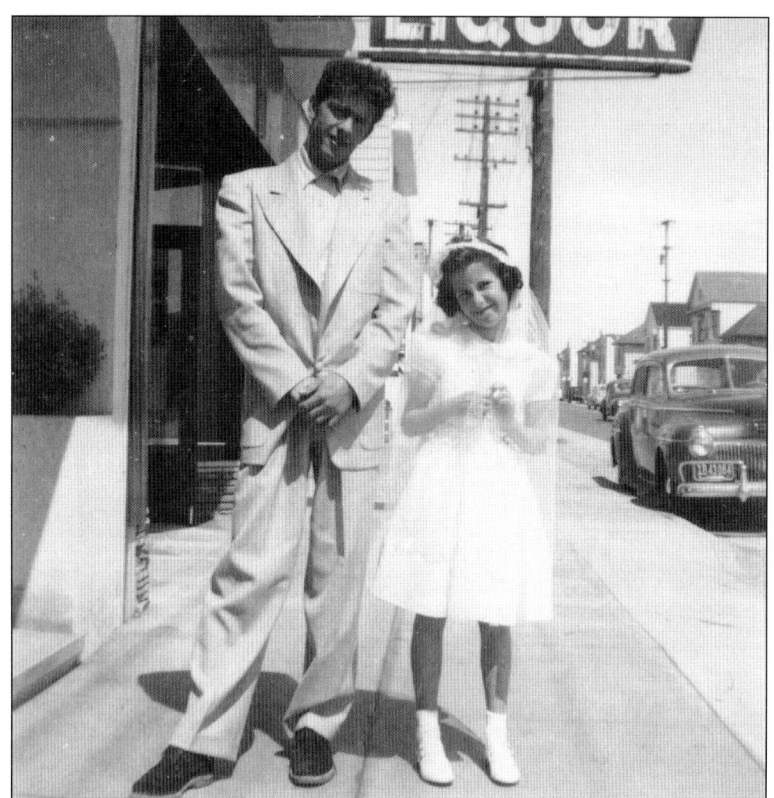

Carol Cenci is pictured outside her grandparent's home on San Bruno Avenue in 1950 on the way to her First Holy Communion Day. Pictured with Carol is her cousin Andrew Brizio. (Courtesy of Carol Cenci Perez.)

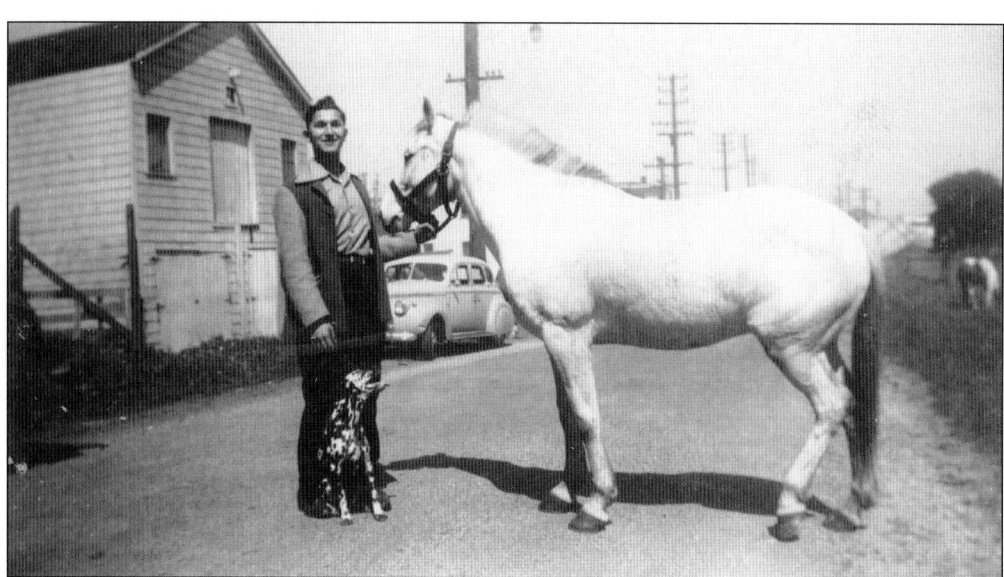

In 1943, longtime Portola resident John Sant is pictured with his horse and Dalmatian on University Street. The barn was located between Burrows and Felton Streets. (Courtesy of the Sant family.)

Georgette and John "Johnnie" Fenech sit in front of 391 Girard Street on August 29, 1945. They are the grandchildren of John Fenech, who opened a grocery store across the street from where this image was taken. (Courtesy of John Fenech.)

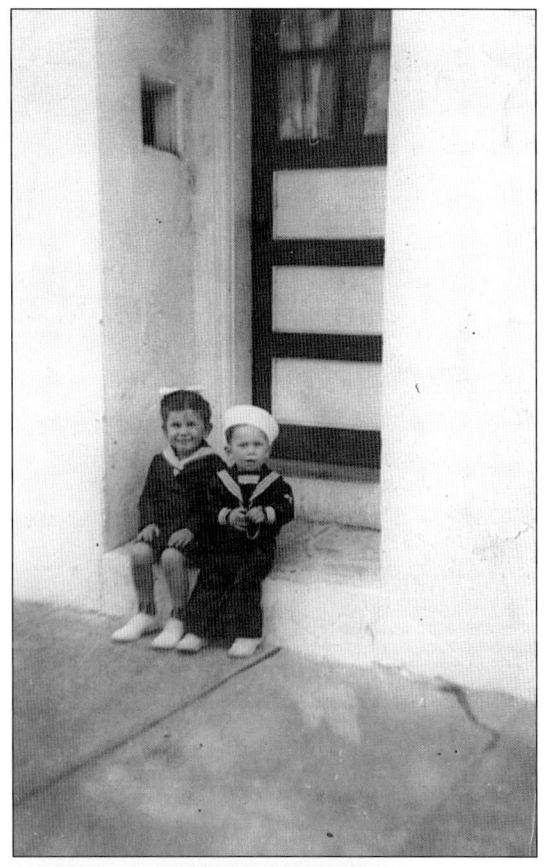

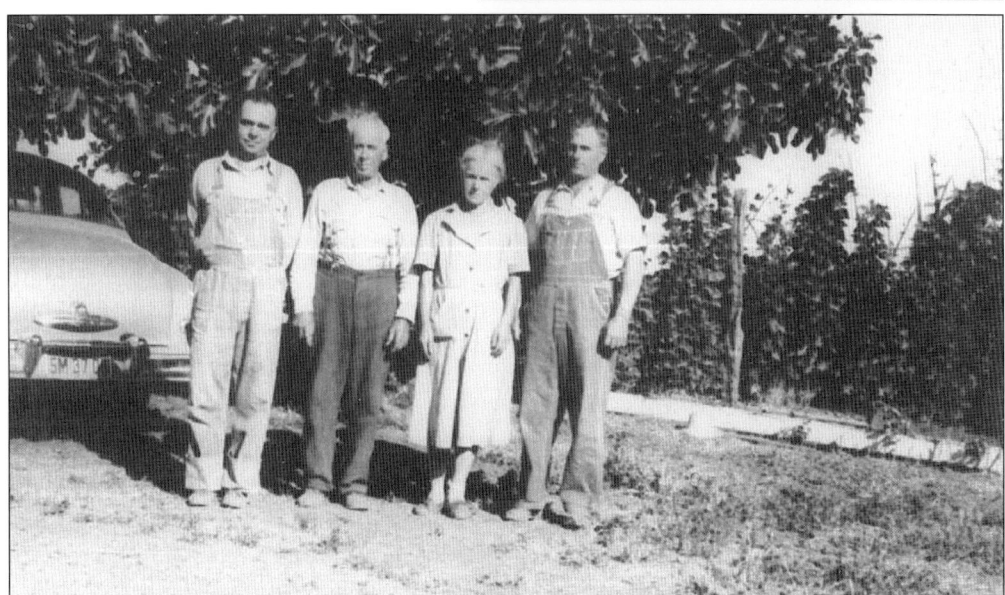

G. Carraro and Sons Contractors and Home Builders at 750 Felton Street constructed many of the homes in the Portola district. Pictured here in 1948 are, from left to right, Frank, Guiseppe, Maria, and Rinaldo Carraro. (Courtesy of the Carraro family.)

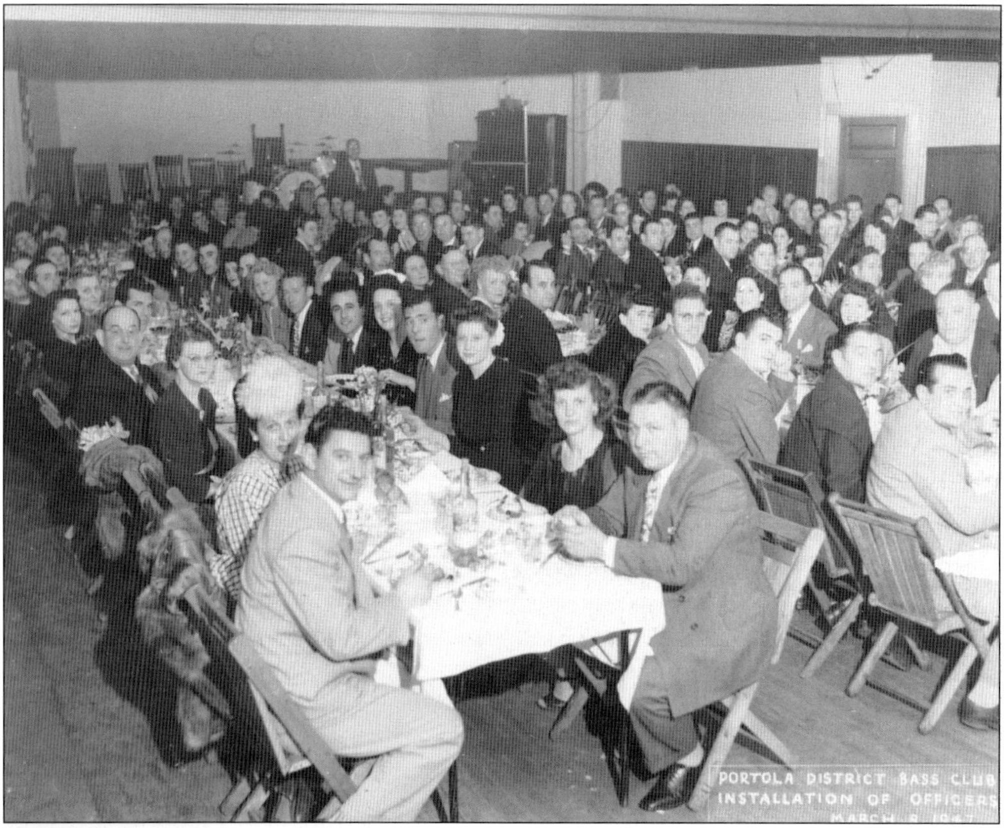

The Portola District Bass Club held an installation of officers dinner on March 8, 1945. (Courtesy of the Gregoire family.)

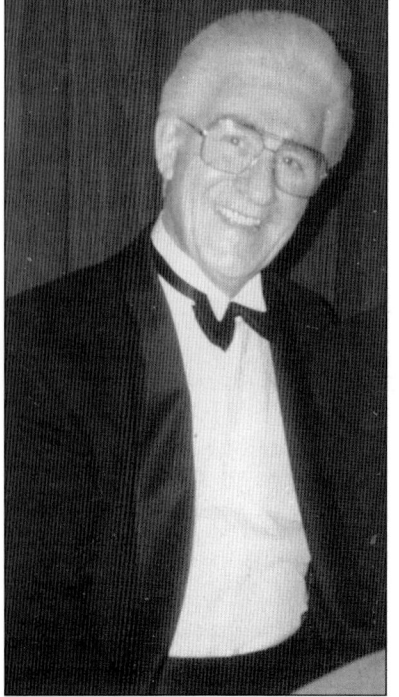

Alfred "Doc" Andreatta was a well-known chiropractor in the Portola, having been in practice since 1948. His first office was located at 2497 San Bruno Avenue. This site would later become the office of Richard Parodi, D.D.S. Doc Andreatta later moved to 2450 San Bruno Avenue (above Golden State Pharmacy). He and his wife, Mary, lived in the Portola since 1949. Doc passed away on September 6, 2004. Mary still lives in their Portola district home. (Courtesy of the Andreatta family.)

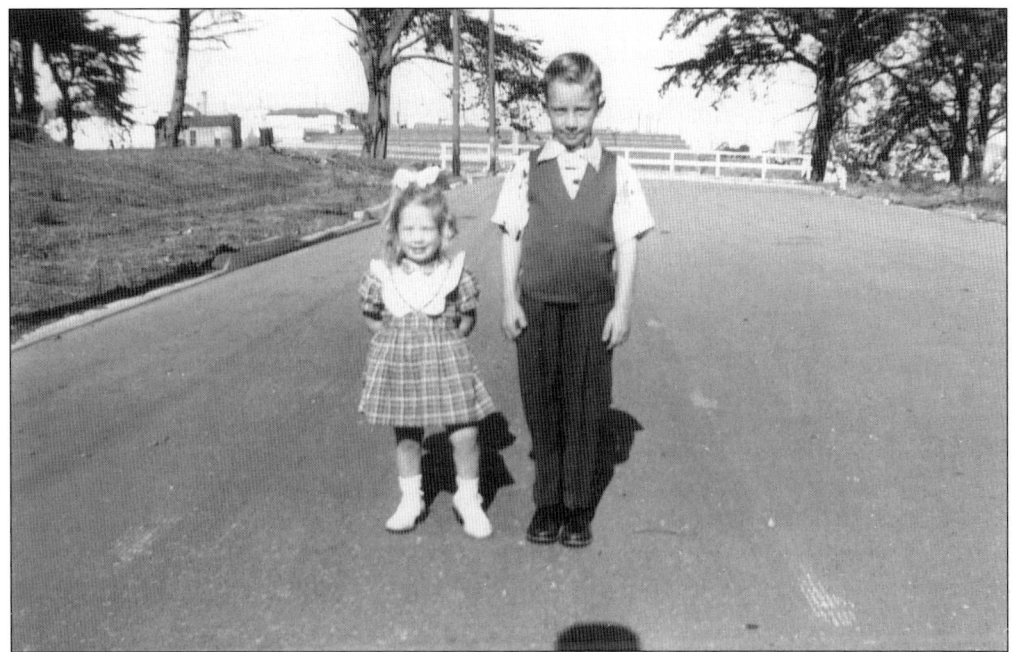
Carmen and Bart Solari are pictured on Princeton Street in the 1950s. The fence in the background was later removed, and stairs were constructed allowing passage through to Burrows Street. (Courtesy of Louise Solari.)

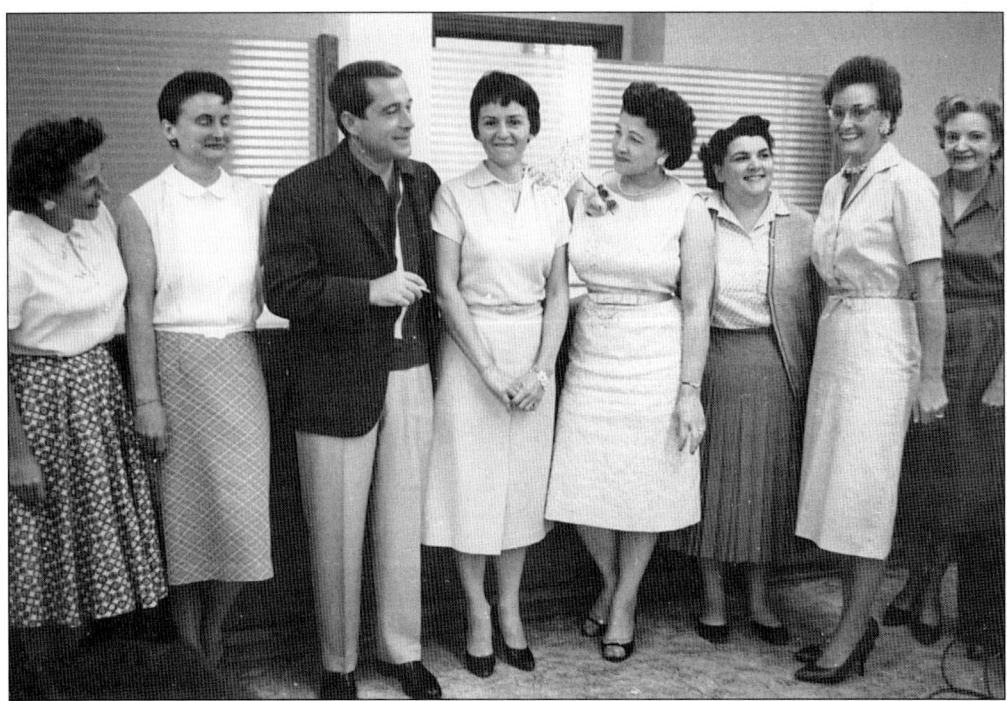
Perry Como (host of the *Perry Como Kraft Music Hall*) visits with Portola residents and employees at the Kraft Foods plant in the early 1950s. (Courtesy of Patricia Semenero.)

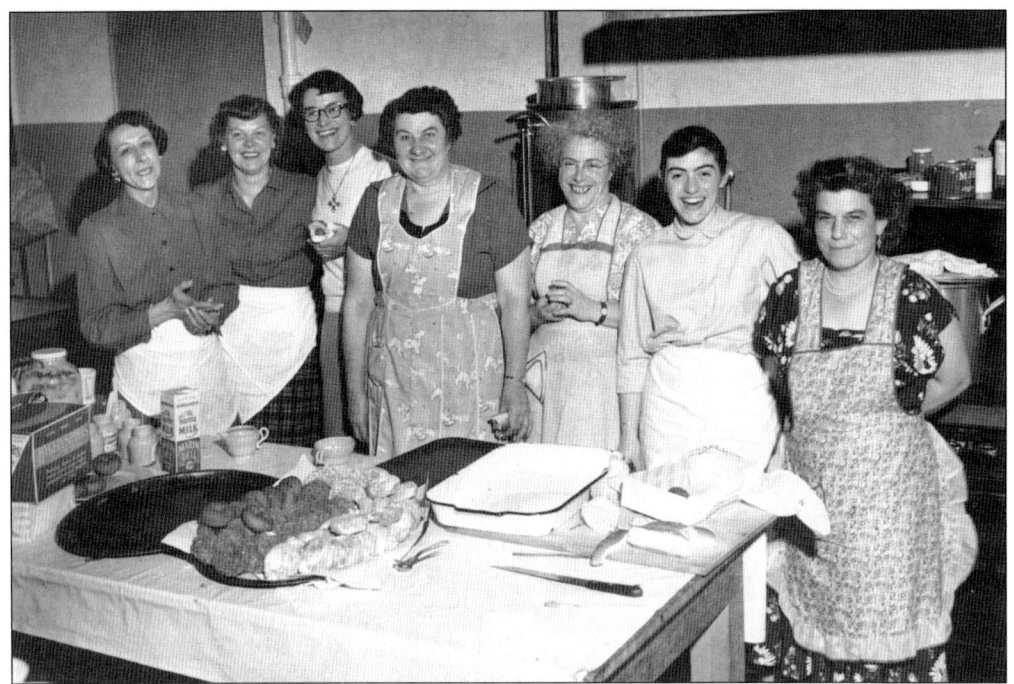

This 1950s photograph shows bingo night at St. Elizabeth Parish. Pictured from left to right are Phyllis Mansfield, Mag Gambelin, Liz Brekle, Birdie, Evelyn Contrero, Mrs. Contrero's daughter, and Jean Fenech. (Courtesy of John Fenech.)

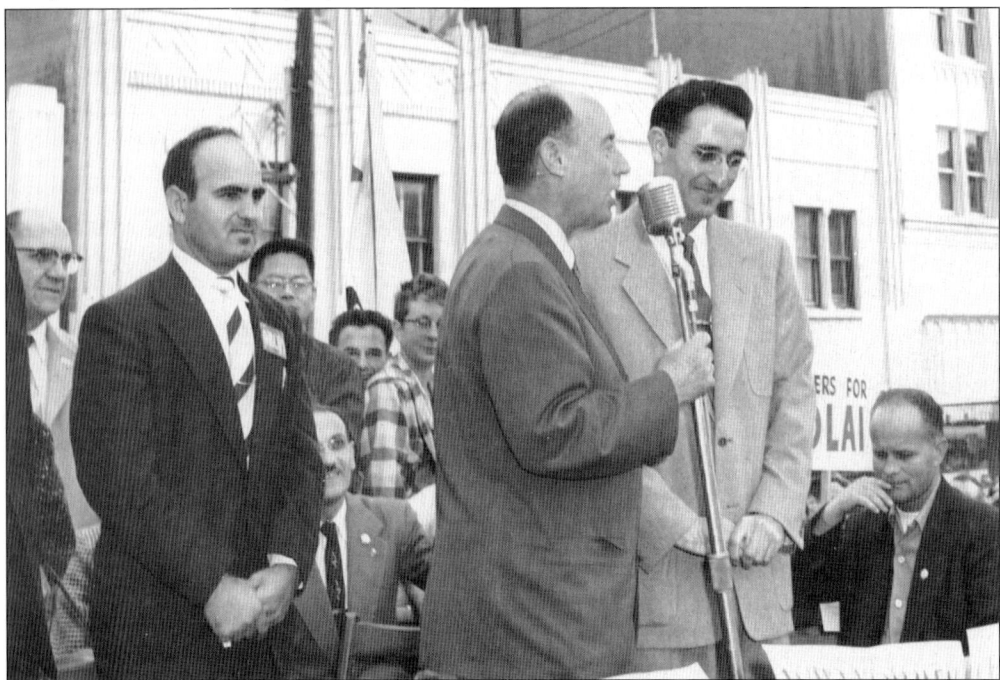

Consul general to Malta and a Portola resident, Charles Vassallo (left) is seen in this photograph with 1956 Democratic presidential nominee Adlai Stevenson (middle). (Courtesy of Charles Vassallo.)

Pictured here are Ray Ferrera (right) and his wife, E. Lilly, at their home. It was built before the 1906 earthquake and survived intact; it was later raised to its current height. Ray owned Ferrera Electric, which has been meeting the electrical needs of the Portola since it was established in 1960. This home and business is located at 108 Wayland Street. (Courtesy of author.)

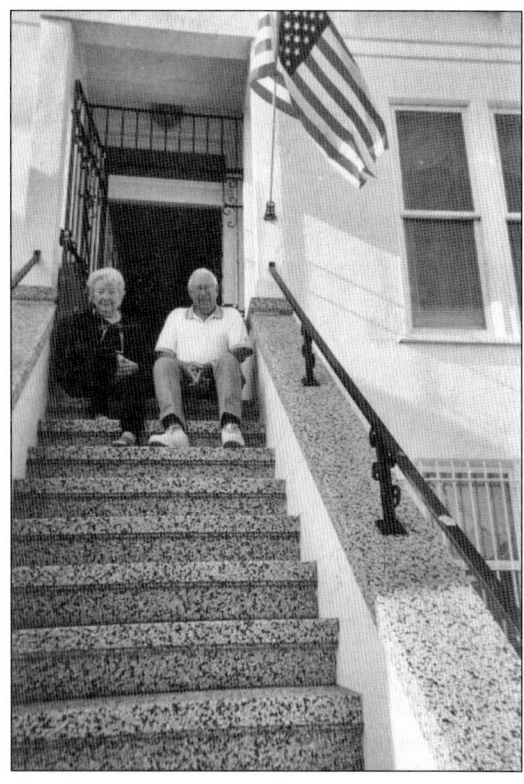

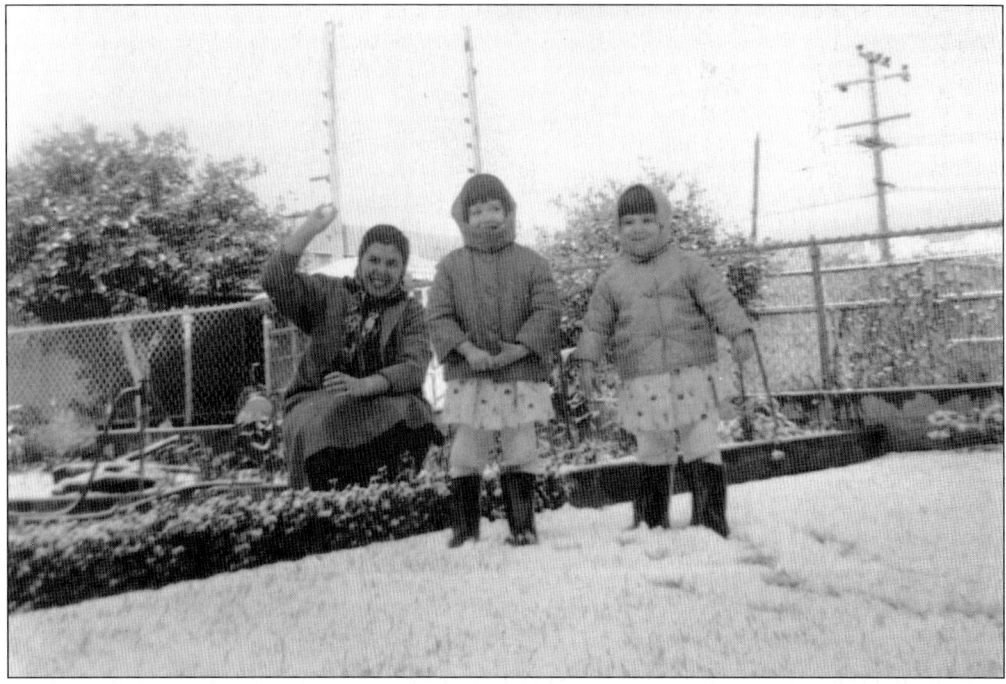

A family makes snowballs in the backyard of their home on Holyoke Street on January 23, 1962. Only a moderate amount of snow fell as indicated by the tracks left by the children's boots. (Courtesy of Mary Lou Garibaldi.)

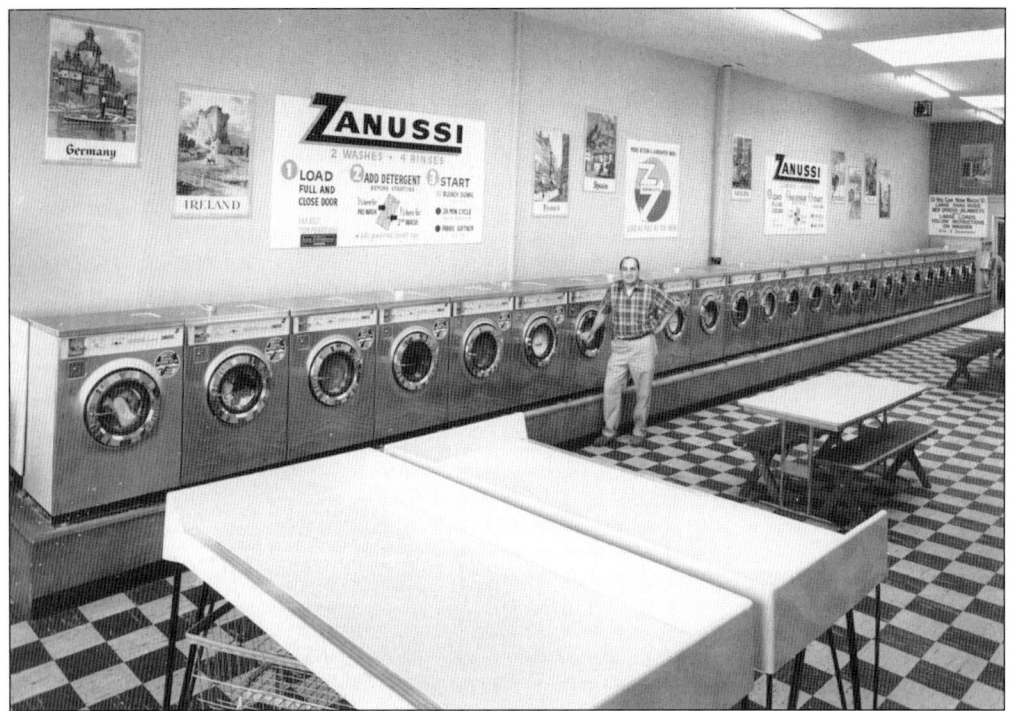

The Lightning Coin Launderette at 1448 Silver Avenue was owned and operated by Ben Papapietro and Frank Barbaccia. In this November 10, 1967, photograph, Ben Papapietro is seen with 25 new Zanussi washers. (Courtesy of the Ben Papapietro family.)

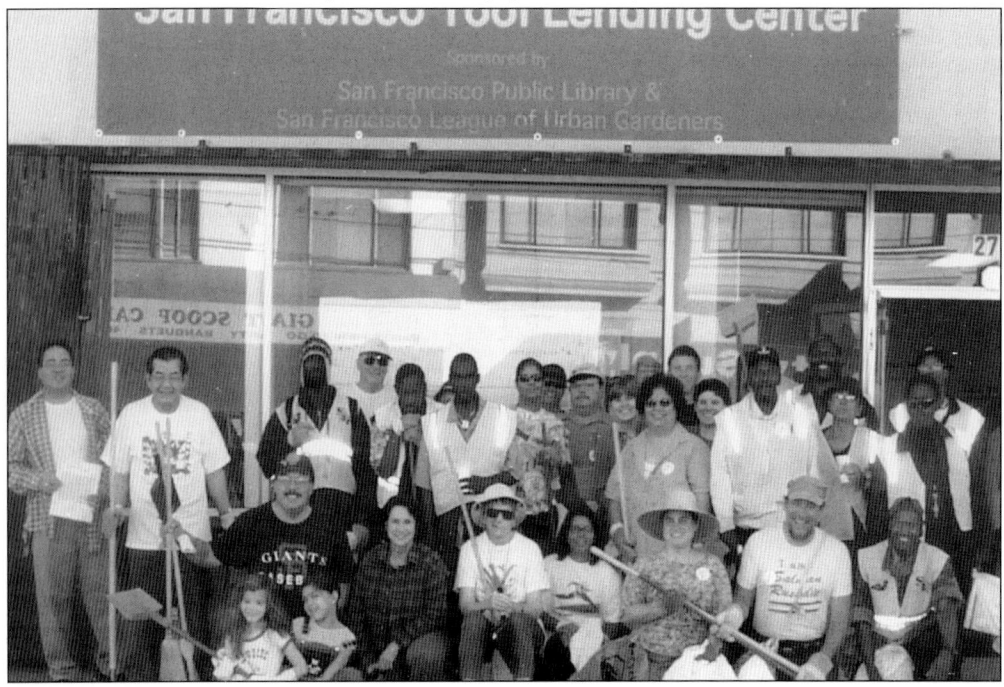

The first San Bruno Avenue Community Clean-up crew poses in front of the now defunct San Francisco Tool Lending Center in 2000. (Courtesy of Dwayne and Terezinha Jusino.)

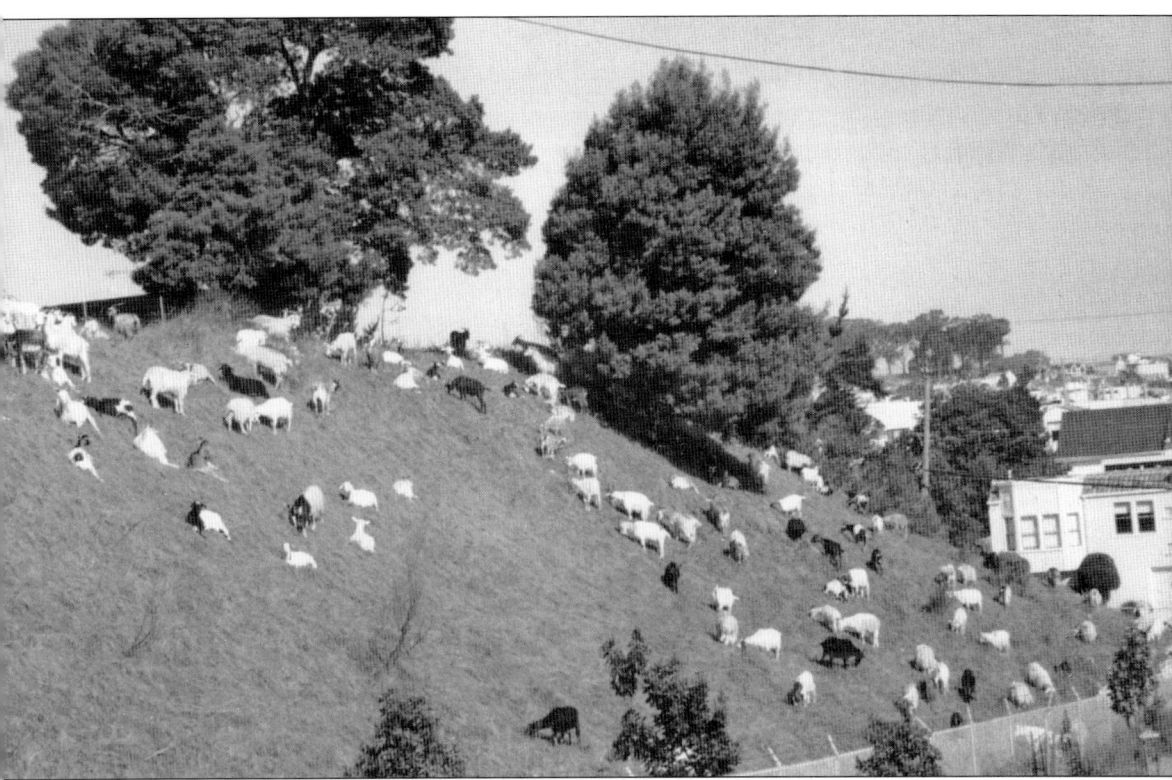

Goats R Us, a family owned grazing company, has been used by the San Francisco Public Utilities Commission to reduce brush in the area. In this 2004 photograph, the goats are pictured doing their work on Felton and Bowdoin Streets. The herd consists of Angora, Alpine, Spanish, Boer, Pygmy, LaMancha, and Nubian goats. (Courtesy of Henni Lara.)

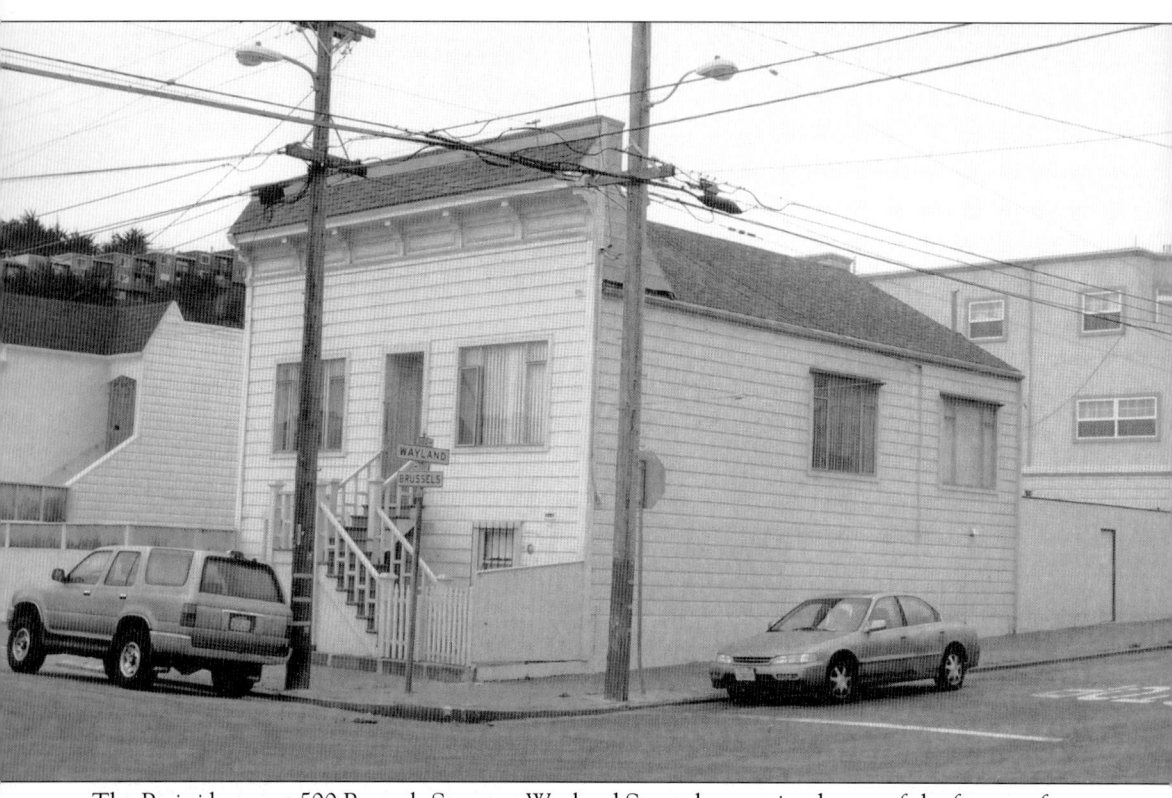

The Perini home at 500 Brussels Street at Wayland Street has retained most of the features from its original 1867 construction. This same home can be seen on page 93 in 1882. Here the building is pictured in 2006. (Courtesy of David R. Mehrwein.)

Five
NEIGHBORHOOD SPORTS

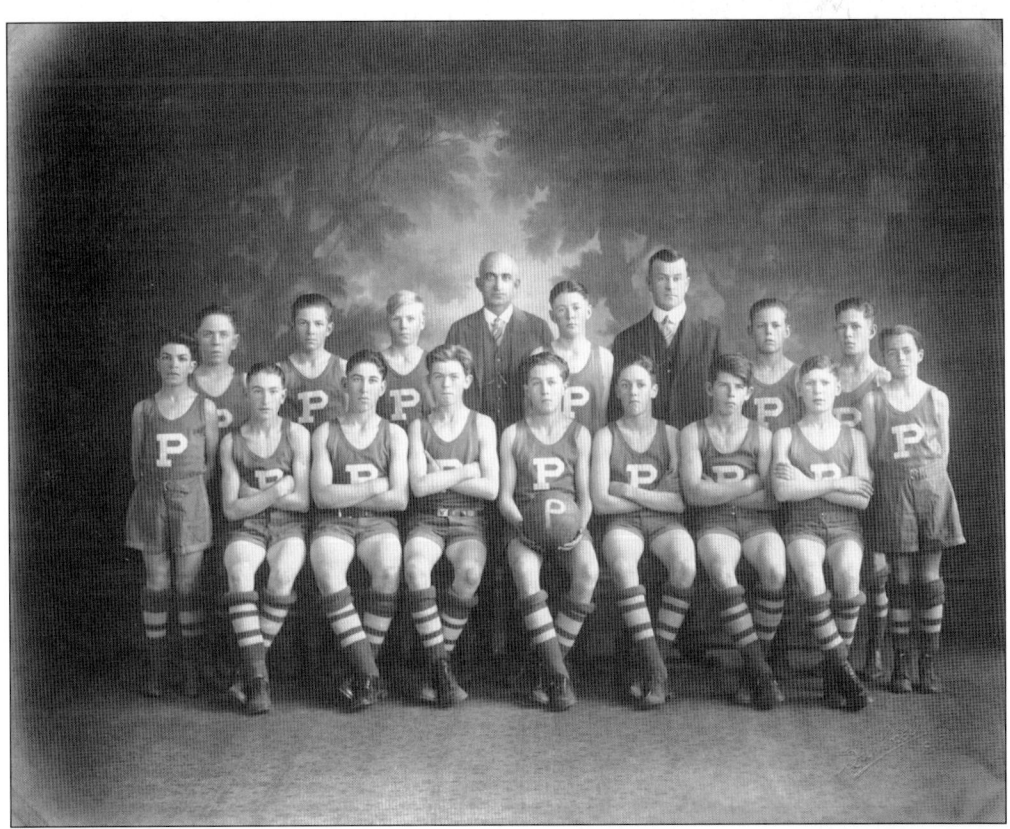

The Portola Junior High basketball team is seen in this photograph from the late 1920s. "Pop" Silvey, who coached the team and also taught mathematics, is at the left of the photograph, and Joe Oeschger, the gym teacher, is to his right. Oeschger was a right-handed pitcher for the Boston Braves from 1914 to 1925. On May 1, 1920, he played in the longest game in major league history—26 innings against the Brooklyn Dodgers. (Courtesy of a private collector.)

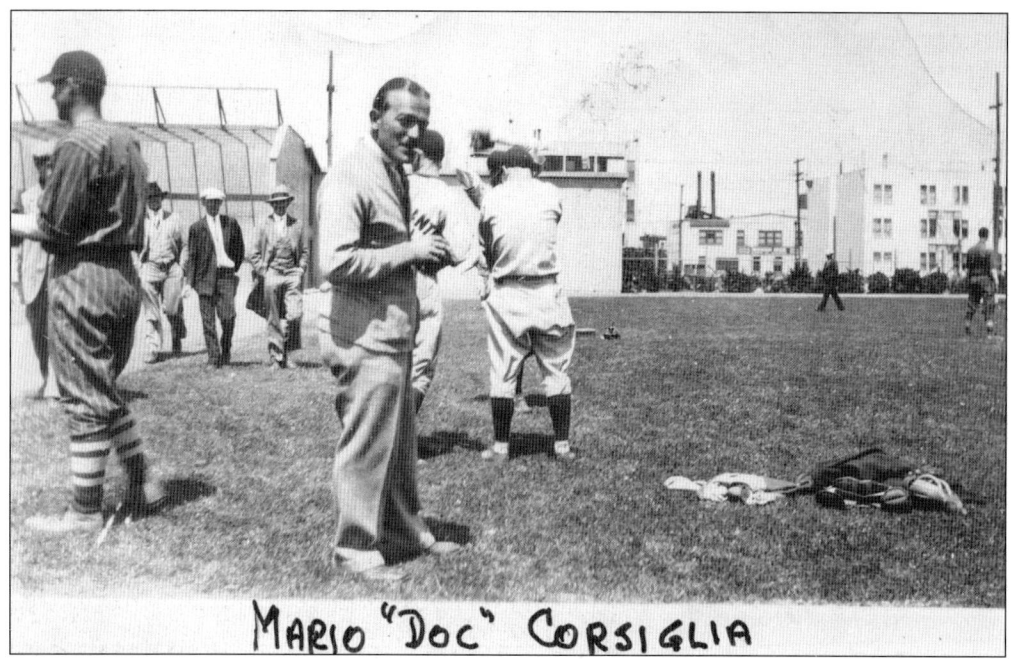

Mario "Doc" Corsiglia, the owner of Mario's Drugs, sponsored a neighborhood baseball team in this undated photograph. Mario's Drugs was located at 2450 San Bruno Avenue. The pharmacy contained a soda fountain and was sub–post office station No. 17. Mario's Drug would later change ownership and be known as Golden State Pharmacy. (Courtesy of Barbara Lister DeMattei.)

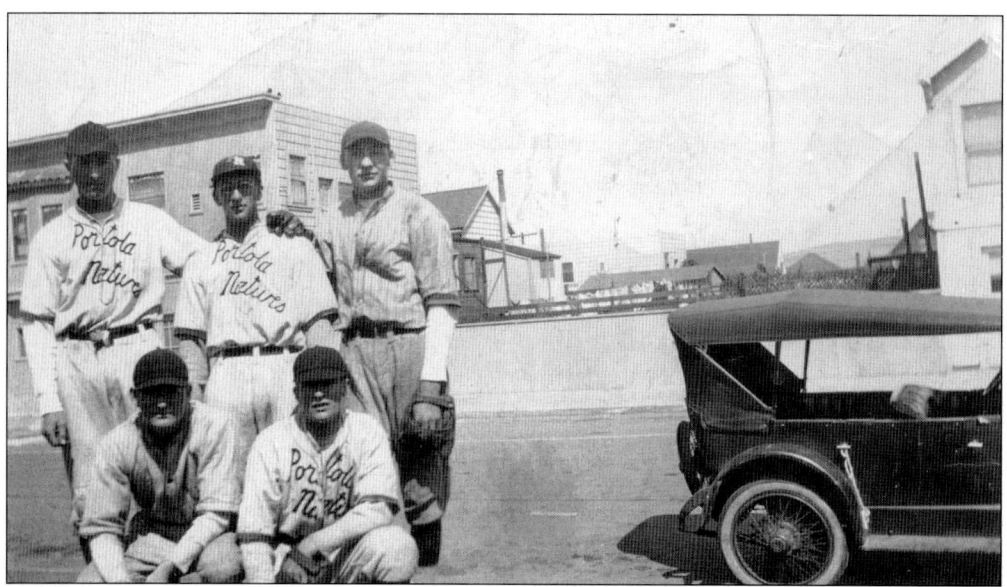

The Portola Natives baseball team poses for a group photograph in this 1920s photograph. They played at Portola Playground. (Courtesy of Barbara Lister DeMattei.)

Portola Natives baseball players Thomas "Tommy" Conlon (right) and "Porky" Sheridan share a moment in this photograph from the 1920s. (Courtesy of the Conlon family.)

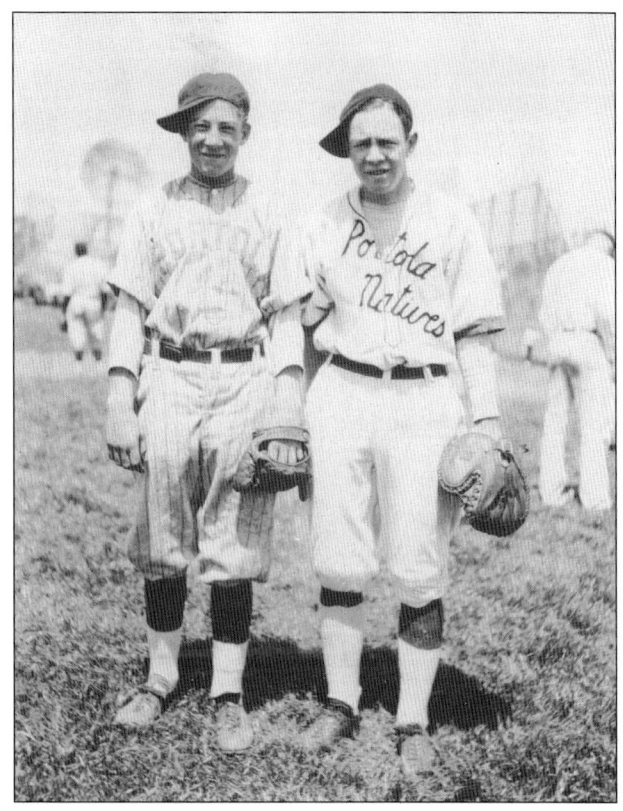

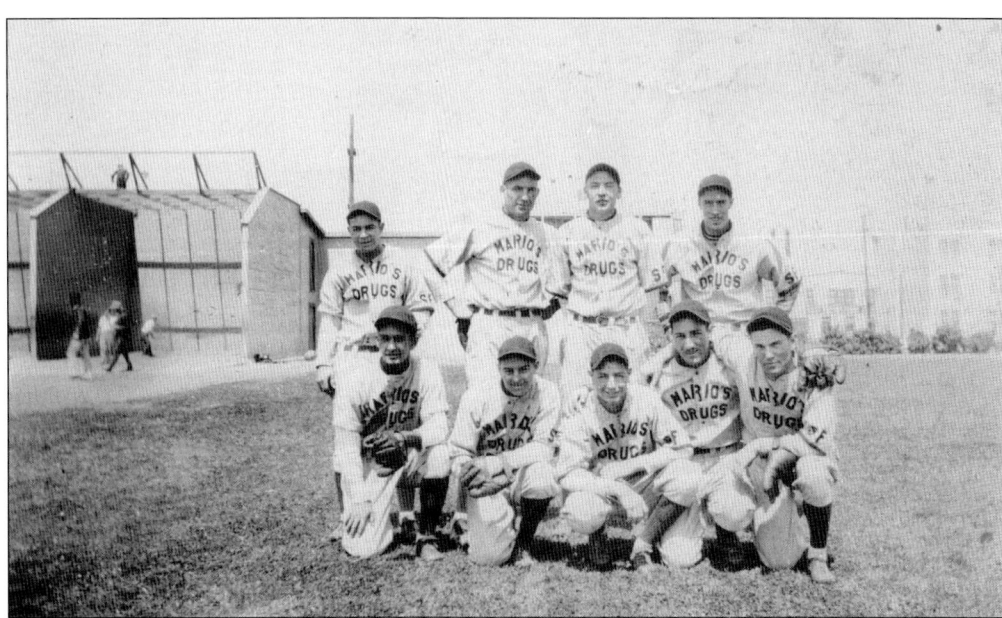

Mario's Drugs baseball team is seen in this photograph from the late 1930s. The team played at Portola Playground. (Courtesy of Barbara Lister DeMattei.)

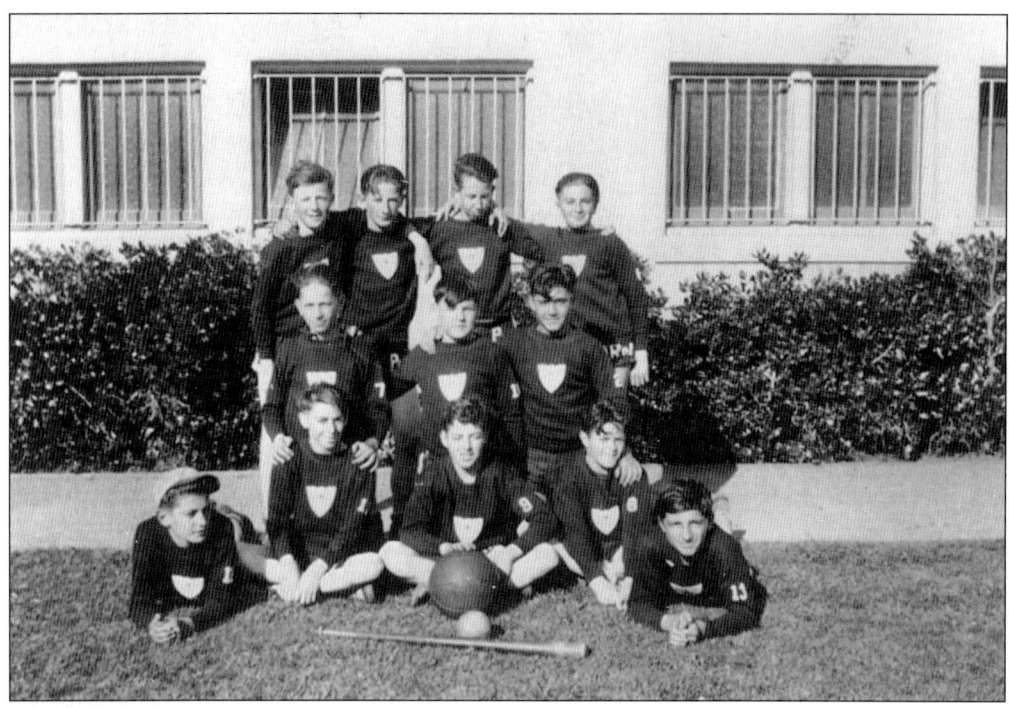

"The Crusaders" are pictured at the Portola Recreation Center in June 1934. Pictured here are, from left to right, (first row) John Larrieu, Adolph Buffo, Fred Del Sarto, Russ Spudone, and Ralph Cataldo; (second row) Mike Ribbota, Jim Grady, and Fred Camacho; (third row) John Houlihan, Ted Katsones, George O'Brien, and Frank Montalvo. (Courtesy of Jim Grady.)

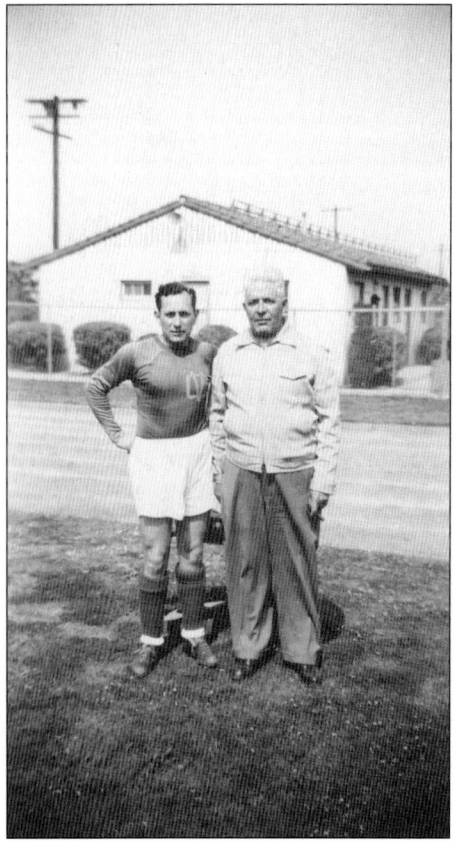

As a 10-year-old child in Vercelli, Italy, John Ardizzone played professional soccer. After immigrating to the United States, he settled in the Portola and continued to play in various soccer clubs until his retirement from the game in 1948. He was inducted into the United States Soccer Federation Hall of Fame on July 10, 1971. In this 1935 photograph, John is pictured at left with an unidentified friend. (Courtesy of Gloria Ardizzone Goggiano.)

Portola resident Sam Fenech played baseball for the Oakland Oaks in 1944. (Courtesy of Barbara Fenech.)

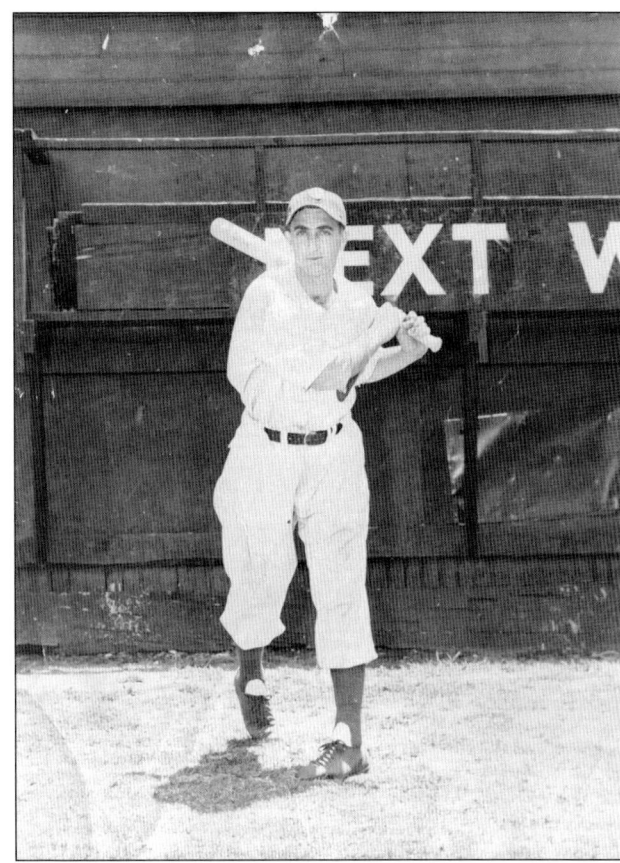

The 1947 Portola Merchants baseball team poses with manager Joe Gaggero in 1947. (Courtesy of Robert Arata.)

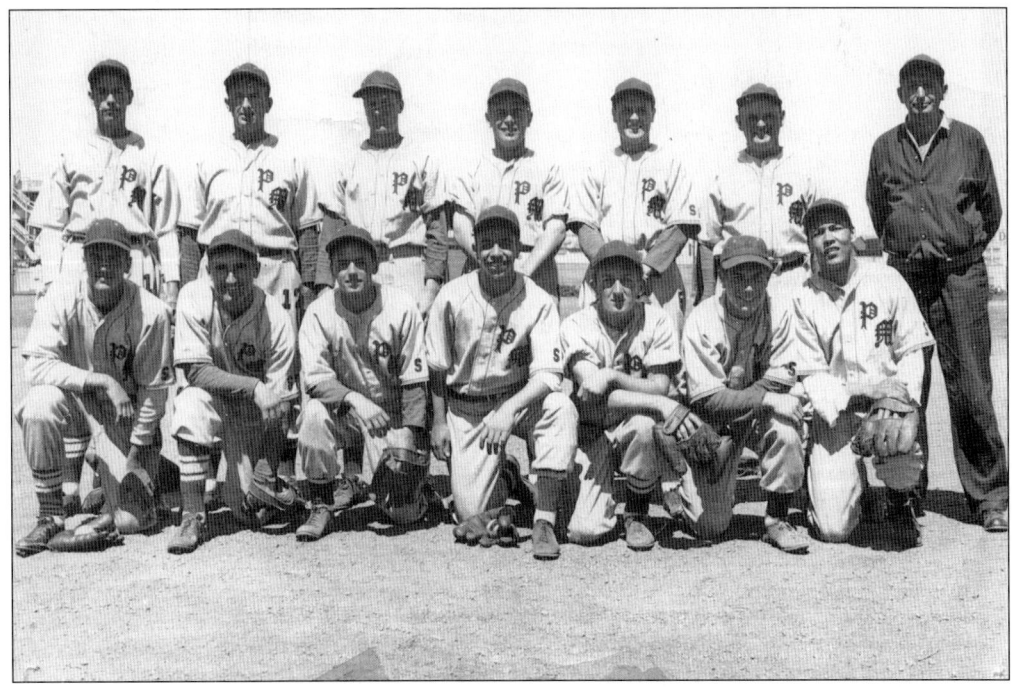

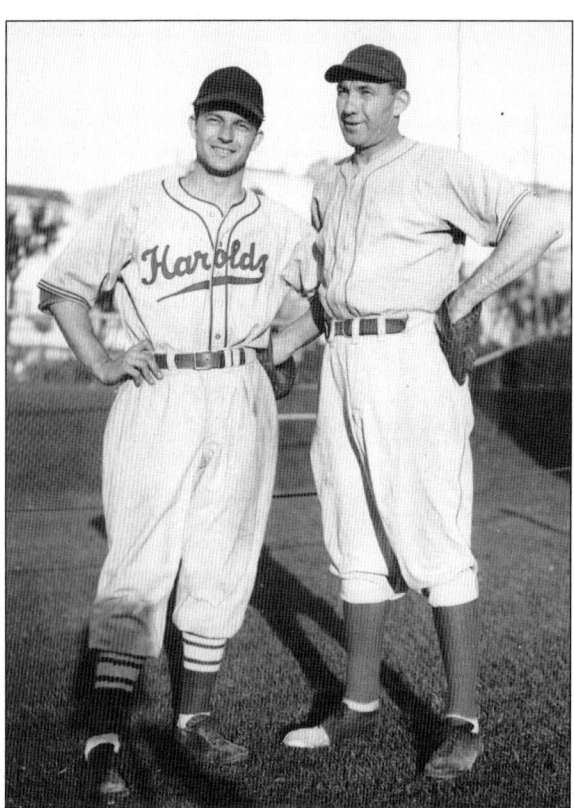

Pictured here on July 17, 1948, Portola residents Walter Lister Jr. (left) and Walter Lister Sr. both pitched for Harold's Club team. (Courtesy of Barbara Lister DeMattei.)

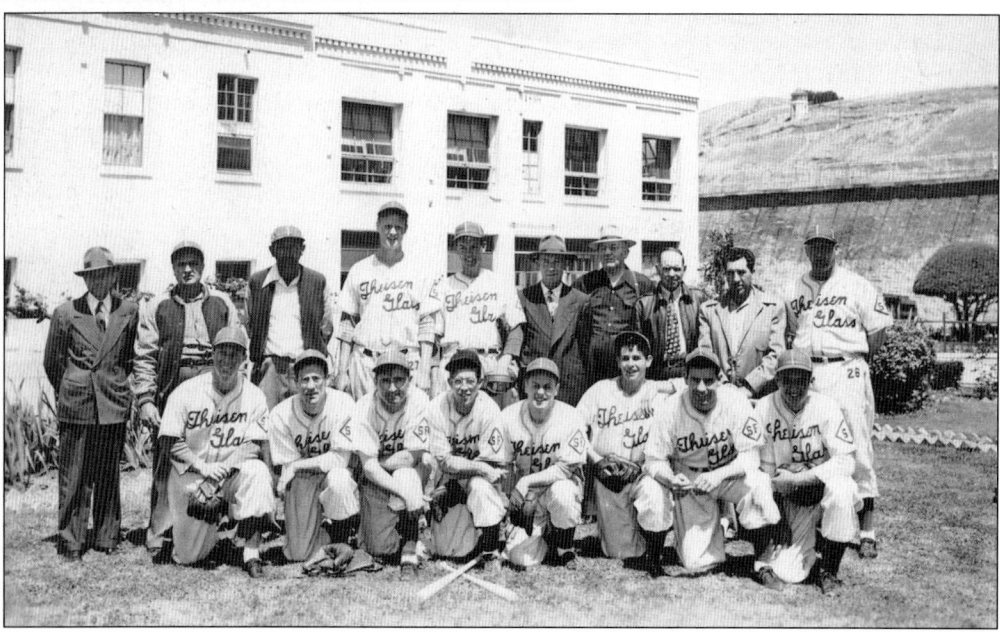

Joe Gaggero became the manager of the Portola Natives in 1944. They later called themselves the Owl Drug Juniors and were sponsored by Owl Drugs. In 1946, 1947, and 1948 they were known as the Portola Merchants. In 1949, the team was sponsored by Theisen Glass Company. Gaggero is pictured in the back row, third from the left. (Courtesy of Ron Gaggero.)

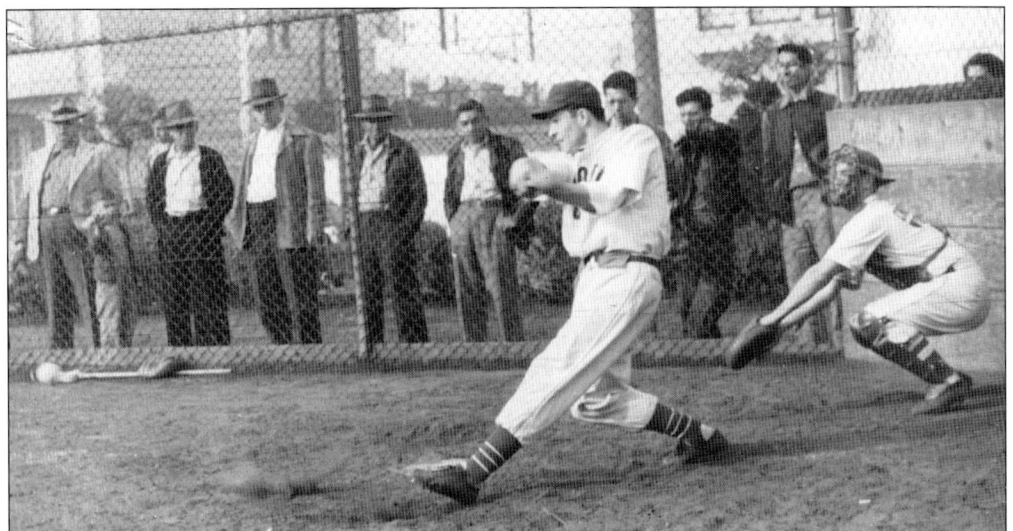

Walter Lister Jr. is pictured batting at Portola Playground in this 1950s photograph. (Courtesy of Ron Gaggero.)

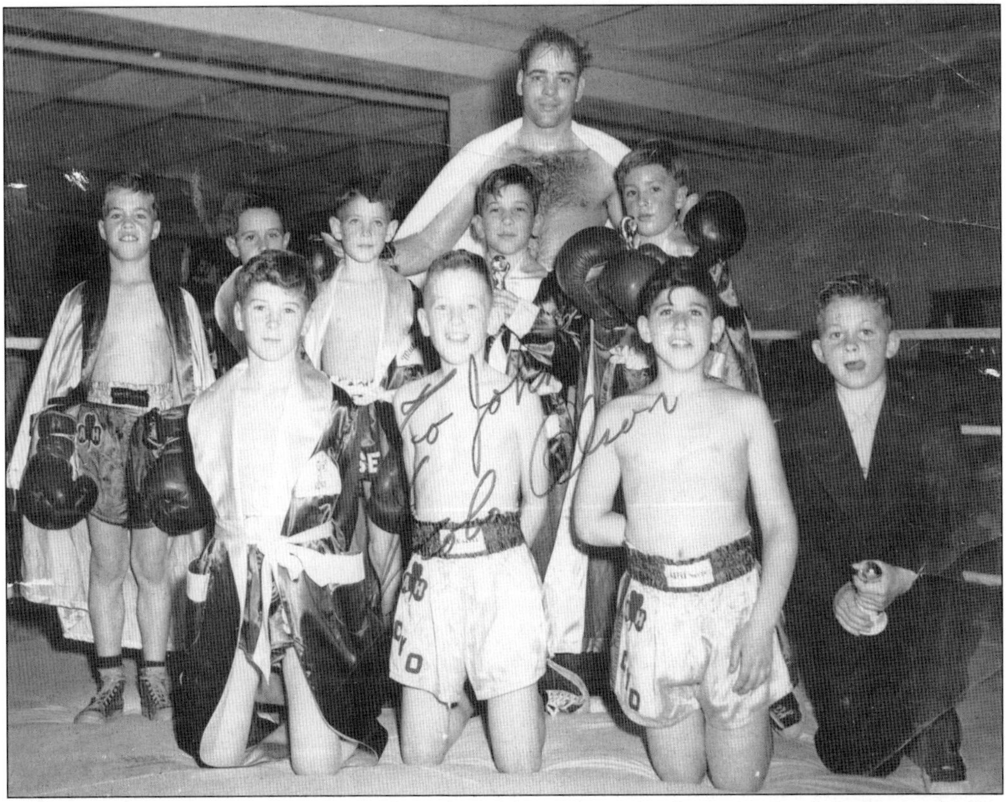

Middleweight boxing champion Carl "Bobo" Olson sparred a four-round exhibition at the St. Elizabeth/All Hallows CYO Boxing show. Pictured with Olson in this 1954 photograph are, from left to right, (first row) Michael White, Jerry Fritsch, Ronald Tomasello, and Eugene Pudlo; (second row) John Shaw, Tony Madrid, Steve Eadni, John Fenech, and John Yerman. (Courtesy of John Fenech.)

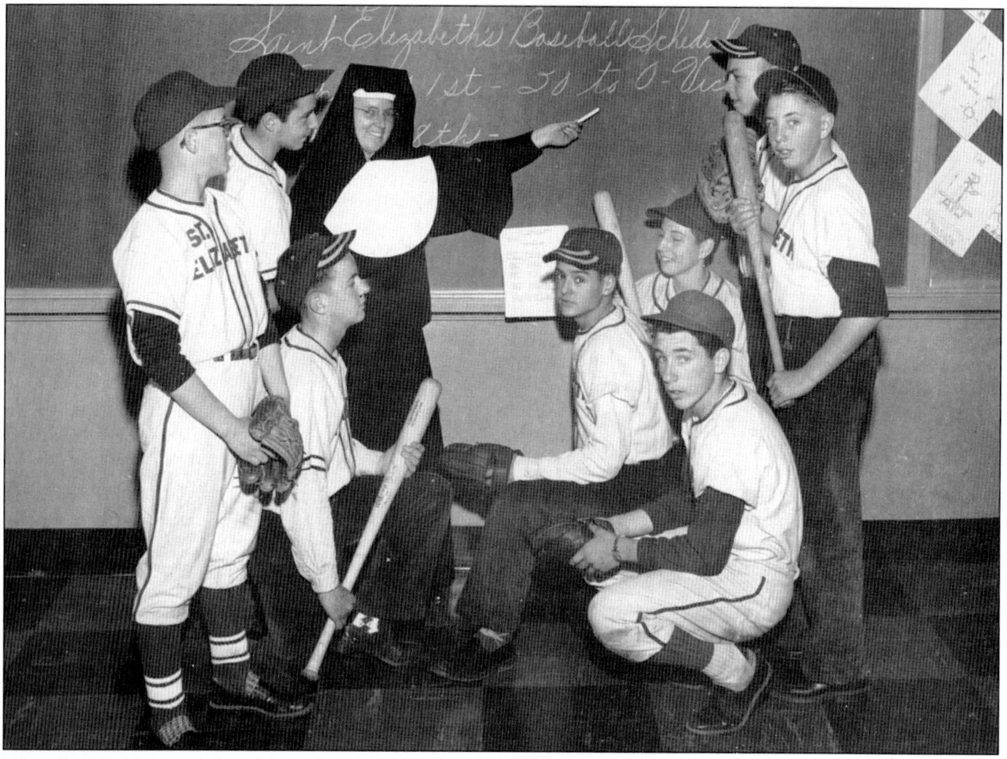

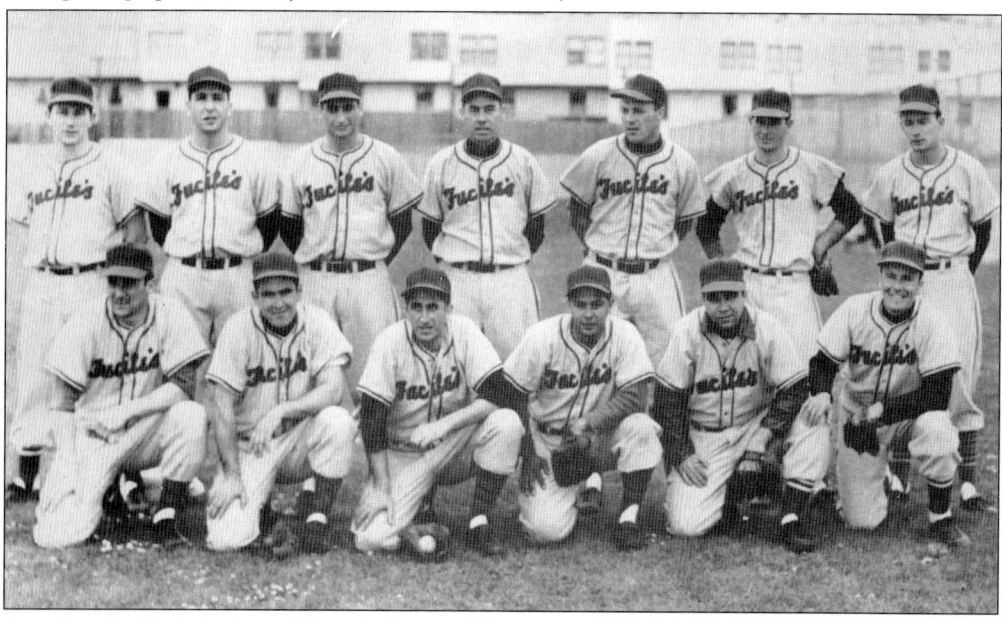

The St. Elizabeth School baseball team gets a pep talk from Sr. Felicitas Cronin, PBVM, in this 1956 photograph. (Courtesy of St. Elizabeth Church.)

Salvadore Fucile Sr., owner of Fucile's Bar at 2470 San Bruno Avenue, sponsored a semiprofessional baseball team made up of Portola residents. This April 1956 team photograph also includes the owner's sons Louis (second from left, back row) and Salvadore Jr. (third from left, back row). (Courtesy of Matt Fucile.)

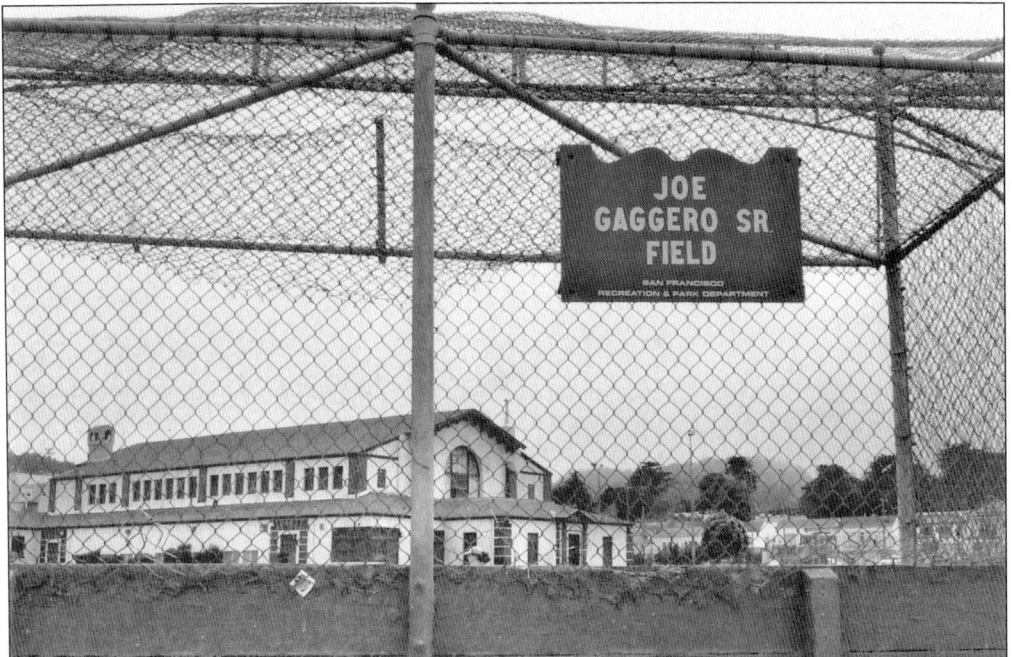

Joe Gaggero Sr. was the best-known Bay Area semiprofessional umpire of his time. Long before Little Leagues and Babe Ruth Leagues, Joe ran his own farm team. He had enough players to manage four or five teams, including the Portola Merchants. If sponsors were not available, Joe financed the team himself. On May 22, 1982, the field at Portola Playground was dedicated in his honor and named the Joe Gaggero Sr. Field. Over 300 people showed up to honor him. Below, Joe Gaggero Sr. is seen with his grandchildren Phillip and Christopher Gaggero at the ceremony. (Above courtesy of David R. Mehrwein; below Ron Gaggero.)

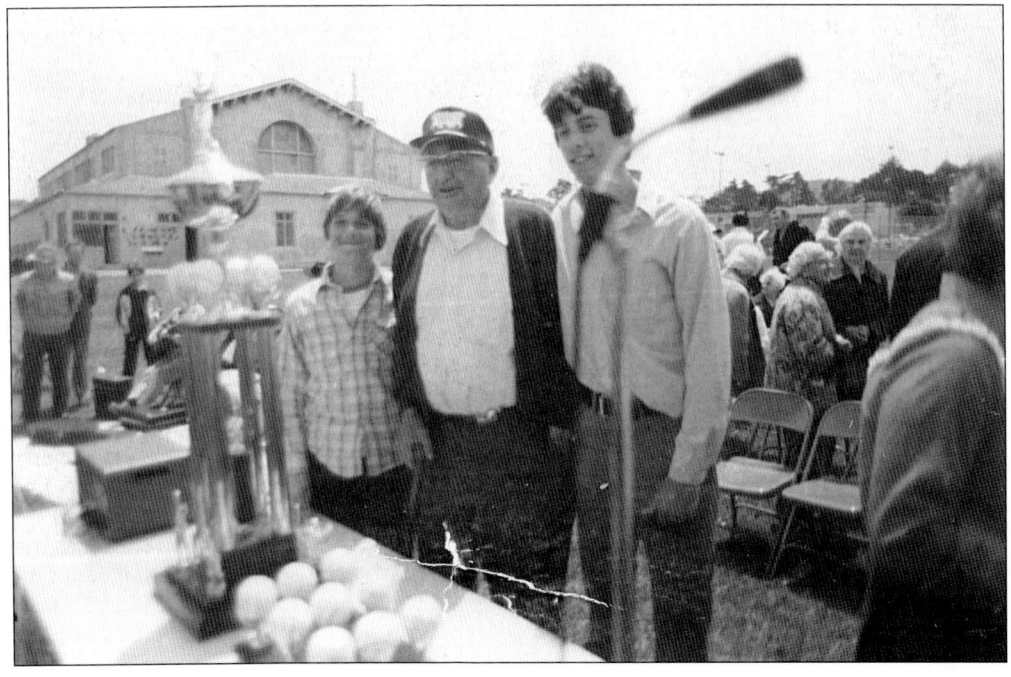

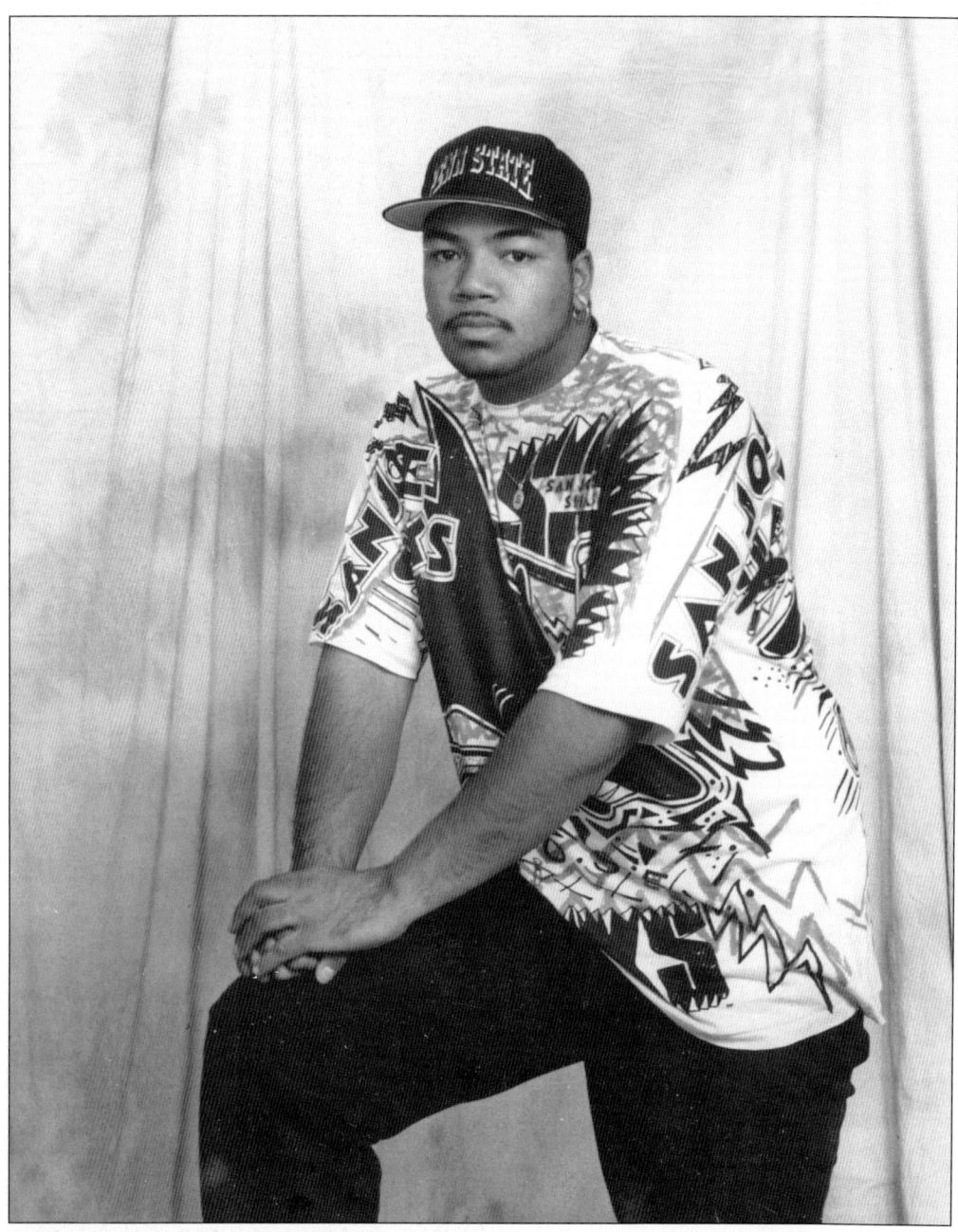

Sululagi M. Palega Jr., a Portola resident active in community service, was also an athlete who could often be found practicing in Portola Park. On March 19, 1994, while in Modesto for a basketball tournament, he was killed in a random drive-by shooting. The city dedicated Portola Park in his honor on August 3, 1996. (Courtesy of Dorothy Palega.)

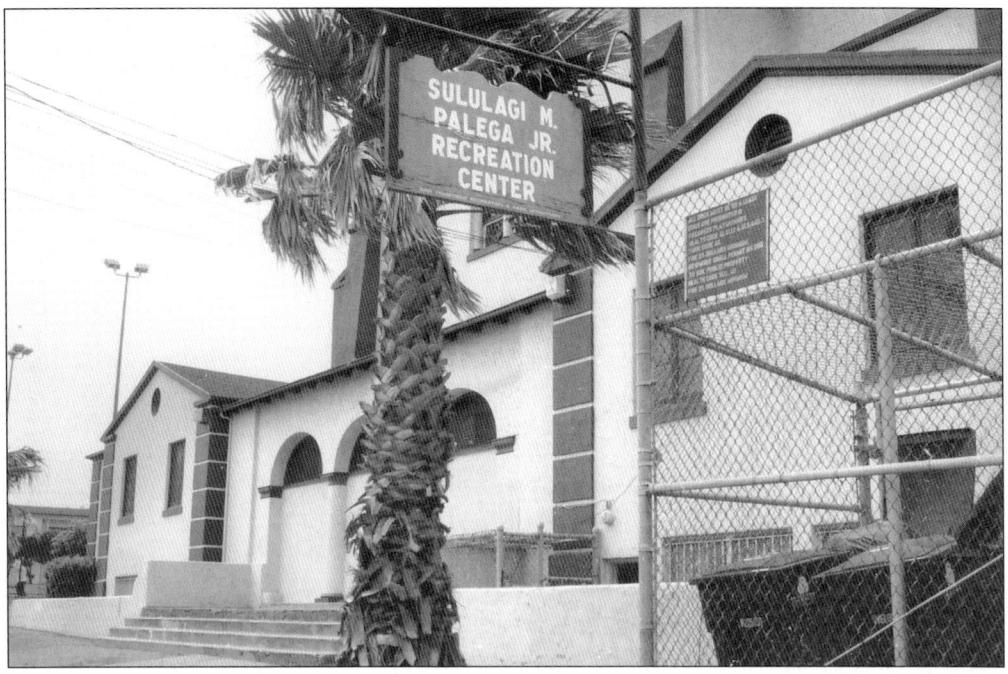

The Sululagi M. Palega Jr. Recreation Center was dedicated in honor of Sululagi M. Palega Jr. on August 3, 1996. The site was formerly known as Portola Recreation Center. (Courtesy of David R. Mehrwein.)

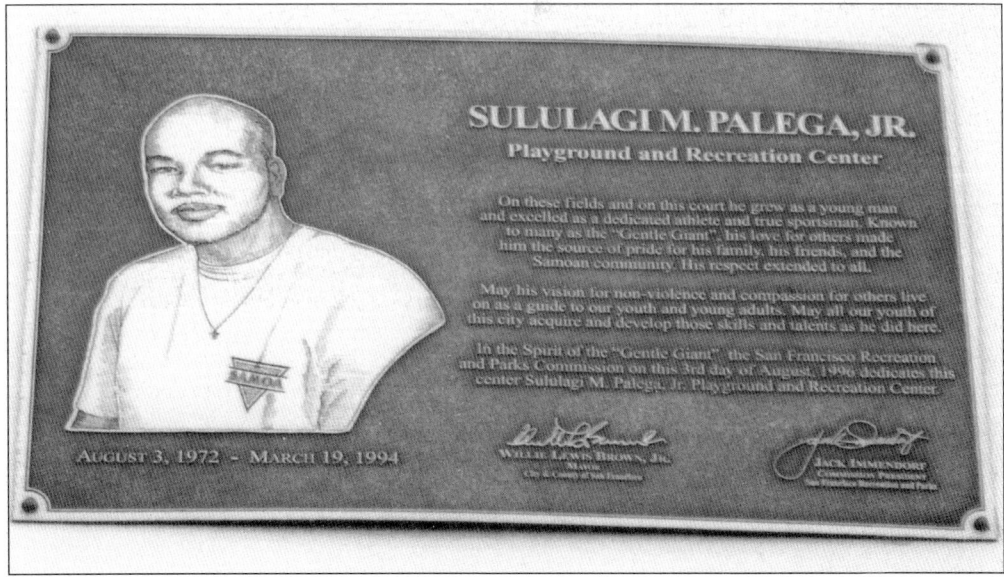

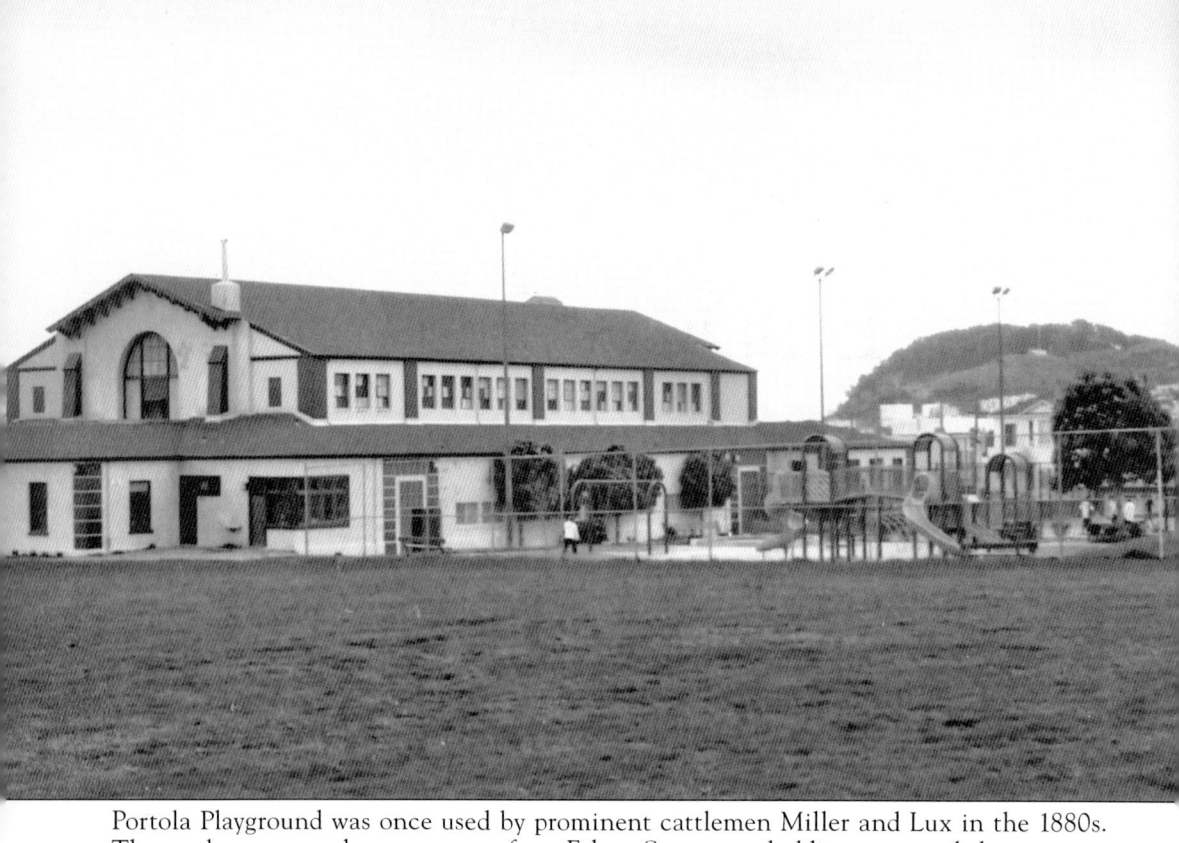

Portola Playground was once used by prominent cattlemen Miller and Lux in the 1880s. The cattle company drove steers up from Felton Street to a holding pen until they went to Butchertown for slaughter. Today the park is known as Palega Playground. (Courtesy of Dwayne and Terezinha Jusino.)

BIBLIOGRAPHY

Application to California Reading and Literary Improvement and Public Library Construction and Renovation Bond Act of 2000. Submitted by the City and County of San Francisco, January 16, 2004.

Breschini, Gary S., Ph.D. *The Portola Expedition of 1769*. Monterey County Historical Society. August 20, 2006. www.mchmuseum.com/portola1769.html.

Hansen, Gladys. *San Francisco Almanac*. San Rafael, CA: Presidio Press, 1980.

http://www.stanford.edu.group/virus/uda/index.html

Isaak, Peggy A. "How It Was Growing Up 'Out the Road.'" Jewish Bulletin.

Leibo, Steven A. "Out the Road: The San Bruno Jewish Community of San Francisco, 1901–1908." *Western States Jewish Historical Quarterly*. January 1979, Volume XI, No. 2.

Lowenstein, Louis K. *The Streets of San Francisco*. San Francisco, CA: Lexicos, 1984.

San Francisco Examiner. San Francisco, CA: 1988.

Across America, People are Discovering Something Wonderful. Their Heritage.

Arcadia Publishing is the leading local history publisher in the United States. With more than 3,000 titles in print and hundreds of new titles released every year, Arcadia has extensive specialized experience chronicling the history of communities and celebrating America's hidden stories, bringing to life the people, places, and events from the past. To discover the history of other communities across the nation, please visit:

www.arcadiapublishing.com

Customized search tools allow you to find regional history books about the town where you grew up, the cities where your friends and family live, the town where your parents met, or even that retirement spot you've been dreaming about.

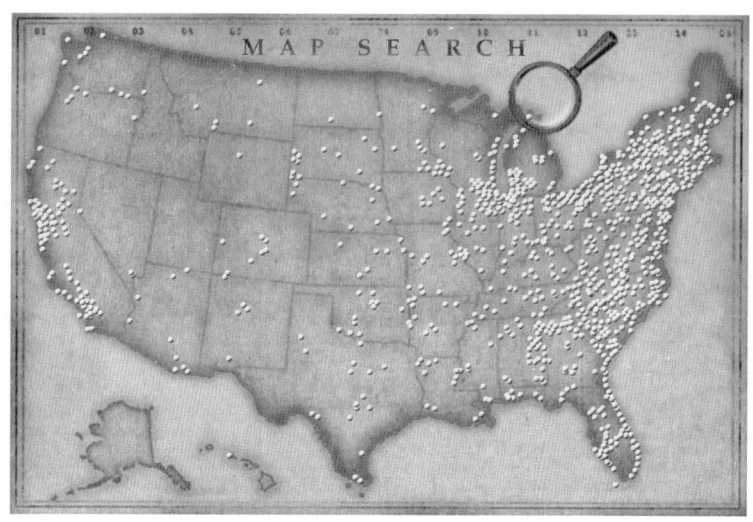